Not only does Christian McEwen help me listen better to the people in my life, as I had hoped she would, she leads me to listening as a practice, a way of paying attention to life itself.

In over a hundred "essayettes" of a page or two each, McEwen speaks of many ways of listening, of many great listeners, of many forgotten sounds. She speaks out of her concern for the raucous world, and her love for the sounds of the world. She gently shows us that to listen is to open ourselves to the life we are living together, to the sounds and the silences of this struggling and beautiful Earth.

The book is the fruit of years of thoughtful work and research, the writing is lovely to listen to with the inner ear, and the extensive list of sources at the end is a precious treasure which I will refer to with gratitude. *In Praise of Listening* is essential for us now, encouraging us to love with our ears this noisy and suffering world we live in.

I will return to this book again and again. *In Praise of Listening* is for everyone who wants to learn to hear the love in the world.

—**Susan Moon**, Zen teacher
and author of *Alive Until You're Dead*

Christian McEwen refreshes our senses through her poetic study of listening. She has found words for seemingly ineffable experiences, from the potency of a "tiny, charged stretch of silence," to the subtleties of tone and rhythm in the human voice. She is all ears! Her capacity for listening extends to friends, family, and colleagues from many creative fields, whose stories she deftly interweaves with her own. Indeed, this is a book for artists, by which I mean curious, sensitive people who wish to tune into their surroundings with an open ear. I will certainly share her book with my piano students. I am always looking for ways to help them develop their listening skills, so they may be fully and expressively present, alert to the music's nuances, and able to hear their own inner voice.

—**Alexandra Gorlin-Crenshaw**, musician,
multidisciplinary artist, and teacher

In Praise
of
Listening

A Gathering of Stories

Christian McEwen

BAUHAN PUBLISHING
PETERBOROUGH, NEW HAMPSHIRE
2023

ISBN: 978-087233-374-1
Library of Congress Cataloging-in-Publication Data

Names: McEwen, Christian, 1956- author.
Title: In Praise of Listening : A Gathering of Stories / Christian McEwen.
Description: Peterborough, New Hampshire : Bauhan Publishing, 2023. |
Includes bibliographical references. Identifiers: LCCN 2023035001 (print)
| LCCN 2023035002 (ebook) | ISBN 9780872333741 (trade paperback)
| ISBN 9780872333758 (ebook)
Subjects: LCSH: Listening.
Classification: LCC BF323.L5 M363 2023 (print) | LCC BF323.L5 (ebook) |
DDC 153.6/8--dc23/eng/20230802
LC record available at https://lccn.loc.gov/2023035001
LC ebook record available at https://lccn.loc.gov/2023035002

www.christianmcewen.com

Cover art by Mimi Robinson www.mimirobinsonart.com

Cover Design by Henry James
Book design by Sarah Bauhan

BAUHAN
PUBLISHING LLC
PO BOX 117 PETERBOROUGH NEW HAMPSHIRE 03458
603-567-4430
WWW.BAUHANPUBLISHING.COM

In memory of
Mariel Kinsey and Parker Huber,
two peerless listeners

CONTENTS

INTRODUCTION

❦

The ear draws forth the story.

Italo Calvino

There'll come a time, say the Anishinaabe, when the world's people will arrive at a fork in the road. The air will be too thick to breathe, and it will no longer be possible to dip a cup into a stream and bring out fresh water to drink. At that time, they say, we'll have to walk back along the paths of our ancestors, retrieving all the many treasures they have left behind. Each of us will find something that we need: some tale, some parable, some crucial story. We'll pick it up and put it in our knapsack—whatever we can carry, large or small—and together we will walk on down the road.

For me, one of those crucial stories has to do with listening.

Most of us think of listening in a fairly literal fashion: human beings listening (or not listening) to one another; the pleasure of attending to a familiar piece of music. The word derives from the Old English *hylsnan,* which means, quite simply, "to pay attention." But *listening* can have a far broader and more capacious meaning, moving out beyond the small apparatus of the ears to the hands or belly or enveloping spirit/mind. When a massage practitioner talks of "listening to the body," or a gardener describes herself as "listening to the land," when writers and artists explain that they are "listening" to their work-in-progress, they are using the word as I would like to use it here—as an extended metaphor for openness and receptivity, less actual than symbolic, less physical than metaphysical, rippling out from the self-centered human to the farthest reaches of the non-human world.

I have been exploring such listening for a number of years, tracking it through literature and literary history, Buddhism, nature writing, science, and sociology, comforted by the echoes and connections between those very different fields. I've also interviewed several dozen expert listeners: writers and therapists; naturalists and storytellers; along with a handful of superb musicians. Some of those I quote are famous and familiar: Montaigne, Chekhov, and Virginia Woolf; Mary Oliver, Barry Lopez. Some are our own magnificent contemporaries: the botanist Robin Wall Kimmerer, the trumpeter Frank London, the avant-garde singer Meredith Monk. Others again are personal friends and colleagues, little known outside their own immediate circle. Their stories are included in the pages that follow, along with memories and impressions of my own.

In Praise of Listening is composed of thirteen chapters, each one made up of a number of short sections or "essayettes," which can themselves be read in any order. It focuses at first on human-centered listening (listening to childhood, listening inwards), and gradually moves out into the surrounding world (listening to the wild, to the little sounds of every day). After a couple of chapters devoted to professional listening (listening to music, writers listening) it reaches a place where listening overlaps with what one might call "the ear of the heart" (communing with the dead, listening to silence or to the spirit), to arrive, finally, at a kind of global listening ("All Our Relations") where there is nothing and no one that is not worth listening to.

In a world of racket and distraction, such generous, expansive listening is increasingly under siege. But it remains a skill worth honoring, worth passing on: a source of clarity and joy and wise embodiment, as well as a vital bridge to those with whom we disagree. "Many an old story begins with the words, 'Long ago, when animals could speak...'" writes naturalist Lyanda Lynn Haupt. "Perhaps the corollary would be just as good an opening ... *'Long ago, when people could listen.'*"

~ 1 ~

Children Listening

Some linguists believe that the oldest word is hist—*listen!*
Kathleen Dean Moore

The Small Sounds of the Past

Long ago, back before adult time began, I remember lying on the rug
beside the fire, with the gray rain pouring down outside and my uncles' voices on the record player: their heavy, grainy, grown-up voices,
familiar and monotonous:

> *Ye Hi'lands and ye Lowlands*
> *Oh whaur hae ye been?*
> *They hae slain the Earl o' Moray*
> *And laid him on the green.*

Years later, as I neared the end of this book, those songs returned to
me in dreams. The house was dark and hunched under a starry sky,
everyone in it fast asleep, but my uncles were still singing those old
folksongs, their voices blazing out into the night.

Many of us turn to images to spark our memories: the childhood
drawings, still stuck to the belly of the old refrigerator, the family album crammed with faded photographs. But sounds too can be powerfully evocative. My friend Eleanor Adams was born in Connecticut
in 1916 and spent her childhood summers on an island called Deer
Isle. Deep into her nineties, she remembered the sound of every local truck, each with its characteristic engine. She liked to wake up

very early, in what, for her, was the middle of the night, to listen to the milkman in his horse-drawn wagon: the clatter of hoofs striking the metaled road, the clink of the glass bottles set down on the stoop.

Children watch and listen, notice, pay attention. They lie on the worn rug in front of the fire and hear the click of a silver needle against the pocked top of the thimble, the soft intake of someone's breath. Nothing is too modest or humdrum to be enjoyed. Mariel Kinsey grew up in China, where her parents were missionaries. She remembered the tall stand of grasses behind the family compound, "sort of like corn," she said, and how the children liked to play there, "rustling through." She described too, a neighbor called Mrs. Hauskke, who used to hand out slices of bread and butter sprinkled with sugar. Kinsey was six or seven at the time, and still recalled how it felt to bite into one of those slices. "White bread slathered with butter and sugar. And the crunching sound of the sugar! Isn't that something!"

In an increasingly noisy and intrusive world, such memories can act as catalysts, reminding us to attend to our own present-day impressions, or "listen inwards" to what our bodies have to say. It is as if in summoning such long lost sounds, we were able to reconstitute the ground underfoot and the sky overhead, the very foundations of our human being.

"Remember to love your sense of hearing," advises the composer W. A. Mathieu, "love the echo of the world calling us awake inside our skulls."

Little Velvet Voice

As a child, I was accused of being dreamy and distracted, of not listening when the grown-ups spoke to me. I was scolded, too, for making too much noise. *Little velvet voice,* my father used to croon, mock-soothingly. As I grew older, he would repeat the description of Cordelia in *King Lear.* "Her voice was ever soft / Gentle and low, an excellent thing in woman."

"*Ha!*" I would respond (noisily, emphatically), shutting the door (hard!) and racing off upstairs. Papa might fancy himself in the role of Lear, but I had no interest in playing Cordelia. My voice was never going to be soft, gentle, and low. But listening was something else entirely. Listening had always been important.

My own memories begin in London, with the pigeons calling from the sill outside the window, and the slap of warmish water in a yellow-painted bath. My mother says I loved being sung to and would coo and gurgle in appreciation. At eighteen months, I was given a giant teddy bear (always known as Big Teddy), who grunted when you turned him upside down, a wonderfully robust and satisfying sound. I loved Big Teddy and thought him very funny and impressive. But best of all was when Mama read to me or told me stories. "She was delicious like that, listening," my mother wrote, in the notes she kept at the time. "And I wished I always had the patience to keep her so."

The summer I turned three, we moved to Wiltshire, to a square thatched house called Coneybury, not far from Stonehenge. My mother pictures me dancing around the house, "interviewing everyone and collecting all the stones (a shoe stone, a bottle stone, a letter stone)," and bringing her information on "the birds and flowers and spiders and life in general." But I liked silence too, and solitude, and calm. I remember crouching in the linen cupboard among the soft heaped towels, listening to the slap of the iron in the nursery, the grown-up music floating from downstairs. Often, I'd lie down flat under the piano, letting my whole body fill up with its thunder, watching Mama's long feet as they pressed the pedals. Or I'd race outside and hide in the tall grass, listening to the bantams squabbling in the henhouse, the harsh cry of the cockerel tearing open the sky.

We lived close to each other in those days, physically close: we heard the intake of each other's breath; my father shaving, spitting out; the water running for a long, hot bath. If "home" is composed in part of such familiar sounds, then Coneybury was made of Nanny's small transistor radio, always tuned to Radio One, and the Beatles singing, *"She loves you, yeah, yeah, yeah!"* It was the glint and crackle of the nursery fire, and our own obedient, fumbling, soft-voiced prayers. It was the board that creaked halfway down the passage, under the thick felt of the McEwen tartan carpet, as someone got up to tend a wailing baby. It was the shrill of Mama's morning kettle, the blackbird caroling outside my father's study window, the crunch of yellow gravel as my bike swerved to a stop.

I sped like a minnow through that wide mesh of sound, hardly distinguishing human from non-human. Just as each bird had its own song, so each plant or animal or insect had its own distinctive sound. There was the cool squelch when you pulled a daffodil from between its long green leaves, the rough *hee-haw* of our donkey, Gypsy, cavorting in the nearby field, the impassioned thrum of a grasshopper in the curl of my closed hand. There were the tall indolent swans sailing down the river Avon, ruffling their feathers, turning their fierce beaks from side to side. Everything spoke to me and steadied me, showed me how to listen.

Not Being Heard

It may well be that things are different now. But when I was a child, the grown-ups seemed to belong to another world entirely. They had their own culture and preoccupations, their own inscrutable jokes and anecdotes, their own way of drawing back and becoming utterly, unassailably, silent. I remember trying to work out what they really meant, beyond the laughter and the kisses and the charged emphatic welcome. Did Papa like that gruff man with the mustache? Was Mama actually interested in what the nice lady at the Post Office had to say? Or were they just pretending? It was hard to tell. I longed to translate those adult words and gestures back into my own vernacular, to get at what I thought of as "the truth."

We were still at Coneybury when I began to ponder this, and there were four of us at home, ranging in age from seven and a half to barely two. It was as if we were in some way interchangeable, a litter of soft-haired, bright-eyed little creatures, lounging on the sofa or across the floor. Papa worked as a barrister in the city law courts, and we only ever saw him on weekends. Our mother, on the other hand, was almost always there. But there were groceries to order, letters to write, flowers to arrange and rearrange. There were calls to make, dinner parties to be planned. I think it was hard for her to see us as individuals, each with an equivalent center of gravity: dark with un-expected angers, rifted with sudden bursts of exaltation.

Only very rarely did she take the time we craved to sit and listen.

A Rush of Memories

In the course of gathering material for this book, I asked many people to describe their early memories of sound. My friend Meg Fisher wasn't sure, at first, that she had anything to tell. Most of her childhood memories were visual ones. But then she recalled the silver bell on her tricycle. "I can *really* distinctly remember the sound that metal bell made. *Tring-tring!* It made that nice satisfying little *tring!* every time you pressed it." Suddenly she could see the twisted handle of the bell and feel her thumb on it, see the handlebar to which it was attached, and the way that handlebar connected to the trike's front wheel. The white cement of the sidewalk, the rather rough, parched lawn—all those details were released by her clear memory of the bell.

"They had been locked away, inaccessible, until the sound freed them."

Gradually she came up with a long catalogue of childhood sounds, from the squeak of her sneakers shinnying up a metal pole to the *whomp!* and hiss of her mother's steam-iron, and the flapping of fresh sheets on the line. She was too small to help, but she remembered her mother pinning up the sheets, and the sun and shadows moving through them. "And there was a sound—the sound of those big sheets in the wind."

There is a strange delight in keeping track of such things, brightening and enlivening each passing day, while also reaching back deep into the past. Where adults tend to focus almost exclusively on the human voice (whether internal or external, sung or spoken), children make no distinction between what is and is not worth listening to. Everything talks, from the spit and crackle of a newly laid fire to the kiss and slurp of raindrops on a distant roof. In *Great Expectations*, Charles Dickens describes his hero, Pip, lying awake in bed, listening to "those extraordinary voices with which silence teems. . . . The closet whispered, the fireplace sighed, the little washing-stand ticked, and one guitar-string played occasionally in the chest of drawers."

Acknowledging this is more than an act of pleasurable nostalgia. It also serves to ground us in the present, encouraging us to pause for a moment—*stop and listen!*—and remind us of an openness and receptivity that are still possible, even now. There are sounds that energize and nourish us, that catch our ears and open up our hearts, sounds that return us to ourselves again. "It makes me so happy," someone said to a good friend of mine, "just to listen to you breathe."

The Big House

When I was eight, we moved to Marchmont, an enormous sandstone palace in the Scottish Borders. There were four of us children, then five, then six, looked after by a nanny and a nurserymaid on an upper floor, while our parents lived their separate lives on the floor below. If the grown-ups sat up late, talking over dinner, their voices did not reach us. If my little sister whimpered in her distant cot, I could not hear, did not get up to soothe her. My room was in the middle of the house, facing the front drive with its long avenue of beeches. On winter nights, I lay in bed listening to the rasp of my own breath; the front door opening, closing; a last burst of adult laughter. I could hear the cars starting up outside; their lights sent dazzling probes across my narrow ceiling.

Marchmont was a metropolis in and of itself, housing a multitude of different voices. There were the squeals and protests of the younger children, and the bright music from the nursery radio. There was the soft rambling chatter of the cleaning ladies as they moved from room to room—rich Glaswegian, Border Scots—the flounce of sheets as they changed a bed, the roar of the vacuum cleaner. A door would swing sharply open, and then sharply shut, and you'd hear the tread of feet in the downstairs hall, and a stranger's voice hallooing up the stairs. Down on the ground floor, in the big old-fashioned kitchen, Mrs. Shirer would be peeling the potatoes, dropping them one by one into a bowl of fresh cool water, while Mrs. Forsythe busied herself with soups and stews and scones and apple pies. One floor up, in what had been my grandmother's boudoir, my mother would be sitting at her desk, paying bills or writing letters, talking on the phone.

At Christmas and Easter, and for most of the summer holidays, the house was crammed with visitors: aunts and uncles and cousins, family friends, visiting nannies, elderly priests. Passionate conversations would unfold in every room, as if each one were a stage set all its own: gossip and stories in the kitchen and scullery; household management and the domestic arts (including children and their education) in my mother's sitting room; politics in the dining room where the men sat late over their liqueurs.

As a child I could drift from room to room, eavesdropping casually en route, communing less with other humans than with the house itself. Each piece of furniture had a voice of its own, from the sagging wheeze of the library sofa to the *shoosh* of the drawing room curtains, composed of narrow strips of ivory-colored silk. On rainy days, I used to wander round for hours, rustling the dried rose petals in the front hall, listening to the faint strains of my mother's Mozart, or the tinkle of the chandelier as the washing machine whirred and juddered on the floor above. Hunched on the stairs, I could hear my world in its entirety: sighs and creaks and shouts and murmurs; laughter, birdsong, distant voices; divided into generous swathes by the great bell which rang at stately intervals throughout the day. And always the hum of the house itself, so large, and so sweet-scented.

Invisible

As a child at Coneybury, I spent a lot of time alone, climbing trees or crouched in the long grass behind the hedge. I watched my mother as she snipped with her sharp secateurs among the flowers; peered through the small-paned windows to see my father at his desk. At Marchmont too, there was a game I played, shadowing some blinkered adult along the corridor and down the stairs. It demanded silence, caution, near-invisibility, the willingness to pause a moment, to stand very still. Later I would move out into the garden, out into the surrounding countryside. I loved it then, in May and June especially, when the rhodies bloomed in sumptuous clusters at the edges of the lawn, and the blue tits rustled from the dark close-woven hedge. It was as if each strand of sound possessed its own individual color: blue and brown and green and silver-grey. There was nothing that did not speak, that could not be spoken, from the creak and swagger of the big old-fashioned wheelbarrow to the twist of water from the fountain splashing sideways in the wind.

Out beyond the garden was a narrow stream, known to us as the Swardon Burn. It ran clear and cool, the water glinting over the stones. Brown trout rested in the deep, slow-moving pools. You could see the frill of their gills turning with the current. I remember the seethe of green as I crouched up to my thighs in the water, reaching forward into the soft, arched hollow under the bank, *listening*, as if my hands themselves had ears. Sun warmed the grass, the leggy stalks of meadowsweet and nettles and rose campion. Under the bridge lurked the dark tire-coil of an eel.

I did not want to be seen while I was doing this. If I caught sight of another human being—one of the foresters, or a keeper's boy, someone perched on a tractor far across the field—I would slip back into the shadows till they passed. The smallest thing was enough to make me freeze: a sudden flurry of pigeons from the little wood, the quick fillip of sound as a troutling leapt upstream. It was as if the wind blew through my hair into my empty skull and the light thrilled in my wrist bones, as if the *chirr* of the grasshoppers whirred in my own chest.

I was invisible, I was listening, I was catching fish with my hands.

Left to Our Own Devices

After she read the passages above, my friend Pat Musick sent me a cornucopia of beloved childhood sounds, from the soaring wind among the pines and the incessant fluttering of the aspen leaves, to the squeak of snow underfoot and the *sssssshhhhhh* of ice skates in a frigid Colorado winter. Another friend, Laetitia Bermejo, recalled the wind in the poplars outside her grandfather's house in France. "It sounded like water," she said. "It sounded like gravel. It's amazing how many things it could sound like. The sound of the sea. The sound of thunder. The sound of rain pouring down. And slapping on the windows, and slapping on the roof."

Bermejo remembered human sounds as well, including the clink and rattle of the rag-and-bone man as he trundled through the streets in his old cart. "He would shout, '*Whaddah maht!*'—obviously some version of 'Rag-and-bones!'" She had clear memories too, of the man who sharpened knives. "There was a very particular whistling sound. *Turr-rrr-tood-le-rroo!* Like one of those little panpipes. It would go *up!* And then it would go *down!* And then it would go *up!* And you always knew, 'Oh, there's the sharpener!'"

Asking people to map or draw these sounds—or just to mimic them—elicited yet more surprising details. My mother recalled the hiss of the gas fire in her childhood nursery, and the cry of the muffin man from the street below. Radio host Daisy Mathias spoke with nostalgic fondness of a particular cement pad near her parents' garage. "And on the cement pad were three metal covers that closed off the garbage pails. That's where trash was put. And that little *scree-click!* when you stepped on the pedal . . . we don't hear that anymore."

I was struck both by the precision of these memories, and by the satisfaction evoked by their retrieval. It was as if each of us were once a miniature John Cage or Native elder, delicately receptive to the surrounding soundscape. But that way of knowing the world is being forgotten, displaced by the gadgets and distractions of the digital age. The first time I saw someone reach for her mobile in the happy hubbub of a family Thanksgiving, I was startled by her rudeness. Now, I am sorrowfully unsurprised to witness a driver backing uphill into moving traffic, her cell phone still pinioned to her ear, or the student strolling across campus under a radiant moon, fixated on the small screen of her phone. "People have always been distractible," writes techno-critic Nicholas Carr. "Minds wander. Attention drifts. But we have never carried on our person a tool that so insistently captivates our senses and divides our attention."

All too soon, not listening to other people becomes not listening to the larger world, and ultimately, not even to ourselves.

What Is Lost

In the summer of 2015, Oliver Sacks wrote a short essay called "The Machine Stops," which later appeared in *The New Yorker.* Sacks was a writer and neurologist, best known for *Awakenings* and *The Man Who Mistook His Wife for a Hat,* as well as for a lively and surprising memoir, *On the Move.* He was, above all, an enthusiast, with a brilliant, original, astonishingly well-stocked mind. But what he saw, as he left his apartment and moved out into the New York City streets, had begun to trouble him. "People peering into little boxes or holding them in front of their faces, walking blithely in the path of moving traffic, totally out of touch with their surroundings . . . young parents staring at their cell phones and ignoring their own babies as they walk or wheel them along. . . ."

At twenty-one years old, I traveled round the States on a Greyhound bus, enjoying many lively conversations along the way. On that same bus now, passengers barely raise their eyes from their tiny screens. The willingness to be open to a casual encounter, to trade impressions with a stranger, has almost completely disappeared. More subtle forms of listening are also under siege, from private wool-gathering or rumination, to communing with the past or the beloved dead, to the many pleasures that reside in silence. "The immediate present is undermined, perforated by a sense of elsewhere," writes Sven Birkerts in *Changing the Subject: Art and Attention in the Internet Age.* Always drawn towards the latest piece of news, the latest *bleep*, our attention is splintered, fragmented, broken up.

In a recent interview, the poet Joy Harjo spoke of trying to protect her own creative focus. She was working at her desk when she heard a *"Ding!"* from her computer, and realized she'd responded like one of Pavlov's dogs. It shocked her, she said. "That's not what I wanted to do. I wanted to stay on my track of listening." It made her wonder why she was reacting in that way. But of course, she knew the reason all too well. "Somebody is hungry for money, so if they keep you there with these sounds . . . then they will have your attention, and your attention means money, for them."

In a world where "the airwaves . . . *all* the airwaves—are increasingly choked with noise," that battle for our attention has now reached a crescendo. Sacks and Birkerts are not alone in trying to sound a warning. Over the last decade, the number of thoughtful "escape manuals" has continued to proliferate. Early classics included Nicholas Carr's *The Shallows: What the Internet is Doing to Our Brains*, and William Powers's *Hamlet's Blackberry: Building a Good Life in the Digital Age*, followed more recently by Cal Newport's *Digital Minimalism: Choosing a Focused Life in a Noisy World*, Jenny Odell's *How to Do Nothing: Resisting the Attention Economy*, Catherine Price's *How to Break Up With Your Phone: The 30-Day Plan to Take Back Your Life*, and Johann Hari's *Stolen Focus: Why You Can't Pay Attention—and How to Think Deeply Again*.

Price states the issue with heartbreaking clarity, "Our attention is the most valuable thing we have," she says. "We experience only what we pay attention to. . . . When we decide what to pay attention to in the moment, we are making a broader decision about how we want to spend our lives."

The New Noise

If the allure of shiny, pocket-sized devices is one reason for *not listening*, another is the ever-increasing noise. The poet Anne Carson describes a date with friends one steamy summer evening. The two couples meet in the street and decide to try a nearby restaurant. The place is "dark, cool, oaken." It is also unbearably loud. But none of them is bold enough to say so. "Our hearts crumble," writes Carson. "We order food by pointing and break into two yell factions, one each side of the table." They try to focus on the meal, as if eating in and of itself could be construed as conversation. "We cover our ears inside our souls."

For most of us in the developed world, Carson's experience has become dauntingly familiar. So-called public spaces are the worst. Muzak™ blasts across the bar, the hotel lobby. Trailers for upcoming movies have their volume turned excruciatingly high. But noise pursues us into our domestic lives as well, in the low drone of the refrigerator and the air conditioner, the screech and rattle of the computer printer, the ever-heightened pitch of voices on radio talk shows and TV.

Meanwhile, airplanes swoop down low above our heads; eighteen-wheelers barrel down the freeway, and the blare of leaf blowers and diesel-powered heavy equipment disrupts our day, along with the shrill whine of pneumatic drills, trash compactors, emergency alarms, and backup beepers. It comes as no surprise that a third of the United States population now suffers from some form of hearing loss, much of it noise induced. There are other consequences too, including compromised immune systems, exhaustion, and high blood pressure, plus increased risk of heart attacks and diabetes. Children perform less well in school; adults are subject to depression, hypertension, and insomnia. In some cases, people's taste buds are affected, making food taste less savory, more bland.

Whether noise is reckoned simply as "unwanted sound," or (more contemptuously), as "garbage perceptible to the ear," it remains a major focus of concern across the United States, generating more than 40,000 complaints per year in New York City alone. There are many different ways to tackle this, from quelling it at its source to installing special "low-noise" paving and replacing delivery trucks with smaller electric vehicles.

Meanwhile, the cacophony continues unabated, from the jackhammer pounding on a local street corner (110 decibels), to the jet engine revving up across the runway (120 decibels), to the threshold of human pain and injury (125 decibels). As the singer Meredith Monk remarked quietly in the early months of the pandemic, there's no question that "The Earth needs a lullaby right now."

Listening for the Muse

> *When you start working, everybody is in your studio—the past, your friends, enemies, the art world, and above all, your own ideas—all are there. But as you continue painting, they start leaving, one by one, and you are left completely alone. Then, if you are lucky, even you leave.*
>
> John Cage

Laetitia Bermejo is a figurative artist, currently living in Mallorca, Spain. The two of us have been friends for more than forty years. She grew up in the English city of Leeds, with a Spanish father and a French mother, and speaks all three languages with equal facility. Perhaps because of that, she has an acute sensitivity to sound. Not long ago, she showed me a painting she'd just finished. A small child was standing with her hands over her ears, surrounded by a circle of ferociously honking geese.

"I wanted to convey *noise*," Bermejo said. She remembers seeing the geese at a farm outside Leeds. They'd been eating brambles, so their tongues were bluish-purple. As a three- or four-year-old, herself hardly bigger than the geese, she had been struck by their menacing tongues and orange beaks, as well as the sheer volume of their cries. For her, the painting serves as a symbol "of the eternal honking of traffic, of mobile phones, *all the machinery of now* that just fills your ears until you can't think straight."

"Why this need to be perpetually connected?" she asks. "Why this terror of—what do they call it? FOMO. *Fear of Missing Out.* I have friends, they're older than me, and they always have this machine on! and they look at it twice a minute, if not more. I see them panic—they even panic on my behalf when I leave mine at home or in the car. And it pings and it pongs, and it bleeps and it blurps—it drives me insane!"

At times she begs them, "Can't you turn that off?" But there's always some excuse to leave it on.

Bermejo was born in 1959, the eldest of three children. Her father was a professor of Spanish language and literature at Leeds University, a tempestuous man with a lively sense of humor. Bermejo remembers him telling the most wonderful stories. "When we were kids, we'd say, 'Tell us a story, Dad!' and he had a whole panoply of invented jungle characters. The hero was Don Gorillo, who was a gorilla. And his very unlikely friends, a donkey, an elephant, a bull!"

Her mother was a more fretful and demanding person, whom Bermejo describes as "riddled with anxiety." "She wanted to be listened to," Bermejo says, "but she didn't have much time to listen." She remembers getting up earlier and earlier each day, so as to have at least ten minutes to herself before her mother woke. "I can't function early in the morning. But I *certainly* can't function when someone's pecking into my ear. And my mother couldn't resist." That too helped influence her goose painting. "Thank God she didn't ask me about it," says Bermejo. "'Cause what am I going to say? 'Mum, it's all about you!' *Mother Goose*. With all that a 'goose' implies! 'Silly person. Loud person. Mother person—noisy, cackling, heckling, interrupting, don't-let-anybody-else-get-a-word-in-edgeways kind of thing."

"I can disguise it," she tells me, "and say it's about 'the noise of now.' But it's like the noise of now reminds me of the noise of then."

Bermejo has always loved to draw—just simply "making marks." She has stacks of sketchbooks filled with spiky, vivid images in pen and pencil and colored ink. She also works with watercolor and pastel. But her favorite medium is oil. "I never actually invent," she says. "I don't think you can. What I try to invent is *the something there that already exists*. When I'm actually doing it, there's a kind of—total absorption."

But even when she starts out brimful of confidence, there's always a moment when the painting doesn't work. "Now that's when—if I'm patient—*the painting will tell me*."

Bermejo doesn't remember when she first came across that phrase, but from the start it resonated with her very strongly. She remembers one piece she struggled with, in which a woman was shouting from her balcony. Bermejo got so bored and frustrated, she turned it to the wall for half a year. But later, when she looked at it again, she saw at once what needed to be done. "'She's far too small! I just need to exaggerate her size!' And suddenly—it worked!" In fact, the painting later sold.

When her work becomes too charged and frantic, Bermejo goes outside to calm down. "I go for a walk, and I'm kind of attentive to everything. 'Oh, new posts! Oh, different colored gravel! Ah, sheep in that field! Oh, strange screeching sound! Oh, saw blade! *Dook-dook-dook!*'" At times, the smallest of excursions—like a quick trip to pick up a bobbin for her sewing machine—can help give her the solution that she needs. It's actually a kind of listening, she tells me, "a listening out . . . not discounting anything that happens to you as a possible nourishment."

During her first years in Mallorca, Bermejo lived in the fishing village of Deia. A quarter of a century later, she can still recite a litany of its characteristic sounds, from the donkeys braying and the cockerels crowing to the wash of sea along the rocky shore. She remembers the sheep too, grazing on the terraces between the olive trees. Because each one wore a bell, she'd hear their distant tinkling as they moved about. The bells themselves weren't especially mellifluous, but because they all had a slightly different timbre, as a "together sound" she found them beautiful. "*How can I paint a painting that would evoke those sounds?*" Bermejo used to ask herself. "The donkey, the cock crow, the bells, the sea, the wind, the thunder. . . ."

She never did resolve that particular composition. But each day, in her basement studio, the same long listening continues.

Consider the following quotations:

Her mother had once told her that childhood was a big, blue wave that lifted you up, carried you forth, and just when you thought it would last forever, vanished from sight. You could neither run after it nor bring it back. But the wave, before it disappeared, left a gift behind—a conch shell on the shore. Inside the seashell were stored all the sounds of childhood. Even today, if Jameelah closed her eyes and listened intently, she could hear them: her younger siblings' peals of laughter, her father's doting words as he broke his fast with a few dates, her mother's singing while she prepared the food, the crackle of the evening fire, the rustling of the acacia tree outside. . . .

Elif Shafak

The soundscape was marked by different sounds that indicated important events such as the arrival of the milkman shouting from his cart, the horn of the kerosene seller arriving in the neighborhood, the flute of the knife grinder, the announcement of the man who repaired mattresses, the horn and grinding of the train's wheels on the rail, the trembling of the earth and the vibration of doors and windows when the train approached; that is, each job or daily experience had its own sound mark.

Fabián Racca

Continue to explore:

Bring to mind an early memory of listening. Who or what were you listening to?

List some of your favorite sounds—and then search out opportunities to hear them in reality. Can you find a way to map or draw them too?

∾ 2 ∾

Listening Inwards

Listen to your life. See it for the fathomless mystery
that it is. In the boredom and the pain no less than in
the excitement and gladness: touch, taste, smell your
way to the holy and hidden heart of it.

Frederick Buechner

Inner Noise

In the center of my chest there is a strange, coiled shape, reminiscent of an ammonite or fossil worm. I experience it as fixed—metallic, bronze—and at the same time, oddly volatile. It sparks and fizzes like a mini-Catherine wheel, gurgles to itself like water disappearing down a drain. The spot it occupies feels bruised and sore, self-doubting, sad. And yet I know it as a latch, a crucial key. I call it "Sorrow's Gate."

The crowd at Sorrow's Gate is restless and unhappy. There is the high whine of anxiety, the low drone of depression and self-doubt. The voices hiss and spit and interrupt each other, replaying conversations from the distant past, rehearsing words and phrases for tomorrow. They rush in a tight posse to defend themselves and rebuke the listener (me). When I am tired and anxious, lonely and preoccupied, my only soundtrack is that crowd at Sorrow's Gate.

Some people never talk to themselves at all. But for those who do, up to a quarter of the day can be spent in such helpless self-communing. The psychologist Robert Sardello writes of the "inner noise" made up of those competing narratives. How to befriend that roaring crowd, and at the same time find a way to disengage, "to allow the pause, the stumbling, the inarticulateness, the gaps, the searching," and, ultimately, make a little space for silence?

Most of us are unwilling even to try. We are too busy, too distracted, too afraid. In a recent study at the University of Virginia, a group of forty-two were given the choice between doing nothing for some six to fifteen minutes or treating themselves to a series of light electric shocks. An astonishing two-thirds of the men and one quarter of the women preferred the shocks. They were afraid of solitude, afraid of looking inward. The opportunity to muse and brood and dream and wonder, to interrogate themselves, pursue the track of their own thoughts, had become not just rare, but actively terrifying. "Listening to their lives" was the last thing they wished to do.

But for those who are willing to brave that incessant racket, there's much to be learned from that crowd at Sorrow's Gate. "The life span of an emotion is only about a minute and a half," says Buddhist teacher Pema Chödrön. "So, if we pause, we need not react to it." *Slowly, slowly.* It can help to feel the body from within, focusing on the breath, grounding ourselves in the immediate present. More often than we might expect, the cacophony dies down, the log jam gradually breaks apart. A certain spaciousness reveals itself, its soft, white petals opening. Steady and attentive, welcoming: we too may hear the still small voice within.

In their classic book *How Can I Help?* Ram Dass and Paul Gorman provide a memorable image of this, suggesting we see our minds as the blue sky, and our thoughts as passing clouds. "The sky is always present. It contains the clouds and yet is not contained by them." It is tempting to identify with each new thought as it appears: pulling it close, holding it up to judgment. But there's no need for this. "We can remain quiet and choose which thought we wish to attend to. And we can remain aware behind all these thoughts, in a state that offers an entirely new level of openness and insight."

In other words, we can begin to "listen inwards," allowing silence to seep up from below, trusting that beyond that raucous crowd the calm self waits. "It is the surface of the sea that makes waves and roaring breakers;" writes the Sufi teacher Hazrat Inayat Khan, "the depth is silent. So, the depth of our own being is silent also." The poet John O'Donohue agrees. "Give yourself the opportunity of silence," he advises, "and begin to develop your listening, in order to hear, deep within yourself, the music of your own spirit."

A Back Shop All Our Own

As a young journalist, Teddy Wayne used to walk, to wait, to rest, to ride the subway—calmly at ease in the immediate moment. Now he describes himself as having almost no downtime. The only place he can count on being alone with his thoughts is in the shower. For him, as for so many of us, it is a struggle to find time for introspection, contemplation, time to focus on one simple, solitary thing.

Each day throws up a new set of challenges, personal, political, environmental, global, filtered through a growing armory of insistent media. Walk into any bar or local diner, stroll through any airport concourse, and catch the glazed faces of the TV sets blasting simultaneous (and contradictory) news. Wander alone beside the ocean—the Atlantic, or Pacific, it matters not. The sun may be shining, the great waves crashing on the shore. Wherever you find yourself, someone will have her head bent as she walks, entranced by her omnipotent gadget and its tiny screen.

If we are to succeed in "listening inwards," to hear within ourselves "the music of our spirit," we need not more external input, but more silence. And we need a refuge too, whether real or imagined, some kind of shelter or protected space where no one else can get to us and interrupt. As a child, I used to crouch on the attic stairs when I was angry or unhappy, bumping down from one dusty step to another as my mood improved. Often, I would slide back the heavy skylight, and climb out onto the roof, strolling between the tall sandstone chimneys, soothed by the *roo-coo* of the pigeons, the soft roar of a distant lawn mower. I was a twelve-year-old giant up there among the clouds, grateful for time to pause and catch my breath and calm my temper, time to be invisible, unknown. That yearning to hide out, to remain unseen, is familiar to most children, and to adults too, if we would only acknowledge it. Montaigne suggests we reserve "a back shop all our own," in which to befriend our various complexities. "Here our ordinary conversation must be between ourselves and ourselves, and so private that no outside association or communication can find a place."

My friend Susan Moon, a long-time Buddhist teacher, gave a workshop on the theme of refuge, asking students to name objects that for them represented shelter or safety. Examples might include a treasured book or fluted shell, the image of a tortoise or a snail. But one woman spoke of "taking refuge" in her disappointment, another of finding shelter in her grief. As Moon told me this, I realized that anything at all can become one's "back shop" or private hermitage—any repeated practice, any time or place, any familiar psychic territory. All that matters is that we should be able to inhabit and befriend it: reading, writing, dreaming, drawing; pausing, exploring, *listening in.*

Sometimes the focus will be on particular words and images. Sometimes what matters is the tone of what we hear—the drone of lethargy, the flare of panic or self-pity, a burst of exhilaration at some long-forgotten joy. The goal is not so much solving or resolving as remaining open, conversing with our own bewilderment and complications, our own wild, multivocal choir. In examining the specific texture of our lives, we change the experience by *not* trying to change it. *Breathing room.* Little by little, as our troubles are made welcome, they are braided into other parts of our own psyche: empathy, intelligence, reflective self-awareness.

"Look at this window," says Chuang Tzu. "It is nothing but a hole in the wall, but because of it the whole room is full of light."

A Meditation on Sound

Mark Epstein is a Manhattan-based psychotherapist, and a well-known writer too: the author of *Thoughts Without a Thinker; Open to Desire;* and, most recently, *Advice Not Given: A Guide to Getting Over Yourself.* He is also a practicing Buddhist, and someone who has thought long and hard about the act of listening.

In a recent workshop, Epstein alternated talk with silent meditation—in this case, a meditation on sound. As soon as everyone joined the circle, he asked them to pull out their cell phones and *to leave them on*. If someone got a call, that would be just fine. The instruction was to listen—to acknowledge the interruption—and then to return to the breath. "I'm trying to show how meditation can be therapeutic," Epstein said. Just as one can attend in a nonjudgmental way to passing sounds, so too, one can listen inwardly to the *basso profondo* of one's thoughts and feelings.

"How will you know the difficulties / of being human," Rumi asks, "if you're always / flying off to blue perfection? . . . Workers need ground to scrape and hoe, /not the sky of unspecified desire."

For Epstein, that ground is the rocky territory of one's own emotions, messy and repetitive as they often are. "Emotional life can be part of the meditative experience," he says. "Not something reserved for one's diary, one's partner, one's therapy—and not something to be ashamed of or squelched in the hopes of a more 'spiritual' experience."

Again and again, he encourages people to befriend their inner worlds, however challenging, to be curious and welcoming, to "simply listen."

Each time someone's phone rang at the workshop, there was a moment of reactivity—a frisson of anxiety and irritation. But this also served as a call to mindfulness, cutting across routine habits of dissociation. As the hours passed, people began to listen differently. Instead of "resisting the unpleasant noises and gravitating towards the mellifluous ones," they became increasingly relaxed, open, and responsive, not just to the shrill of cell phones but to their inner noise as well. And that, of course, was precisely what Epstein had intended. Because as he himself continues to emphasize, "Meditation is not just about seeking peace, it is about being present with everything."

The Ear in Fear

Meditation offers one way of self-befriending, but there are numerous others too, including such ordinary practices as reading, writing, dreaming, and drawing, even going for walks. Over time, any of these can help return us to ourselves again, restoring the calm and clarity we had imagined lost. One of my favorite accounts of this is related by the artist Paulus Berensohn.

Paulus Berensohn was a trained dancer and professional potter who also loved to sew and practice doodling. Halfway through his life, around the age of forty, he came down with a mysterious illness, possibly cancer. Healers told him that fear was at the root of it: somehow, he had to let go of that fear and replace it with love. Berensohn had no idea how to accomplish this. He did, however, possess a "small and stubborn intuition" that the fear might contain something of value, "something to embrace."

> So, I took the word fear and doodled it. I wrote it over and over again. I drew it by echoing the lines of my own handwriting writing it. I wove its letter forms in and out of each other. After a long time, more than a year, I finally saw what was then obvious, that every time I drew the word fear, three-quarters of that time I was drawing the word *ear*: f.EAR. There's an *ear* in your *fear*, Paulus. Open it, listen. But how?

He realized too that "EAR" was right in the center of the word, hEARt. "Was ear a bridge between fear and love? Drawing heart . . . I discovered the word art in heart and was profoundly encouraged, heartened, to see that in heart, ear and art overlapped, becoming one."

Some years later, Berensohn spent six months in Tasmania, studying Deep Ecology. While he was there, he noticed that his doodling of heart had taken on another form. "The "h" that begins heart in the western hemisphere of my brain had made a dyslexic shift in the southern hemisphere." HEART had become EARTH. Later, a second H attached itself to HEART, just as he began to include ritual and altar-making in the classes he was teaching.

> A movement of imagination from FEAR to EAR to ART to HEART to EARTH to HEARTH to ALTAR— to thanking and praising and gratitude doodled into the tissue of my subtle body.

None of this was an accident, he said. Nor was it a fantasy. He didn't make it up. "There it was. It came towards me. It captured my imagination."

The Joy of Reading

Paulus Berensohn wrote and drew and kept an illustrated journal; he was also a committed reader. As little as six minutes, concentrated reading has been found to slow the heart rate and ease tension in the muscles, reducing stress levels by as much as 68 percent. It is better at calming our nerves than listening to music, going for walks, or even—that universal panacea—reaching for another cup of tea. But reading is not just a matter of relaxation, or the delights of character and plot. It also permits a certain interiority or inner listening, a certain shapely, ordered time. For the writer Sven Birkerts, the novel is "a field for thinking, a condensed time-world parallel (or adjacent) to ours. . . ." More than anything else, he says, such reading "tunes up" and "accentuates" his inner life.

I think of myself at five and six, when, after months of struggle, I first wriggled through the scratchy briar patch of torn-up words into the ease and luxury of silent reading. Books were the doorway to a marvelous new world: each one a small, tip-tilted house, a private hermitage: hideout for eyes and heart and breathing brain. By my seventh birthday, I was already reading seriously: Victorian classics by E. Nesbit and Frances Hodgson Burnett, and new books too, like *Mary Poppins, Finn Family Moomintroll,* and *The Children of Green Knowe.* It was as if each book were a bright comfortable person eager to make your acquaintance. "Take *me!*" they called in warm, appealing voices. "Take *me* down! Look at *me!*"

Birkerts says that in reading Nabokov, Woolf, or Bellow, he finds himself "perfectly mapped to that other mind." I know just what he means. Head bowed over a book, it is as if I am myself inventing it – decorating the different rooms, mimicking the voices – in a strange act of simultaneous translation. In listening to the author, I am also listening, deeply, to my own most private self. As a child, I almost never mentioned this to my younger siblings, certainly not to the other girls at school. Even now, I find it hard to believe that such an experience might be shared. I taste the words, and savor them under my breath, rub my thumb against my lips and turn the page. My tongue shifts like a little animal inside my mouth.

"A book is a magic carpet that flies you off elsewhere," writes Jeannette Winterson. "A book is a door. You open it. . . . Do you come back?"

Questions Without Answers

If reading is one form of treasured refuge, drawing us into alignment with our inner lives, writing—especially creative writing—can free us to explore those lives in depth. Where adults brood and dither, afraid of what they might discover, children are at times remarkably fluent.

One summer, I taught a poetry workshop at the Edinburgh Book Festival, working with a mixed group of seven- to thirteen-year-olds. The classes were held in an open tent with two long trestle tables and a scattering of folding chairs, and our theme was "Questions Without Answers." I told the children about my brother James, then aged three or four, staring at the slime inside a broken daffodil. "Why do flowers have silver blood?" he'd asked. I talked about my old friend Daniel, raised in a literary London household, and his anxiety on seeing a crucifix for the first time. "Who is that very sore man on sticks?" Then I flipped through Neruda's *Book of Questions,* and read out random lines: *"What happens to swallows who are late for school?" "Does smoke talk with the clouds?" "How old is November anyway?"* and encouraged them to come up with similar questions of their own.

Some of the children had trouble understanding the assignment. They were used to ordinary questions with ordinary humdrum answers, and my enthusiasm for these unlikely queries baffled them. But one bright-eyed little fellow seized his paper and started writing straight away:

> *What is nothing?*
> *Can nothing be something?*
> *Is it true God is greater than words?*
> *Can we explain something that can't be explained?*
> *How big can a question be?*

I thought he would run out of steam, but the questions grew only more astonishing. Does the devil have a God? he wondered. Can you color a word? Can you write a color? Do questions breathe?

His poem was twenty-six lines long: lucid, calm, impeccably spelled, without a single erasure or a crossing-out. Where had all this come from? The boy seemed startled that I'd even asked.

"I just wonder about things," he told me, "every night before I go to sleep. I think about things like that all the time."

"Questions Without Answers" by Ruairidh Irwin, aged 8

What is nothing?
Can nothing be something?
Is it true God is greater than words?
Can we explain something that can't be explained?
How big can a question be?
Can you do things that can't be done?
Does the devil have a God?
What is a question that can't be answered?
What does the universe do for fun?
Can a number be a word?
Why do we count the alphabet?
Can we use a question as an answer?
Do questions breathe?
Can you fill the universe with questions?
Can we eat time?
Is the past like food that has been eaten?
Can you color a word?
Can you write a color?
Why do we name not explain?
Why do you forget?
How can you break a promise?

Dream Work

I've been attending to my dreams for more than fifty years: writing them down as soon as I wake up, making time to draw them all, however clumsily, and talking them through with friends. I find them almost magically sustaining. One New Year's Day I dreamed a one-line poem, containing only the color blue. Another time, I woke up with the words—in my own voice or someone else's—"*A listening breath, yes, that's right.*" On a third occasion, I was given what I thought of as a leaf meditation. Broken bits of leaf were falling down inside my body, fluttering from head to heart, gusting down each arm and separate leg. The instruction was to watch them as they fell.

Night after night, behind our closed eyelids, we watch a piece of theater designed specifically for us: playful and mysterious, deeply wise. Dreams delight and surprise us, calm us down, offer knotty little koans to set us on our way. In an ever more intrusive, literal-minded world, they return us to our own interior riches, infusing ordinary waking consciousness with a darker, more mysterious kind of knowing.

Soon after my younger sister was diagnosed with ovarian cancer, I woke from a dream about my teenage niece, Susanna. We were sitting together at the kitchen table, in the midst of an impassioned falling out.

"*I hate you! I hate you!*" she cried.

"You don't have to like me," I told her calmly. "You have full permission to hate me as much as you want. But would you like to lie down?"

She leaned against me, light as a blown seed, then pulled two chairs together under the table, lay down and fell asleep. Next thing I knew, she'd slipped sideways off the chairs, smashing her face on the hard floor. I began to sob uncontrollably. The squabble with Susanna (made literal in her "falling out" of the two chairs) felt almost unbearably momentous. When the dream continued, and I joined the family in the Emergency Room, I saw that each had a huge bruise on their pale cheek.

Weeks later, given the chance to shape a dream in clay, I knew at once which one I wanted to explore.

The clay was silky-soft, elastic, malleable. I rolled it out onto the table, shaped a head, the rough chrysalis of a body. Then I shaped the family: five narrow watching figures, each with the same stark print across their cheek. Across the table, one friend made a tree and then a treehouse, a nest, a wide-spread hand; another shaped a dolphin in mid-leap.

There was clay left over, moist and promising.

I hesitated for a moment, closed my eyes. It was as if the clay were leading me, showing me what to do. In my journal I found the image of a house that at the same time was a bird with outspread wings. I shaped that too. And then I saw that if I wadded it together, I could turn the bird into a peacock, and the "roof" would become its tail. I pulled out a curvy neck, a proud and jutting head, recut the zig-zag patterns on its sides. The bird was large and authoritative, towering over the little human tableau, my own hunched and weeping self. A line from Wallace Stevens came to me. "Do you remember the cry of the peacock?"

It echoed back to childhood, to the noisy birds screeching on the lawn behind our house, the outraged flutter of wings when we came too close. But it was yet more potent, as if I were being reminded of some older story I had half-forgotten or had never known. *Do you remember the cry of the peacock?* The peacock was sacred to Juno/ Hera, and before that to Saraswati, Indian goddess of wisdom, and to the great Goddess herself. It is a guardian being, deeply maternal. The tail alone carries one thousand eyes.

My family was in peril, wounded, stricken, each with the mark of death on their pale cheek. The peacock was miraculous, a divine protector. And the hands had understood—had listened inwards—had somehow known what needed to be done.

And There Was Light

"When you take the time to draw on your listening-imagination," writes John O'Donohue, "you will begin to hear this gentle voice at the heart of your life." A number of excellent books have now been published with listening as their theme. But in terms of attending to that gentle voice, my clear favorite is *And There Was Light* by the French writer Jacques Lusseyran—a radiant memoir, in which he describes his early, sighted childhood, and what happened after he was struck blind at the age of seven and a half.

Lusseyran was a lively, energetic child, who loved to run and to explore. But one April, as the family prepared to return to Paris after their Easter vacation, he was overcome by a powerful foreboding, and began to cry. He could see the sunlight on the path, the rows of vegetables, and somehow knew that he was seeing them for the last time.

Three weeks later, Lusseyran was at school. When the bell for recess sounded, all the children raced towards the door. In the crush, someone pushed against him from behind, knocking him into the sharp corner of the teacher's desk. One arm of his glasses gouged deep into his right eye, and the second eye was also traumatized, and had to be surgically excised. By the time he returned to consciousness, he was completely blind.

The shock, of course, was tremendous. But Lusseyran recovered with astonishing speed. Blinded on May 3, by the end of the month he was already walking, clinging to the hand of one of his parents, "but still walking, and without any difficulty." In June, he began to learn Braille. By July, he was running and playing with a crowd of other children, hanging by the trapeze, and sliding down the slides, building sand castles on a broad Atlantic beach.

Grown-ups told him that to be blind meant "not to see." But for Lusseyran, that simply wasn't true. After a short struggle to use his eyes in the old way, he realized that he was looking "too far off, and too much on the surface of things," and began to change course, looking more closely "from an inner place to one further within." Almost immediately, his surroundings were transformed. From that time on, and even in his dreams, he described himself as living "in a stream of light."

Lusseyran saw light, and went on seeing it, although he was blind. And not only light, but color too. Everyone he met had their characteristic color. This was true of his family and his friends, and in particular of a little girl called Nicole, who for him was "like a great red star, or . . . a ripe cherry." When she came to sit by him, he saw "rosy reflections in the canvas of the awnings." The sea itself took on a purple tinge. He followed her by the red shadows that trailed in her wake.

Still, there were times when both light and color faded, almost to the point of vanishing. It happened every time he was afraid. Anger and impatience had the same effect. He would see "black butterflies everywhere," or, worse, see almost nothing. The only way to move around the house or garden, he writes, "was by not thinking at all, or thinking as little as possible." Then he slipped between obstacles "the way they say bats do."

Lusseyran had always loved to listen, but now his listening became essential, helping to orient his every move. He heard the floorboards creaking as he crossed a room, the chink of the plaster statue on the mantelpiece, the tiny sounds as the window panes shifted in their plaster frames. When he entered his bedroom, he heard "the bed, the wardrobe, the chairs . . . stretching, yawning, and catching their breath."

His parents (both musicians) left him free to multiply sounds to his heart's content, tossing pebbles, singing, ringing bells, leaning back against the trunks of trees. "Everything talked," he writes. Oaks, poplars, hazelnuts, and willows all had their own distinctive voice. Soon, Lusseyran could walk down a country road, and describe the shape of the trees to either side, even if they were not spaced at regular intervals. Each tree revealed its height and bulk and looming presence: short and scrubby, elegant and tall.

Rocks too, could be distinguished from a distance, likewise the shape of the surrounding countryside. "Just look!" Lusseyran would tell his good friend Jean as they climbed a hill. "This time we're on top. You'll see the whole bend of the river, unless the sun gets in your eyes!" And to Jean's amazement, he would be entirely right.

Listening was a practical necessity for Lusseyran—a physical skill honed to the point of genius. But it was also metaphysical. In order "to live without eyes," he had to remain attentive and alert, to refuse all irritation, anger, and impatience. Six years later, when the Germans invaded Paris, and he became a member of the youth resistance, that clarity of purpose, that absolute moral stamina, were to resonate through everything he did.

Consider the following quotations:

It is easier to sail many thousand miles through cold and storm and cannibals . . . than it is to explore the private sea, the Atlantic and Pacific Ocean, of one's being alone.

Henry David Thoreau

The mind's ear is as potent as its eye.

Robert Bringhurst

Continue to explore:

Make time to listen to your own inner voices. What do they have to say?

Commit to keeping a dream journal, in which to write or draw or paint your dreams.

~: 3 :~

The One Who Listens

I want to talk about everything with at least one human being as I talk to myself.

Fyodor Dostoevsky

Arthur's Aunt Annie

Arthur Strimling is in his eighties now, a sturdy, handsome man with a head of silver-grey curls. He grew up in the Midwest, the son of progressive Jewish parents, and as a small boy, he loved listening to them talk. "My parents were really terrific conversationalists, so there was always good—lively!—smart talk in my house, and I really loved it." But they themselves were not good listeners. Strimling always had the sense of being judged, of being obliged to supply what were seen as the right answers. "I learned as a child to go underground, to be like a cockroach, you know. Just run out in the dark, grab what you need, and get back in your hole, fast."

His parents believed that love consisted in saying the worst thing you could possibly say to those you cared about, and defended their behavior in exactly those terms. But for Strimling such fiercely qualified affection was not enough. He was hungry for more generous and capacious listening. And he found it in his mother's sister, Annie Klein. "I first found someone to listen to me in my Aunt Annie," he says now. "She's the first adult I ever trusted in my life. And the revelation was that there was so much inside of me to say."

Annie Klein lived in upstate New York, in a big, old, pre-Revolutionary house with an enormous kitchen. The Strimlings would drive out from Minnesota two or three times a year, and stay with her for days, or even weeks. Arthur remembers sitting on a counter while his aunt was cooking, and *talking, talking,* all day long. "I didn't know what I knew until I could start talking to somebody who listened. It was revelation, it was ecstasy. And it was terror. Cause I was very afraid of what would come out. But Annie was there. And I could talk to her. And I loved that."

How We Listen

The human ear is a marvelously intricate mechanism, made up of the outer ear or pinna, the tiny bones of the middle ear, and the fluid-filled cochlea, crammed with sensory hair cells. When someone speaks or sings, the sound is gathered by the pinna, then travels down the ear canal, and hits the eardrum, causing it to vibrate. That vibration is amplified by the ossicles, the so-called hammer, anvil, and stirrup, each one as minute and delicate as a piece of finely carved netsuke. These in turn vibrate the oval window, opening into the snail-shaped cochlea of the inner ear. Here sound is translated into electrical signals and sent on to the brain. Because human beings have no "ear lids," we have no way to muffle the receptivity of our eardrums, or to still the tremulous connectivity of those tiny bones. We simply can't *not hear.* We catch the shrill of a chickadee outside our morning window, the long resonant purr of a contented cat. In a darkened theater, we recognize the intake of our lover's breath.

Or rather say, that such refined and conscious listening is available to most of us: a bodily option, a simple human pleasure. Which does not mean we always take advantage of it. As most of us understand only too well, *hearing* is one thing, and *listening* another.

"Listening is receptive," says the composer W. A. Mathieu. "You allow something outside your body to come inside, into your deep brain, into your private of privates." And again, "Learning to listen takes time and patience, like training a small muscle."

44

The One Who Listened

By the time I was eleven or twelve, I would be summoned downstairs to make up the numbers at grown-up dinner. I was expected to talk to the gentleman on my left for five or ten minutes, and then turn to the gentleman on my right. I listened with attention to their huntin', shootin', fishin' talk, marveled at their raucous politics. Some were dry and formal; others did their best to make me laugh. I almost always tried to be polite. But when my painter uncle came up from London with his paramour, the beautiful Lady Egremont, I knelt on the carpet between them, drinking in their energy and intimacy, listening, shamelessly, to their tales of the Far East. This was what conversation was *supposed* to be. I wanted to dissolve into the little space between them, to be translated, magically, into another life.

Of the few who really listened to me in those days (among them my sister Kate, our nanny, Cathy Ainsley, and a couple of girls at my new boarding school), the one I remember best is my father's mother, my beloved Grandmama.

Grandmama lived by herself in a little house called Flourish Walls, not far from Marchmont. Her husband had died a few years earlier, and she was then in her sixties, a slim upright woman with forget-me-not blue eyes and soft curly hair ("mouse's hair," she called it) most often tinted lavender or grayish blue. She had a distinct presence, some quality of clarity and decisiveness, and what some saw as an altogether too-well-developed sense of class and caste. But as her "darling favorite eldest granddaughter" (the eldest of the McEwen grandchildren, and for a while, the only girl), I early on found favor in her eyes. She would have me to stay for the best part of a weekend—Friday night, all of Saturday, most of Sunday—and I rejoiced in every precious minute. Grandmama was mine, blissfully mine, and I was entirely hers.

When I was sent away to boarding school in Sussex, she wrote to me almost every week. Whether she was remembering her own boarding school in 1915—"We were supposed to wear an apron in our baths (though I don't think anyone put them on)," or describing my cousin Hugo and my brother John (then barely five) walking "very slowly by themselves, talking like two old bachelors" as they collected fir cones for her fire, her letters were always vivid and engaging. I read them as one would read a sheet of music, her voice sounding directly in my ear. Here, for example, she records for me her joy in witnessing a lunar rainbow. "There was an almost full harvest moon, and the air was full of tiny raindrops, and this silver ghost of a day-time rainbow stretched, a perfect arc, over the glimmering fields." It was, she said, "very strange and lovely and magical."

Every time that Grandmama wrote to me, I responded with a letter of my own. "I always like seeing your handwriting on an envelope," she told me. "So neat and prim, rather like a Jenny Wren might write." Not that she saw me as a Jenny Wren. "More like a stormy petrel," she decided, "with dashes of kingfisher." Such endearments made their way into the letters themselves. "My darling Miss Pussy Cat," she called me, or "My darling Squirrel Nutkin," signing off in equally lavish style, "Dearest love, my little Greek sea urchin," or "Dearest love, my darling Jenny-Wren-stormy-petrel-kingfisher, Your doting Grandmama." Perhaps she hoped her kindness would protect me, at least a little, as I moved out into the larger world. "Only three years till you are grown up," she noted, the month I turned fourteen. "What a sobering thought."

Because my letters to her have not survived, it is impossible to reconstruct the full flavor of our correspondence. Like me, Grandmama had been the eldest of four sisters; like me, she had been seen as moody and bossy, quick to take offense. *What did I mean to her?* I wonder now. *Had she been something of a stormy petrel too?* I only know that I felt safe with her, and deeply loved, allowed to criticize and make connections, to read and write, luxuriate, explore. I could give voice to my homesickness far away at boarding school, my struggles with math and chemistry and physics, my growing anxiety about my father's health. Grandmama had patience for all of it. She sheltered me and made me welcome, spoiled me, gave me time.

For several crucial years, both in person and on paper, she was the one who listened.

Katie's Letters

Grandmama died in September 1971, when I was only fifteen. For a long time, it seemed as if there were nobody to talk to. But as my sister Kate grew older, and was herself sent off to boarding school, each of us became for the other the one who listened—if not in person, during the holidays, then, once again, through letters. Hers were lengthy and detailed and lavishly embellished: a beautiful washy waterfall tumbling over blue rocks under a crescent moon, a Merlin figure scattering stars. One letter had a tiny illustration for each line of the address: a McEwen tartan scarf (for my surname), knives and forks and spoons (for the street name, Sheffield Terrace), the outline of St. Paul's and a policeman's hat (for London). Another was written almost entirely in her own invented hieroglyphics.

Turning them over now, I realize just how much got named between us, from country pleasures like guddling (catching fish with one's hands) or collecting beech-nuts to a prolonged consideration of what it meant to be a woman. We were intensely interested in each other's lives, not just what we were seeing or doing, but the interior journey too, the private tale of books, thoughts, revelations—what Kate once called *the beautiful, almost imperceptible progression.*

But there were deeper issues too, which we were able to broach only with each other, like Kate's difficulty in talking to our mother, or her questions about the family house and Papa running it.

> I mean what do you think? Is it right? Children begin
> by loving their parents, then they judge them. . . . I was
> wondering what my judgment here was—and will I
> forgive him? I hope you understand. I am referring to
> the twenty years he spent making sure that Marchmont
> would not go—. . . . Aren't there BETTER things he
> could have done? He is really clever—talented. That is
> why I want to ask you.

It was exactly the sort of question I might have raised myself. At some point I must have said to Kate how grateful I was for such talks, and how pleased I was that we were sisters. She shrugged off the compliment in her own sweetly oblique fashion:

I'm glad you're glad I'm your sister. I'm probably glad
you're mine as well but being someone's sister or
brother or having sisters and brothers—well, they are
so bound up in yourself that you can't really say about
them—if they hadn't been born who would you be?

It was a fair question. By then our character and interests were so intricately intertwined that neither of us could have said who was influencing whom. Our worlds meshed far down into dreamland:

Last night I dreamt that you had written poems of your
own in the back of *The Prophet*. I was disappointed on
waking to find that of course you had not.

And again:

Dearest MC, Whenever I lose a thread and get a letter
from you, I find that you still have it. Goodness, it is
good to have someone to write to. . . . I have only to
write one word and you know *where* I mean, not just
what I mean.

We trusted one another's take on things, each other's judgment and sensibility, at a time when we trusted absolutely no one else's. Other teenagers—the children of our parents' friends—baffled and dismayed us. *I have come to the definite conclusion*, Kate wrote, *that I simply can't stand girls of my own age*, however *nice, interesting, whatever*. Neither of us had read Adrienne Rich at that point, but we both sought androgyny, seeing it as refuge from the usual female roles and expectations: cashmere jerseys, high-heeled shoes, a poised sophistication. Meanwhile we kept on writing to each other, kept on listening, doing our best to create a private enclave where our work could flourish: my poems, Katie's paintings, our mutual exploration of the larger world. Half a century later, the letters track our talk: the only praise that really mattered was our own.

Gifted Listeners

Kate and I were both big readers, making our way through the black-backed Penguin Classics, devouring Tolstoy and Chekhov and Dostoevsky. We were especially fond of Alyosha in *The Brothers Karamazov,* "a clear-eyed young man of nineteen, radiant with health." His looks satisfied us immediately: "very handsome, graceful, moderately tall, with dark brown hair . . . a rather long, oval-shaped face, and wide-set dark gray eyes." But it was his temperament that attracted us most. He was described as "bright and good-tempered . . . very thoughtful and serene." Above all, he was a careful listener.

Alyosha is, of course, a fictional character. But there are superb listeners to be found in nonfiction work as well, among them the grandfather of the Israeli writer, Amoz Oz, and the father of the American writer, Brian Doyle, all, alas, now dead. In his memoir, *A Tale of Love and Darkness,* Oz explores the secret of his grandfather's charm, which, he says, he only came to understand years later:

> He possessed a quality that is hardly ever found among men, a marvelous quality that for many women is the sexiest in a man.
>
> He listened.
>
> He did not just politely pretend to listen, while impatiently waiting for her to finish what she was saying and shut up.
>
> He did not break into his partner's sentence and finish it for her.
>
> He did not cut in to sum up what she was saying so as to move on to another subject . . .
>
> He was in no hurry, and he never rushed her. He would wait for her to finish, and even when she had finished, he did not pounce or grab but enjoyed waiting in case there was something more, in case she was carried along by another wave.

Oz's account is so deft and affectionate one can imagine offering it as a brief instruction sheet on "generous listening." The same is true of

Doyle's essay on his father. Here Doyle explores the crucial stages of his father's listening: first the listening itself, the pause, the encouragement, and then (and only then) the commentary.

> And he did this not once but many thousands of times
> . . . so that the number of times he listened patiently
> and attentively and scrupulously, and then politely
> waited a few beats to give a speaker a chance to dig
> deeper into or clamber hurriedly out of the hole he had
> just dug himself, and then said something gentle and
> encouraging before tacking finally toward the subject
> at hand, surely was a million or more. . . .

Unlike most people, for whom "the jockeying, the topping, the shouting of self, the obviation of the other, is the prime work in conversation," for Doyle's father, that tender, scrupulous listening was what mattered most. Deep into old age, he remained for Doyle the most gifted listener he had ever known.

Tell Me a Story

Long ago, when I was already living in the United States, somebody I loved died back in Scotland. Her name was Mrs. Shirer. She was short and stout, with pure white hair and mischievous black eyes. For years she had worked for my family, peeling onions, scouring potatoes and carrots, making thick nourishing broths and serviceable stews. I remembered her worn cotton pinafore, pulled tight around her middle, her cobwebby wrinkles, the soft dewlaps on her neck and upper arms. I remembered sitting with her over tea and biscuits in her tiny house, how well she'd listened, how deeply kind to me she'd always been.

And now she was dead, and I was far away in western Massachusetts, with nobody to remember her with, nobody to mourn. Until my friend Arthur happened to call, and I mentioned she had died. "Tell me a story about her," he said. And so, I did. I told him about her busy hands and smiling wrinkles, how generous she'd been, how very kind. I told it all. And at once the grief was lightened. He didn't need to know Mrs. Shirer in order to provide solace. He only needed to know me. He only needed to offer me a listening ear.

Distant Neighbors

Biography and autobiography, literary and social history, personal memoirs, letters and journals are all rich sources for the study of close friends—those who, in Gertrude Stein's lovely phrase, possess "the skillful audacity required to share an inner life." I am especially fond of *Words in Air*, the complete correspondence between Elizabeth Bishop and Robert Lowell, and of *The Element of Lavishness*, a gathering of letters between Sylvia Townsend Warner and her editor, William Maxwell. But my current favorite is *Distant Neighbors: The Selected Letters of Wendell Berry and Gary Snyder*, first published in 2014.

The two men first met in the early 1970s, introduced by the Bay Area publisher Jack Shoemaker. By then, they already knew and admired each other's work. Both were passionately committed to their own home ground, and had parallel interests in writing and literature, philosophy, anthropology, economics, and the environment. Snyder was a radical, a practicing Buddhist; Berry, a committed agriculturalist, and a Christian. But their differences were energizing. "If we agreed about everything," writes Berry, "what would we have to say to each other? I'm for conversation."

In 1977, they did a reading together at the San Francisco Museum of Modern Art, each reading a poem dedicated to the other. Afterwards, Berry and his wife visited Snyder at Kitkitdizze, the family homestead in the Sierra Nevada foothills.

> Our arrival at Gary's place . . . was like coming out of a tunnel. We were with the people we had come to see, and for a day and a half had no appointments. Natural and human events took place around us because of their own necessities—a kind of generosity in that, permitting rest. We had the deer stepping unafraid through the clearing, the windy light shimmering in the pines, good food, fire, laughter, the company of friends."

They were neighbors, Berry decided, *distant* neighbors.

In the years that followed, the two men visited at intervals, but mostly stayed in touch through letters, consistently inspired by one another's life and writing. Here, for example, is Gary Snyder, writing in response to Berry's "Three Memorial Poems:"

> Brave poems—they send me back to my own life refreshed; work joyfully in impermanence!

And here is Berry, complimenting Snyder after reading a recent interview in *East West Journal:*

> Your words, everywhere I find them, give me the sense of being spoken not just to, but *for.* What a relief! . . . In what you say, I don't hear you speaking as a poet, but as a friend and fellow worker.

Children were born, marriages made and broken, more books were written, and somehow there was always more to say. "The longer I go without seeing you, the more things I think up to ask you and tell you," Berry writes. "You'll never hear the half of it." Once again, the differences were generative. "Sometimes my awareness of where you are standing gives me a sort of binocular vision," he tells Snyder. And Snyder too pays tribute to all he's learned from Berry. "My Occidental hat is off to you," he writes, "and my Oriental side is making a deep namaste bow to you." And again, emphatic, as if underlined in light, "*I love our long distance friendship.*"

The Harpist and His Friend

Among the many stories compiled by Paul Reps in the tiny classic, *Zen Flesh, Zen Bones,* is this one, about a harpist and his friend.

Long ago, in ancient China, there were two friends, one of whom knew how to play the harp—oh, so beautifully!—and another, who knew how to listen.

When the harpist played a song about a mountain, his friend would say, "I can see it rising up before my eyes."

When he sang and played a song about a river, the listener would cry out, "Now I see the waterfalls, the slow deep pools."

But the listener fell ill and died. And after that, the harpist cut the strings of his harp, and never played again. *Why not?* people asked. Because, he told them, there was no one left to listen.

Chekhov's "Grief"

Jessica Beckham lives in the California coastal city of Alameda and teaches at a school in San Francisco. She has an hour-long commute each way, involving the BART train and two buses. As she struggles to find herself a seat, she looks round at her fellow passengers, some busy with books or magazines, most bowed over the slim rectangles of their phones. "I wish I could carry a sign," she says. "*I'm reading a book. You're reading a book. Please be my friend.*" Or, "*I'm trying to get off my phone. Please talk to me.*"

Beckham is not alone in her hunger for embodied company. In a survey of 20,000 Americans, conducted back in 2018, almost half said they lacked "meaningful, in-person social interactions on a daily basis," and that, of course, was prior to the pandemic. We tend to see this as a contemporary issue, exacerbated by digital distraction, by what one might call "hurry sickness," and by the rise in human-generated noise. But it also reaches back deep into the past. One of my favorite examples is a tiny six-page parable by the nineteenth-century Russian writer, Anton Chekhov.

It opens at dusk on a winter evening, with thick wet snowflakes swirling under the newly lighted lamps and settling on the hats and shoulders of the passersby. A cab driver, Iona Potapov, sits on his box waiting for a fare. He and his little mare are white from head to foot with falling snow.

As the mist gathers over the city of St. Petersburg, the lights grow brighter, and the street becomes rowdier and more crowded. "Cabby!" someone calls, and Iona jumps. An officer in a greatcoat is looking for a ride.

Iona picks up the reins and smacks his lips at the mare. The officer gets in, Iona flourishes his whip, and the sleigh is on its way. But a coachman swears at him, a pedestrian glares at him, and the officer berates him for his careless driving. Iona hardly seems to know what he is doing. When the officer tries to chaff him, he stares back, open-mouthed.

"What?" asks the officer.

Iona's voice is gruff. "My son, sir, he died this week."

"What did he die of?" asks the man.

But when Iona turns and starts to explain—the high fever, the three days in the hospital—the officer loses patience. "Turn back round!" he orders. "Use your eyes! Keep moving!"

Iona settles back in his seat, and once more flourishes his whip. He glances round at his fare, but the man has closed his eyes, and it is obvious he doesn't want to engage. Iona lets him down just north of the river and stops to wait outside a tavern. Two more hours go by.

At last, three young men appear out of the darkness, two of them tall and thin, one short and hunchbacked. Again, Iona tries to talk to them, but to no avail. He delivers them safely to their destination, and looks around, desperately, for just one person who will listen. But the crowds hurry by without noticing him.

Iona trundles the sleigh a little further and abandons himself to his grief. But after barely five minutes, he gives a sharp tug at the reins. "The stable," he says, and the little mare starts off at once, as if she understood.

An hour and a half later, he is sitting by a big dirty stove. A number of other drivers are snoring all around him, and the air is fuggy and hot. There's a young cab driver over in the corner, and again, Iona can't resist mentioning his grief. But the young cabby wraps his head in his arms and goes to sleep. Iona sighs. It's almost a week since his son's death, and he hasn't been able to talk about it properly to anyone. It needs to be told slowly and carefully: how his son fell ill, how he suffered, what he said before he died, how he died. Every detail of the funeral needs to be described, plus the journey to the hospital to fetch his clothes. It is an enormous thing he has to tell.

Finally, he pulls on his coat, and goes out to the stables, thinking about the corn, the hay, the bitter weather. "I can sleep later on," he tells himself.

"Are you enjoying yourself?" he asks the little mare, looking into her bright eyes. "Go on, dig right in. We may not have earned our corn, but we can certainly eat hay. Yes! I'm too old to drive," he adds. "My son could have done it. If only he had lived."

He is silent for a moment, then continues, "That's how it is, my friend. There's no more Kuzma Ionitch. He's left us on our own. Now, let's imagine that you had a foal, you were that foal's mother, and suddenly that foal died, and left you to live on after him. It would be hard, wouldn't it?"

The little mare munches, listens, and snorts warm breath into her master's hand.

Iona's feelings are too much for him, and he tells the little mare the whole long story.

Consider the following quotations:

A student came to her teacher, the writer, Grace Paley, and told her, "I have nothing to say." And Paley said, "Yes you do. You just don't have anyone to say it to. Say it to me.

Christian McEwen

My whole life, I've been waiting for someone to find me and I would tell them everything . . . and they would keep asking, 'And then what? And then what?'

Svetlana Alexievich

Continue to explore:

Remember a time when you felt completely listened to. Who was doing the listening? What did that person do?

Is there anyone with whom you maintain a long-distance friendship? What form does it take? (e-mail, letters, phone calls, Skype or Zoom . . .)

~ 4 ~

The Beloved Voice

I thank you for your voices. Thank you.
Your most sweet voices.

Shakespeare

Vocal Nourishment

Hearing is the first sense to develop in the human fetus, as it is the last to depart the dying body. The tiny ossicles, or inner ear bones, reach full size half way through the second trimester. Five months after conception, the fetus hears little more than the rush of blood through the uterus and the gurgle of its mother's digestive system, along with the double murmur of their paired heart beats. But as it continues to grow, the womb grows with it, and the outer world becomes increasingly audible. Tucked in its own domed amplifying chamber (curled, oddly enough, in the shape of an ear), it can make out the whine of the refrigerator, the roar of the vacuum cleaner, and always, the pure, familiar cadence of its mother's voice.

Then comes the cacophony of labor, the aural assault of the delivery. For the first six months of life, sight, touch, and hearing are bewilderingly intertwined. But little by little, the infant learns to separate and savor each of the different senses, and half a lifetime later, the adult harkens back to those first remembered sounds. "I'd be conducting a score for the first time," said the conductor Boris Brott, "and suddenly the cello line would pop out at me." He had no idea why. It took his mother, a professional cellist, to provide an explanation. All the pieces he "recognized" were ones she'd played when he was still a child in utero.

For those lucky enough to receive calm and affectionate parenting, the mother's voice remains a steady source of energy, causing oxytocin to be secreted in the brain. Each time the little one is fed or changed or sung to, he drinks in his mother's warmth and touch and smell, and most crucially, the unique timbre of her voice. Surrounded by a random group of adults, each greeting him by name, the child will not respond at all until his mother speaks—at which point he will turn towards her, like a plant turning eagerly towards the sun. "The vocal nourishment that the mother provides . . . is just as important to the child's development as her milk," writes ear specialist Alfred A. Tomatis.

Music may in fact "have a developmental . . . priority over language," notes the archaeologist Stephen Mithin, given how strongly human infants are drawn to melodious *motherese*, much preferring it to ordinary adult speech. Such baby talk or IDS (infant-directed speech) includes a much higher pitch than normal, as well as hyperarticulated vowels, shorter words and phrases, and considerably more repetition. Its slow singsong patterns of intonation can be found, virtually identical, across the globe. A correlation has been found between the amount of IDS a child receives and the degree to which he grows and thrives. "I dozed on and off listening to my mother's voice," writes the novelist Elizabeth Strout. "I thought: All I want is this."

Coming to Our Senses

It was the week before Christmas, and my six-year-old niece had joined the other carolers in the town square. I watched her as she danced from foot to foot, her whole small body filled up with the sound. What was she singing? Something with a merry rollicking tune and a persistent beat. Something she loved to sing, and already knew by heart. The grown-ups towered above her in their winter coats: black and grey and brown and navy blue. She danced among them like a wood-sprite in the darkness of the woods. Her clear child's voice rang out, a living flame.

What Susanna could achieve unselfconsciously at six, losing herself in sound, in full embodiment, comes far less easily to most adults. Most of us identify almost entirely with the small fortress of the head, not realizing that we have a second brain in our gut: a dense web of neurons lining the intestinal tract, the so-called "pelvic intelligence" or "mind palace." Learning to honor that belly wisdom can be powerfully transformative, especially when combined with music, played or sung. One of my favorite examples of this is a little story about listening told by the depth psychologist Carl Jung.

Jung had had a new patient referred to him, suffering from what her doctor called "incurable" insomnia. She was a woman in her mid-twenties, from a very modest background, who had recently qualified as a teacher. But she was tormented by anxiety in her new role, afraid of being found unworthy or of making some irreparable mistake, and had worked herself into a tremendous state of nervous tension.

Jung saw at once that she needed to relax, and began by using himself as an example, explaining how much he liked to go out sailing, letting himself fly with the wind across the lake. "We all need some form of recreation," he told his patient. But he could tell by her eyes that she didn't really understand what he was saying.

Then, as he continued to talk about sailing and the wind, Jung somehow "heard" his mother's voice. She was singing a lullaby to his younger sister, a story about a little girl in a little boat on the river Rhine. Hardly knowing what he did, he began to hum his own words, about the wind, the waves, the lake, and calming down, to the tune of his mother's lullaby.

"I hummed those sensations," he said later. "And I could see she was 'enchanted.'"

The hour came to an end, and the session was over. Jung never saw the young woman again. But her story stayed with him. Years later, he met her referring doctor at a conference, and asked what had become of her. The man reported that she'd come back cured, though he himself had no idea why. "Because all she could tell me was some story about sailing and the wind, and I never could get her to tell me what you really did. . . . Of course, I know it's impossible that you only hummed her a song about a boat."

And yet that was exactly what Jung had done. He had known to attend to something deep inside himself, some belly wisdom, some pelvic intelligence, and had understood what best to do.

"How was I to tell him that I had sung her a lullaby with my mother's voice?" he wondered. "Enchantment like that is the oldest form of medicine."

The Family Voice

Tucked away in one of my many boxes is a cassette tape made by my father in the early seventies. He'd been given a tape recorder for his birthday and was trying it out for the first time. There on the tape is Papa's warm, dry voice, the breathy voices of the younger children. My brother sings a snatch of "Boney was a warrior," my sister emits a burst of nervous laughter. Someone squeals. Papa presses the buttons on his brand new gadget, rewinds the tape.

My father died in 1980, and James and Katie three years later. I have not heard their voices for more than forty years. And yet I'd know them anywhere: a single word would do it, a sharp intake of breath. We are all of us hard-wired to recognize the family voice, even in its minutest manifestations: our sweetheart's murmur at a crowded cocktail party, our grandson calling on a crackly cellphone. We've heard them so often that we've actually reworked the synapses in our brain.

Our mother's voice is, of course, especially resonant. Each time a pregnant woman speaks or croons or hums, her unborn child receives a mini massage. The fetus' heartbeat will quicken when its mother reads a poem, and slow down when a stranger's voice is heard. As long as a year after birth, babies are drawn to the songs and music they first heard in the womb. "My first conscious memory is the singing of ballads," wrote the naturalist, John Muir, "And I doubt not they will be ringing in my ears when I am dying."

Neuroscientist Seth S. Horowitz points out that such listening concerns itself less with the content of what is being said than with the flow of tones or "prosody." This is processed by the brain's right hemisphere, which has to do with context and emotional issues (as opposed to the Wernicke's region, which deals with speech comprehension). Just as a child is soothed by lullabies and repeated rhythmic movement (his mother rocking him, or patting him on the back), so the voice alone has power to soothe and heal.

After Julian Bell was killed in the Spanish Civil War, Virginia Woolf visited his mother, Vanessa, almost every day. "I cannot ever say how Virginia has helped me," Bell wrote to their good friend, Vita. "Perhaps someday, not now, you will be able to tell her it's true."

The word "conversation" comes from the Old French, via the Latin *conversatio*, from the verb *conversari*, "to keep company (with)." It implies familiarity, intimacy. Nested in there too is the word "verse," from the Latin *versus*, "to turn." When we talk, we tend to turn towards one another and look into each other's eyes. Neuroscientists explain that such a gaze draws our voices into a similar pitch or rhythm, while also enhancing empathy and intuition. But at times the experience can be even more delicious when the voice alone is heard.

I think back to a spring evening ten or twelve years ago. Some friends and I were sitting around the dinner table when all of a sudden, the electric power went out. Instead of the usual panicked rush for candles, we sat on into the gloaming, listening, telling stories. There was a palpable relief, even among ourselves, in becoming for a time invisible, freed from the pressure of the public gaze. It was as if we were all tucked up in a giant bed together, dreamy children, traveling through the dark. Voices murmured quietly around the table, glasses clinked. It was an hour before anyone got up to find a light.

Another Self

James Lees-Milne was an English writer and architectural historian who worked for many years with the National Trust. He wrote a number of biographies, including a study of his good friend, Harold Nicolson, and several volumes of architectural history. But he is best known for his diaries—wry, outrageous, catty, self-revealing—and for his eccentric autobiography, *Another Self.*

Most of this engages what is now familiar territory: the philistine father and flighty mother, with Lees-Milne as the sensitive misfit son. His father raves at art and artists (his most damning adjective is the word "artistic"), and his mother abandons the family, literally taking off in a balloon. The tale reaches a peak of awfulness at a grand house outside Oxford, during a drunken party, when the host takes potshots at a statue of Apollo, and slashes at the family portraits with a hunting crop. Then and there, Lees-Milne vows to devote himself to preserving the country houses of England—as indeed he goes on to do with huge success.

So far, so predictably engrossing. But *Another Self* portrays another self than that Lees-Milne. Or perhaps one might say that it unfurls a surprising kindred spirit, at least towards the very, very end. Tender, heartfelt, utterly unironic, the last four pages describe a wartime love affair conducted entirely on the phone.

Lees-Milne served as an officer in the Irish Guards during World War II, until he was caught by a bomb in Battersea, and invalided out. He spent months in a series of different hospitals, returning to London in the gaps between. Late one night he was trying to ring a friend, when his line was crossed with a stranger's, also trying to make a call. "My line is Grosvenor 8527," he heard her tell the operator. She had asked for a Hampstead number. "Instead of which you've hitched me up with Flaxman something. This poor man doesn't want to talk to me at all."

"Oh yes, I do," Lees-Milne broke in, immediately charmed by her voice, which he thought sounded harmonious and clever. They both apologized. But when he rang back a moment later, and got the same crossed line, they talked for twenty minutes. The woman had been trying to reach her elderly mother, who suffered from insomnia, and Lees-Milne had been trying to contact a particular friend. After explaining this, they went on to discuss books (she'd been reading Balzac), and of course the war. "I don't remember enjoying a talk so much for years," said Lees-Milne, before hanging up. And the woman agreed. "It was fun, wasn't it?"

All next day, Lees-Milne found himself preoccupied by the conversation. He remembered the woman's spontaneity and enthusiasm, and the "musical modulation" of her voice. Usually, he forgot other people's phone numbers. But for some reason, he remembered hers: Grosvenor 8527. He repeated it to himself as he walked the city streets, and even took the time to write it down.

That night, as he lay reading, he could hardly keep his mind on his book. The woman's number played over in his head. At last, he couldn't bear it any longer. He got up, went to the phone, and dialed the number. "Hello, it's me," he told her. "So sorry to be a bore, but may we continue our conversation where we left off last night?"

At once the woman launched into an account of Balzac's *Cousin Bette*, and soon the two of them were laughing and joking as if they had known each other for years. They talked for a full three-quarters of an hour. The late hour and their anonymity broke down all conventional reserves, and again they both spoke freely, spaciously, without restraint. "Perhaps we should introduce ourselves," Lees-Milne suggested at one point. But the woman liked the fact that they were strangers. If they'd had friends or family in common, they could never have discussed their lives so openly. After the war, she said, they could reveal themselves to one another. In the meantime, she agreed to make a note of Lees-Milne's number.

The connection only deepened in the months that followed. Twenty-five years later, when he came to write about it, Lees-Milne described it as "perhaps the most intimate and delicious friendship" of his life. He learned very little about the woman he came to call Egeria (named for a legendary Roman nymph)—just that she was thirty-six years old (not much older than he was himself) and had been married at seventeen to a man from whom she was now separated. Her only son, Billy, had recently been killed in action, and she spoke of him as if he were still alive. Lees-Milne, too, came to think of Billy as a son, and referred to him with great fondness and familiarity. But there were no subjects they did not discuss. They even took to reading the same books, borrowing them in turn from the London Library. When he was finally discharged from his last hospital, Lees-Milne rented a small house in Chelsea, and the two of them talked to each other every night, no matter what the hour.

Still, there were times when Lees-Milne found the situation almost intolerable. He would threaten to rush across town and show up on Egeria's doorstep. "We know each other now better than any couple in the world. And we love each other as much. Let's stop this pantomime." But she refused to give way, afraid of the consequences if it turned out they didn't love one other after all.

London was still under regular bombardment, and during especially bad raids, Lees-Milne would ring up to check on his beloved. He had grown used to the "swift, disengaged purr" of the bell at the other end, and felt able to tell by the very first ring whether or not she was there. "If she was at home, the ring was warm and joyous. If she was away, it took on a hollow sound. . . ." Sometimes too, of course, the line would be busy.

But one night, when Lees-Milne got back late from the country, he was greeted by a new sound, achingly different from the usual engaged signal, or the cheery ringing tone. This time his ears were shattered by a prolonged and piercing scream. That same "banshee scream" was repeated the next day, and the next. Finally, Lees-Milne called Information to find out what had happened. The number was unlisted. But a kindly operator gave him the hard news. The house to which that number belonged had received a direct hit three days earlier.

The perfect interlocutor, his other self, was dead. The operator offered to provide Egeria's real name. But that was more than James Lees-Milne could bear. "Thank you for your help," he said. "I'd much rather that you didn't. So, please, please don't." And he rang off.

The Beloved Voice

If it is true, as some psychologists believe, that "our lives are peopled by those who have really mattered," it comes as no surprise that we should treasure, and recall, the particular vocal qualities of those we love. Each of us has a distinctive tone and rhythm, a unique grain or timbre to our voice—and, equally, a specific way of listening.

I experienced this for myself during the first weeks of the coronavirus, tossed between Skype and Zoom and crackling cell phone lines. I spoke with my sister in London, my brother and his family in Scotland, close friends and allies across the United States. Again and again, I found myself cheered and steadied by the mutual act

of listening. Most of us recognize that we need "witnesses for wonder," witnesses too for an immense transition like that global shut-
down. Old friends can help you with a few wise words, often hearing
you more clearly than you can hear yourself. Twenty minutes on the
phone with my good friend Amy Pulley was as nourishing as a fifty-
minute session with a kindly therapist. We had, after all, been talking
to one another for years.

More structured exchanges were helpful too. The local chapter
of Extinction Rebellion, an environmental advocacy organization,
hosted an online listening circle, at which each of us took turns to
respond to the following questions:

> What is challenging for you about this time?
> What is precious?
> What do you wish would continue once the lockdown ends?
> What are you especially looking forward to?

I felt glad of the chance to engage with such questions; grateful, too,
simply to be heard. It was as if the fact of our gathering together—even
in cyberspace—helped restore what British poet David Whyte once
called "the conversational nature of reality," clarity and consensus (and,
indeed, community) flourishing in the space between the words.

But along with the practical and psychological support came something else: the lilt and sway of one another's voices. When we listen
deeply, we *take in* someone's voice, allowing it to vibrate in our own
ears and nose and throat, our own chest cavity, as if for a brief moment
it were truly ours. That intimacy, that shared music, is what matters
most, far below the surface of ordinary, literal-minded human speech.

In Doris Lessing's novel, *The Golden Notebook*, Ella recognizes
from Paul's voice alone that he will ultimately become her lover. "She
knew it from the pleasure his voice gave her, and she was full of a secret delight." I remember a similar experience as I came to know my
good friend Simon, wrapping myself in the rich golden brown of his
voice. Years later, I read of a Native American elder who approached
a visiting Quaker and laid a hand on his chest. "I like to feel where
words come from," he said.

At times the voice alone can serve as a medium of exchange, even without the added freight of meaning. I think here of the wordless *motherese*, universal across human culture, and of Jung humming to his anxious patient. And I remember an afternoon in Bhutan, when some friends and I came upon a group of Indian women laborers, busy repairing the dusty, rocky road. We had no languages in common. But we had smiles and gestures, tone and pitch and rhythm. Our interest and curiosity, and their answering warmth, was entirely apparent.

Poet Mark Nepo reminds us that the Japanese ideogram for "the heart of listening" is composed of three different pictographs: the *ear,* the *eye,* and the *heart,* suggesting that all three should work in unison if wholehearted attention is to be achieved. But if the coronavirus taught me anything, it was that the ear alone could often be enough. My friend Gwen talked on the phone to her elderly mother every other day, love and gossip slipping back and forth across the miles. Her mother apologized when she had no "new news," but Gwen didn't care so much about the content of what was said. Often, she put her mother on speakerphone, while she herself went on about her daily chores. What mattered most was that beloved voice.

Moral Music

"The voice is not only audible, but also visible to those who can see it," writes the Sufi teacher Hazrat Inayat Khan. Jacques Lusseyran would concur. Blinded by the age of eight, he became a gifted listener, most especially to the human voice. At times he heard nothing in class, neither the teacher's questions nor the students' responses, because he was so entirely absorbed in what he "saw" of their voices, ranging from the surreal to the angelic. "There were people whose teeth seemed to fill their whole face, and others so harmonious they seemed to be made of music." This "moral music" was immediately comprehensible to him, as if through a kind of aural X-ray. "When a man's voice reaches me," he wrote, "I immediately perceive his figure, his rhythm, and most of his intentions."

In 1940, when Lusseyran was still in his teens, the German army invaded Paris. He experienced the military music and the Nazi voices as if they were aimed at him "point-blank like loaded pistols," not least because he had been studying German for two hours every day and was already remarkably fluent. For him, the Occupation felt like a "second blindness."

The following spring, still not yet seventeen, Lusseyran founded a Resistance group called the Volunteers of Liberty, made up primarily of students from two local lycées. Fifty-two young people attended the first meeting; within a year there were nearly six hundred. Lusseyran was put in charge of recruitment because, as his friends testified, he had "the sense of human beings." In other words, he knew how to vet possible members, how to listen for their moral music. When he heard in their voices a certain clarity and confidence, he knew they would be fit to join the group. "The light which shone in my head was so bright and strong that it was like joy distilled."

In the months that followed, the Volunteers of Liberty spread out across Paris, "nearly invisible" because of their extreme youth. They listened to British and Swiss broadcasts and compiled a reliable news bulletin which they themselves distributed. They exposed the existence of political prisons and concentration camps, and were among the first to report on the Jewish Holocaust. They even published a photograph by way of illustration, showing an open pit of bones at the edge of a German concentration camp.

Lusseyran meanwhile remained a tower of strength. He possessed a prodigious memory, which easily absorbed the 1,050 telephone numbers he needed for his work. For almost two years he continued to vet every new candidate to join the Resistance. And then, in the summer of 1943, he was betrayed. The culprit was a man called Elio, himself a member of the Volunteers of Liberty. Lusseyran had been uneasy about him from the start—"Elio spoke in a low voice, too low. . . . It lacked clarity and straightforwardness." But for once, his judgment had been overruled. Early on the morning of July 20, Lusseyran was arrested.

In the months that followed, Lusseyran was interrogated thirty-eight times by the Gestapo, and in January 1944, he was transferred to Buchenwald. But even there, "the little blind Frenchman" became a central figure, the official newscaster for the 30,000 prisoners in the camp. A clandestine radio had been set up in one of the cellars, and here news was received from France and Russia and the British Isles. Lusseyran would go from one block to another, translating the official German broadcast, explaining what it meant, and including crucial snippets from the receiving station. "When I went into a block, I took its pulse," he writes. "A barracks was a spirit shared, a collective body. . . . So then, according to the state of things, I gave out more news of one kind, or less of another."

The wonder of it was that taking this role almost completely freed him from anxiety. As "the little blind Frenchman with the happy face," Lusseyran was encouraged by his own encouragement, comforted by his own act of consolation. Moral music indeed. When Buchenwald was finally liberated, in April 1945, of his original group of two thousand, he was one of only thirty who survived.

A Poetry of the Senses

> One day I had a revelation that the voice could be an instrument like the body . . . and that my voice could move like a spine or a foot. I understood in a flash that within the voice are male and female, all ages, different characters, landscapes, colors, textures, and ways of using the breath, limitless possibilities of producing sound. . . . From that point on, I began a deep exploration of the voice as the first human instrument, an exploration that continues to this day.
>
> Meredith Monk

Meredith Monk is a composer, choreographer, filmmaker, and theater director, with an extraordinary singing voice. The sounds she makes are often very strange and at the same time, eerily familiar. With her clicks and wails and syncopated sighs, her sudden jolting shifts in pitch and tone, she calls us back into an unremembered past. It is as if she could recreate the flare of sunlight on the prairie grasses or the tiniest root nudging its lone way between the stones; as if, through the pure channel of her open throat, the very cosmos could be given voice.

Monk is in her eighties now, an elfin figure in a neat high-collared jacket, with bright brown eyes and a long, elegant, high-cheekboned face. She was born with a condition called strabismus—meaning her eyes could not come together to focus—and was somewhat uncoordinated as a child. But she sang back to her mother before she was able to speak, and could read music before she could read words. At three and four, she used to gather all the neighborhood kids together, and regale them with the latest pop songs. "My ear picked up things very early," she says. At night she would lie in bed and sing, soothing herself with half-invented lullabies.

Monk's mother was a professional singer, "the original Chiquita Banana, Muriel Cigar, Schafer Beer, Blue Bonnet Margarine, and Royal Pudding Girl," and her father ran a lumber business in the Bronx. Because both parents worked, Monk spent a lot of time out on the street. As she sees it now, her mouth (she calls it "the Mouth") was her chief source of protection and defense. It was not until high school, and later on, at college, that she felt listened to without having to yell. She remembers her teachers with tremendous gratitude. "Their listening saved my life."

For more than fifty years, Monk has worked with voice, composition, dance, and film, sometimes alone, more often as part of an ensemble. For her, the voice is the first instrument, "the very beginnings of utterance." Often, she starts alone in the studio, singing and improvising at the keyboard. Later, she brings those fragments into rehearsal, and works them through with the ensemble. The process can be slow. It's as if the piece she is working on already exists in some other dimension, and it is her task to figure out the rules. "*What is the voice of this sound-world?*" she asks herself, working, as she says, like a shoemaker, "*working-working-working*—and then all of a sudden, it makes itself known."

Although so much of her work commences with that inner listening—"uncovering the invisible and inexplicable"—Monk knows how to listen to the outer world as well.

As a small child, she used to lie in her mother's bed, listening to the roar of the garbage truck progressing down the street. Nowadays, she spends much of her time listening from her loft in Lower Manhattan, translating what she hears into her own vocabulary. She finds it exhilarating to work with the dissonances and tensions and jagged asymmetrical rhythms of a modern city, as she did in "Urban March (Shadow)" from the opera, *Mercy*, as well as in several other pieces. But in general, she says, her work is very pastoral, echoing the rhythms and repetitions of the natural world.

Some fifty years ago, when she was in her early thirties, Monk went to stay with her younger sister in Placitas, New Mexico. Every day she walked up into the hills and sat for hours, simply listening. Months later, back in New York, she realized how much the New Mexican landscape had infused her work. There was a piece called "Descending," which she had worked on as she walked down from the hill, and another called "Prairie Ghost" in which she could somehow glimpse the local animals and flowers, and far above, the overarching sky.

Years later, Monk bought some wild land of her own, at a little township called Cañones, not far from Abiquiú. She set up camp there along with her partner Mieke, and a number of other women. But this was still wild land. Not far from the campfire there were rattlesnakes and bears—and a pack of very vociferous coyotes. Monk remembers them calling back and forth from cliff to cliff. At night, they woke the women up, they were so loud.

One afternoon, Monk set off alone into the hills. She chose a piece called "Offering" with a high, pure melody, from a project called *Volcano Songs*. She sang it to the coyotes, and the coyotes roused themselves and answered back. "Sort of like my sisters," Monk says, still gratified. "My singing sisters."

Long before she bought the land in Cañones, Monk already had a second home, in the wonderfully named East Meredith, New York. The little house is set right on the road. But she sits there "for hours," she says, listening to the shifting sounds of the landscape: the wind in the trees, the call of the birds, the pulsing rhythm of the crickets, all marvelously rich and interwoven. "Eat your heart out, humans!" she wants to say. Artists, writers, singers, musicians: none of us can hope to compose such dazzling music.

Despite her age, Monk is still performing, though the "two little wisps" of her vocal cords require great care. At times she misses the stupendous high notes, what she calls "the soaring." But she also loves the chance to explore the bottom range, which for her is brand new territory. Meanwhile her mid-range feels stronger than it ever did, and she can still manage solo concerts lasting an hour and a half.

In creating her pieces, Monk aims for what she calls "a poetry of the senses"—a chance to rest the discursive mind and return to full embodiment. She believes our nervous systems are actually being modified by our current devices, and jokes, uneasily, that future generations will only have webs for hands, "with these giant thumbs!" At its best, her work serves a ceremonial and ritual function, weaving together all the senses, and providing an antidote to that incessant bombardment: a chance to slow down and savor the simple fact of being alive. Monk describes this in terms of the infinity sign or figure eight, weaving back and forth between the various performers, and then again from the performers to the audience and back.

Not long ago, when she sang at the Library of Congress, she realized that some members of the audience had never heard music like hers before. So, she described her revelation of the voice as instrument, and talked about each song in turn. "This is a song where the melody repeats. But I'm using different vocal textures each time." Or, "This is a piece two of us are singing together, where we're trying to make it so you can't hear whose voice is whose."

By the end of the concert, the entire audience was on their feet, delirious with applause. Monk was delighted. She sees singing as a vehicle—"but really, what we're trying to offer is our radiance as performers. . . . Because we're so in tune, there's this generous quality, this very shining quality. You see people's insides. And it just shines out."

Consider the following quotations:

Anybody knows how anybody calls out the name of anybody one loves.

Gertrude Stein

It is possible for a blind person to hear the voice of a man or woman speak just three words to recognize that man or woman as if they had been speaking for hours.

Jacques Lusseyran

Continue to explore:

Take the time to listen to the work of Meredith Monk, especially, "Impermanence," "On Behalf of Nature, " "Cellular Songs," and "Indra's Net

Most of us taste much more if we shut our eyes while eating, and hear more if we shut our eyes while listening. Explore the act of listening with your eyes shut.

ᴄ5ᴄ

Learning to Listen

To talk with someone
ask a question first,
then—listen.

Antonio Machado

Checking In

I'd been asked to supper at a good friend's house. My life was in tatters at the time, and I'd been looking forward to the warmth and company: good food, lively conversation. The meal began with a silent grace: breathe in, breathe out, a quiet clasp of hands around the table. So far, so good, I thought. Soon we will begin to talk. But once everyone was settled with their soup in front of them, no one said a word. Instead, the host announced that we'd be starting with a check-in. Each of us was to talk in turn, "checking in," describing what was happening in our lives.

And for the next three-quarters of an hour, we did just that.

I was amazed by this procedure, so slow and so self-conscious, so brutally truncated. It was like seeing a row of little flowerpots set out side by side, each containing one small bloom. Everyone had the same amount of time in which to speak. Each of us told one or two brief anecdotes, provided a short list of recent activities, and then our time was up. There was no chance of linking one experience with another, of intertwining interests and ideas, no questions or elaborations, no laughing, expansive storytelling. It was so humorless, so flat, so achingly predictable. How I longed for dessert, when check-in would finally be complete, and we could turn to the person sitting next to us, and actually converse!

In the last few years, I have read a number of books and articles on the art of listening. Deep listening, active listening, compassionate listening, generous listening: each has its own trademarked identity, and checklist of essential practices. "Don't interrupt when someone else is speaking." "Listen empty." "Try not to judge or fix." "Show the other person that you're paying attention." "Look them in the eye." "Be patient, silent, wait."

But whichever practice is being promoted, I find myself resisting. The rules proliferate, earnest, literal-minded. For me, it feels like trying to dance in iron shoes. When will the soup be finished, and the good green salad and the sensible brown rice? When can we actually talk, actually listen?

True listening, joyful listening, delighted, ardent *tell-me-more*-ish listening, has less to do with keeping quiet while someone talks than with the questions you're inspired to ask, the welcome you extend, the quality of interest and encouragement. What I think of as "open-ended listening," (yes, I too have my proprietary brand) begins with a sense of spacious sufficiency, a way of setting the scene, framing the purpose, meeting the gaze. The listener knows how to pay respectful attention to the one who talks, and asks good (thoughtful, curious, branching) questions. The speaker has something to say and is eager to share it. Cadence matters here, and a shared sense of pace, a foundation of trust and equality—a willingness to let the arc of the conversation swing back upon itself, confident that the talk will find its way, and that both listener and talker are equal cocreators.

It matters too, for someone to be able to say, "I'm not up for this right now. I just don't have the clarity, the energy, the strength of mind to listen properly at the moment. Can we make another time to talk? Tomorrow, next weekend?"

With the escape route well marked, it is possible to assume that your friend—or your neighbor at the dinner table—is as hungry for conversation as you are yourself. This eases the mind considerably. At once you are free to move beyond a routine "checking in" to something infinitely more expansive and surprising. A massive door creaks open. Several walls fall down. No one can predict what happens next.

A Space to Be Explored

I grew up in Scotland, in the country, in what now seems a remarkably self-contained, old-fashioned household. My brothers and sisters and I were brought up to be polite, to say "please" and "thank you." But we talked one way upstairs in the nursery, and another way downstairs with the grown-ups; one way with our parents, and another way with the women who cleaned the house or scoured the vegetables. There were subjects that we never thought to raise, questions that we simply did not ask. Class, however muffled, quiescent, maintained its own authority.

At sixteen, fresh out of boarding school, I set off hitchhiking for the first time. In the years that followed, I hitched from Dublin to the west of Ireland, from Amsterdam to the South of France, from Cambridge back and forth to London, talking and asking questions all the way. I was curious about everyone and everything, and for the first time that curiosity was being seen as welcome. People *wanted* to respond. I remember sitting high up in the cab of an enormous lorry, barreling across Ireland, while the driver told me the story of his life. I remember the young couple who picked me up in France and drove me almost to my door—the warmth and hilarity inside their tiny car, the smell of coffee and fresh air and cigarettes. And I remember the joy of those transient exchanges, the sense that even as strangers we could find a way to talk to one another, that there'd always be something more to be explored.

Half a lifetime later, gathering material for a new book, I thought again about those marvelous, free-ranging conversations, and how they might differ from more considered kinds of listening, in particular the formal interview. I was meeting with lots of people at the time—writers and artists, storytellers and musicians—and asking them to talk to me about their work. To start with, I hardly knew what I was trying to accomplish. But gradually I came to see that whatever my final purpose (a handful of lively quotes, a lengthy interview), it was up to me to create a certain ease and spaciousness, a certain level of courtesy and respect. Only then could I hope for the kind of exchange that pleased me most: rich, exploratory, ultimately transformative, not just for me as interlocutor, but for the speaker too.

"When we are listened to," writes Brenda Ueland, "it creates us, makes us unfold and expand. Ideas actually begin to grow within us and to come to life."

I experienced this for myself both in my initial project (*World Enough & Time: On Creativity and Slowing Down*), and in the one that followed, later published as *Sparks from the Anvil: The Smith College Poetry Interviews*. For the most part, I was ridiculously well prepared. But often there was such a hunger to tell on the part of the poets, that all I had to do was hold the space as each one descended ever deeper into his or her own story. Our small recording booth became a magic portal through which they spoke to the future, claiming their legacy, addressing readers and admirers they would never meet. They could perhaps have done this on their own, supported only by the microphone and its associated machinery. But there could be no doubt that my company, my listening ear, helped provide some of the impetus they needed.

I think especially of my conversation with the African American poet Aracelis Girmay: how she would pause a moment before responding to my questions, "listening inwards," discovering what she had to say. I myself was almost dissolved inside her process. When I opened the door of the recording booth, the two of us looked back at one another, dazed and grateful, as if we'd been spinning off together into outer space.

Hearing Each Other into Speech

Sherry Turkle is a professor at MIT and a licensed clinical psychologist, with a special expertise in culture and therapy, mobile technology, and social networking. She is also the author of several books. In the course of her recent research, Turkle asked people to tell her about their most important conversations with friends and family, colleagues and acquaintances, even complete strangers. Everyone was eager to respond. They told her about the first time they fell in love, or when they realized that their children were no longer children. They remembered how inspired they'd been by someone's encouragement, coming just at the right moment, how it had helped start them on the path towards their subsequent career.

Whatever the length or intensity of these conversations, they all had one thing in common: they had less to do with information and advice than with opening up and slowing down, offering a space for different themes to be explored. "The human soul doesn't want to be advised or fixed or saved," says the writer and educator Parker Palmer. "It simply wants to be witnessed—to be seen, heard, and companioned exactly as it is."

It wants, above all, *to be listened to*, because in the course of such deep witnessing, we hear one another into speech.

I first came upon that phrase in a book by Adrienne Rich: *hearing each other into speech.* Years later, I discovered Rich had borrowed it from the feminist theologian Nelle Morton. This is how Morton lays out what she means, in a little essay called "Beloved Image." Clearly, she is describing one of the early consciousness raising groups.

> It was in a small group of women who had come together to tell our own stories that I first received a totally new understanding of hearing and speaking. I remember well how one woman started, hesitating and awkward, trying to put the pieces of her life together. Finally, she said: 'I hurt . . . I hurt all over.' She touched herself in various places as if feeling for the hurt before she added, 'but . . . I don't know where to begin to cry.' She talked on and on. Her story took on fantastic coherence. When she reached a point of most excruciating pain no one moved. No one interrupted. Finally, she finished. After a silence, she looked from one woman to another. 'You heard me. You heard me all the way.' Her eyes narrowed. She looked directly at each woman in turn and then said slowly: 'I have a strange feeling you heard me before I started. *You heard me to my own story.*'"

At first Nelle Morton understood this experience as astonishing and rare. But then it happened a second time, and a third. It happened to her. And she realized she had witnessed something very precious. What the woman was describing was, as Morton put it, "a depth hearing that takes place before the speaking—a hearing that is far more than acute listening. . . . *The woman had been heard to her own speech.*"

When the first Rape Crisis Centre opened in London in the 1980s, women of all ages lined up to tell their stories. A friend of mine was working there at the time, and she reported that many of those stories had gone untold for decades: stories of childhood abuse, of date rape, of casual brutality, reaching as far back as World War II. They had festered in the memory, frightening, deeply shameful. But until the Centre opened, there had been nobody to listen, nowhere to lay the story down.

"Every liberation movement rises out of bondage with a new speech on its lips," writes Nelle Morton. But first we have to recover the details of our own experience, however bruised and flattened and obscured. To do this, she says, we need to create "a great Listening Ear . . . an ear that hears without interruption down through our defenses, cliché-filled language, pretensions, evasions, pervasive hurts, angers, frustration, internalized stereotyped images until we experience . . . that we are sustained."

Such hearing is essential to empowerment, Morton says. It deepens when the speaker pauses, or the pain grows too intense, accompanies her to the blazing center of her tale, "all the way down to her most excruciating agony." Only then—when that story has been fully told and fully listened to (often, many times)—can the speaker rise like a phoenix from the ashes, realizing her own clarity and strength, her own authentic voice.

Just Listening

In 1933, at the height of the Depression, Eleanor Roosevelt took off across America, listening to ordinary people tell their stories. In three months, she traveled more than forty thousand miles. While her husband, Franklin Delano Roosevelt, was tethered to his desk in Washington, Eleanor became "the voice of the dispossessed," sharing what she learned through radio talks and newspaper articles and hosting regular meetings with the press.

In a world where the rich and powerful consistently set the terms of the discussion, shaping public discourse to better suit themselves, such listening can be an act of resistance, transformative and inspiring. "One of the simplest paths to deep change is for the less powerful to speak as much as they listen," writes Gloria Steinem, "and for the more powerful to listen as much as they speak."

I first met Susan von Reusner at the Zen Mountain Monastery in upstate New York, where both of us were on retreat. She is a practicing attorney in the nearby town of Kingston and is also a committed listener. In 1987, at the age of twenty-two, she set off for Southeast Asia, supported by a Thomas Watson Fellowship. She wanted to talk to women textile workers in Hong Kong, Thailand, the Philippines, and China, and to find out what they had to say about their work.

At that time, the textile industry was being touted as a tremendous success story. But von Reusner was wary of what felt like "a very ethnocentric—almost an imperial—feminism," and of prevailing economic theories too. "*Sweat shops!*" she says emphatically. "Women working fourteen, sixteen hours a day for under a dollar. And the use of child labor." She wanted to investigate, to spend a year just listening, living and working alongside the textile workers, and the fellowship was happy to support her. All that mattered was her ability to follow through. Von Reusner herself had no doubts on that score. "When I know I need to do something, that's it. I just know I need to do it. I'm unstoppable."

Von Reusner arrived in Hong Kong in the early summer, right after graduation. She taught ESL classes to Vietnamese refugees and to illegal Chinese immigrants, and lived for a while on a silk plantation, run by one of Thailand's most successful women entrepreneurs. This woman had a factory dormitory for her workers, and von Reusner was allowed to stay there, clerking part-time in the office by way of payment. "So, I interviewed not only the workers themselves, but women politicians and entrepreneurs, women in very powerful positions. Both ends of the spectrum."

What she found was that the experience of *being listened to* was almost entirely foreign to most of the women. But spending convivial time together, everyone chatting happily back and forth, was for them very comfortable and familiar. So, von Reusner masked her research by presenting it as an English lesson. She'd announce, "We're going to develop our conversational skills," and invite the women to ask her questions, freeing her to question them in turn, starting with safe topics like their family or their village, and moving on to more charged and personal matters. "What is it that *you* want? What are *your* dreams? Do you worry about what life will be like for your daughter, if you have one?"

Such questions required subtlety and patience. But von Reusner never doubted it was worth it. Even now, she is overcome by what she learned from those freewheeling conversations—things she would never have heard from male economists, or from western feminists. "How powerful women are! How intelligent and self-aware! How—*aspiring!*"

What struck her most was the women's hunger, not for wealth or security or a better future, but simply to be able to choose. Many saw education as crucial. "And, oh my goodness, the amount of longing I encountered, both to actualize their own potential, and to be of service to others!"

It was a yearning that had been completely absent from the books she'd read, upending corporate strategies, and emphasizing health and education and personal development rather than exports and profits and the bottom line. "The cure for poverty is not just bank capital," von Reusner says. "It's investment in human capital. And that came across *so clear!*"

A couple of years later, when von Reusner was at Princeton, and found herself pregnant, both her male and female professors tried to convince her to have an abortion. Why would she turn down such a superlative education? "Women have *fought* for this right," they told her. As they saw it, she could either retreat into domestic life, or embark on a career: it was impossible to do both. But von Reusner went ahead and had the baby, and managed to finish her degree. Her year of listening gave her the confidence she needed, modeling enterprise and courage, and helping her commit both to her family, and to her own professional path. It influenced her subsequent work with the UN Development Program, and later as a public attorney. As a New York assistant attorney general, she found she "could really get to the heart of things quickly. I think it's because I am a good listener. I can issue-spot really well."

Each time von Reusner listens to another person, she tries to set aside her preconceptions and allow the speaker time to reveal themselves. "*Take a minute*," she tells herself. "*Really, just look and listen.*" Even now, she feels that her year in Asia has helped her live her life in a more intimate and skillful way. In the decades since, she has never felt lonely or alone. "The better I get at listening," she says, "the more interesting everything is. Words have become a lot less important. I hear so very much—between the words."

The Power of the Pause

When the writer Pico Iyer came to visit Leonard Cohen at the Mount Baldy Zen Center in California, the two of them would sit together in the garden saying nothing. By then, Cohen had been practicing Zen for more than thirty years. His name in the monastery was *Jikan*, which is to say, "the silence between two thoughts." For a poet and songwriter, it could hardly have been more apt. That tiny stretch of silence is a charged thing, brimful of energy and anticipation. Brain neurons spark and fire, trying to predict what will happen next. It is then that the mind performs some of its most vital work: both maintaining attention and encoding memories.

The best, most thoughtful listeners understand this very well.

They not only listen carefully while somebody is speaking, but they also wait, allowing a little moment afterwards—a breath, a spacious pause—lest there should be anything the speaker wants to add. Only then do they themselves begin to speak.

In a world of rush and overwhelm, such courtesies have grown increasingly rare. It is as if even the smallest pause had become suspect—even culpable—with both partners in a conversation expected "to get to the point" as fast as they possibly can.

And yet as friends have always known, a good conversation depends less on speed and efficiency than on ease and harmony and flow, which necessarily include "holes" or "pauses" in our speech—the times when silence has a chance to enter.

"When two people are conversing with one another," wrote the Swiss theologian Max Picard, "a third is always present. Silence is listening. This is what gives breadth to a conversation; when the words are not moving merely in the narrow space occupied by the two speakers, but come from afar, from the place where silence is listening."

That attention to pause, to white space, has long been a commonplace among musicians. The pianist Arthur Rubenstein was once asked how he handled the notes as well as he did. "I handle the notes no better than many others," he responded. "But the pauses—ah! That is where the art resides."

Listen Empty

In a poem by Patricia Lee Lewis, "While talking with her on the phone," the narrator makes a pasta supper while someone weeps long distance down the phone. She fills the cast iron pot with water, adds the salt, lights the burner, and settles the pot on the stove, all while listening closely to the desolate person at the other end:

> *. . . I say I love you, tearing*
> *cellophane. You are perfect in my*
> *eyes. Did you dream last night?*
> *The pasta sticks. And when the woman*
> *in your dream picked up the knife?*

The narrator barely speaks; she asks only a couple of questions. And yet her voice is enough to soothe and steady the other person—her daughter, perhaps, or sister, or beloved friend.

> *I add some virgin olive oil. She isn't*
> *crying now. She says, I think I'd better cut*
> *it off with him. I'm looking for the*
> *colander, the one with larger holes.*
> *. . . Yes, I say,*
> *and take the grater from its nail.*

Is the speaker of the poem *really listening*? *Yes,* I'd answer. *Yes.* Eckhart Tolle writes of the power of centering oneself "in one's own inner energy field, sensing the inner body," even while listening to someone else. And that is what is being modeled here. Certain meditative tasks—walking, weeding, knitting, simple cooking—actually serve to deepen one's attention. So, the narrator continues with her preparations—first one task, and then another—but she's also focused on the distant speaker. A gentle, trusting energy connects the two of them. And there's no question that the consolation works.

If William James is right, and what we call our experience "is almost entirely determined by our habits of attention," then the wise or generous listener is someone who is able to set aside their own preoccupations—at least momentarily—and extend that gift of uninterrupted focus. A number of people have written well about this, including the psychotherapist Abraham Maslow, and the British doctor Rachel Pinney. Maslow, for example, encourages us to corral or "bracket" our own thoughts for the duration of a talk, resulting (if all goes well) in what he calls *real listening*:

"To listen . . . without presupposing, classifying, improving, controverting, evaluating, approving or disapproving, without dueling with what is being said, without rehearsing the rebuttal in advance, without free-associating to portions of what is being said, so that succeeding portions are not heard at all."

Pinney too, advises us to gather ourselves, and pause. In her view, one cannot listen deeply to a speaker, and at the same time marshal one's own forces in order to respond. Such "double attention" is doomed to fail. What she calls *creative listening* has at its heart the instruction "to listen empty," grounding oneself in one's own calm presence, without trying to judge or fix or interrogate what is being said.

The marvel is that if someone is allowed the time they need to do just this—time to do their own naming and explaining—they will often talk their way into their own solution, just like the woman in the poem. The mind alone will not suffice for this. As Leslie Jamison writes in *The Empathy Exams,* "The Chinese character for *listen* is . . . a structure of many parts: the characters for ears and eyes, a horizontal line that signifies undivided attention, the swoop and teardrops of the heart."

Generous Listening

Rachel Naomi Remen is the author of *Kitchen Table Wisdom* and *My Grandfather's Blessings,* both of which made the *New York Times* bestseller list. Her teaching curriculum, "The Healer's Art," is used in medical schools across the United States. Listening to people's stories—"listening generously"—is central to her healing practice. It is a rarity in her profession, where doctors tend to interrupt their patients after eleven seconds of speech, and the typical appointment is only fifteen minutes long. But Remen knows just how valuable it can be. "When you listen generously to people, they can hear the truth in themselves, often for the first time."

Instead of trying to solve someone's troubles, she reminds her students of the power of their own presence, asking them to consider a loss or sorrow of their own, and to bring to mind somebody who helped them. *What did that person do?* she asks. *What did they say?* The students write down everything they can remember. Then she asks them to think of a friend who wanted to help, but somehow failed. *What did that person do? What did they say?* The students make a second list, and the two sets of answers are put on display for everyone to see. *What helped? He listened to me for as long as I needed to talk. She sat with me and touched me. Brought me food. What didn't help? She blamed me, made me feel the loss was my own fault. He gave advice without knowing the full story.*

Then the students break up into small groups, and for the next six hours—two three-hour sessions—everyone shares a story of loss from their own lives. The only instruction is: *Listen generously.*

Such listening can be challenging, as the Buddhist teacher Thich Nhat Hanh makes plain. But it can also be powerfully transformative.

> Compassionate listening has one purpose: to help
> the other person suffer less. You have to nourish the
> awareness that no matter what the other person says,
> you will keep calm and continue to listen. You do not
> judge while listening. You keep your compassion alive.

It is easy to believe that we're not wise enough to do this well; even the most experienced have their doubts. Carl Rogers was a famous psychotherapist, honored for his active listening skills. But he, too, felt the need to center himself before he met with patients. "There is no experience this person has had that I cannot share with them," he told himself. "I, too, am vulnerable. And because of this, I am enough. Whatever this person's story, they no longer need to be alone with it. And that is what will allow their healing to begin."

No one, whether therapist or client, doctor or patient, friend or family member, forgets the experience of such deep and concentrated listening. Forty years after working with Oliver Sacks, an old student of his came back to visit. He recalled how Sacks would ask him to see a patient, say, with multiple sclerosis, to go to her room and spend a couple of hours with her. After that he had to provide the fullest possible report, not only on her neurological problems and ways of coping, "but on her personality, her interests, her family, her entire life history." All those years later, when the man came back to visit, that three-month apprenticeship was the only part of medical school he still remembered.

Saying No

In our combative and noisy world, the practiced listener is made welcome almost always: a calming presence at a rowdy party, a genial and attentive host. But some warnings are in order too. "When someone listens to you, it can feel so much like love, some people may not know the difference," notes the journalist Kate Murphy in a recent book. There is compassion, and there is idiot compassion. *Audiens cave*: listener beware! The too-skilled, too-willing listener can leave some knotty complications in her wake.

At times, the listener herself may be to blame for this. Not all good listeners listen from a place of strength. Some listen out of fear or shyness or self-doubt; some from a desire to remain anonymous, unseen. If that's the case, it can be easy to find yourself taken for granted—or worse, treated with casual contempt—by the usually dominant (usually male) speaker. But it can be easy too, to be misunderstood—treated as someone's "new best friend" (or even lover)—simply because you have chosen to offer them a listening ear. A woman may consent to listen to a (shortish) story, which then metastasizes into a stout blockbuster memoir, exhausting both her interlocutor and herself. And her listening may be generous and attentive, without signaling either agreement or belief—a fact the rabid speaker often fails to recognize, intoxicated by the sound of his own voice.

Listening, after all, is a form of hospitality, and there are times when it is wise to shut the door. However kindly or compassionate, the listener must remember that she (and it is almost always she) has the power and the authority to say no. "No, I can't listen to you now. Just because you're lonely/angry/drunk/unhappy/overwhelmed/fill-in-the-blank—it doesn't follow I'm obliged to listen. Yes, you're older/whiter/stronger/richer/male—but still, I can refuse. I'm no longer thinking clearly. I'm tired. I need a break. You've been talking to (at) me for forty minutes straight and have failed to pause or ask a single question. I've had enough!"

I think here of a story told me by an old close friend. Her husband died of Covid-19 early in the pandemic, and soon after she moved with her brother and sister-in-law to their house upstate. She was grieving and depleted, but grateful for their company and spacious guest room. Meanwhile, the couple were at what seemed like a breaking point in their own lives. Their marriage had reached what the *I Ching* calls "a crescendo of awfulness," and because she was close to both of them, she was privy to all of it. Every time one of them left the house, the other would fill her in on the latest developments: the agonies, the infidelities, the looming prospects of divorce. She listened, she said, till she felt as if she had blood running out of her ears, until she literally had nothing left to give. And the pair of them listened to her—hardly at all.

The fiber artist Sue Montgomery knitted her way through months of meetings at the Montreal City Hall in Canada, changing her yarn from red (when men were speaking) to green (when women took the floor). No one was surprised at the end of her project when the scarf was loudly, disproportionately red.

Just as men out-talk women, so, in mixed company, the rich and entitled tend to out-talk the poor and middle class; the stalwart middle-aged to out-talk old and young alike; and users of the dominant language to out-talk second-language speakers. *Who listens? Who listens more, perhaps, than is entirely comfortable?* The Catholic priest, hidden behind the grille of his confessional. The stranger on the plane. The barman or barista, the waiter or waitress, the secretary, the nurse, the children's nanny. The cab driver, the beautician, the hairdresser and barber and psychotherapist.

And you too, gentle reader, tender listener—unless, that is, you remember to say no.

Walking to Listen

> *Most people . . . they just want to tell their story.*
> *That's what they have to give, don't you see? And it's a*
> *precious thing to them. It's their life they want to give.*
>
> Ram Dass and Paul Gorman

Andrew Forsthoefel is in his thirties now, long bodied and limber, with soft brown hair, mustache and beard, and a dazzling white smile. He has an air of wholesome integrity, like a young preacher or a present-day Transcendentalist: warm and personable and outgoing, comfortable in his own good company. He is very much a writer, and what Gertrude Stein once called "a village explainer," someone who, in no uncertain terms, knows how to walk his talk.

In October 2011, at the age of twenty-three, Forsthoeful set off from Chadds Ford, Pennsylvania, carrying a fifty-pound pack on his back, along with a handwritten sign: WALKING TO LISTEN. And for the next eleven months, he did just that, walking south to the Gulf Coast, and up in a long sweep through New Mexico and Arizona, stopping to converse along the way. By the time he arrived at the Pacific in September 2012, he had worn out five pairs of shoes, and recorded more than eighty-five hours' worth of interviews. These later became the basis for his book, *Walking to Listen,* which was published by Bloomsbury in 2017.

Forsthoefel wasn't the first person to accomplish such a trek. Some sixty years earlier, in 1953, a woman known as "Peace Pilgrim" had set off walking in the Pasadena Rose Bowl Parade and kept on walking for the next twenty-eight years. She never used money and carried with her an absolute minimum of supplies: no more than a comb, a toothbrush and a ballpoint pen, along with a small bundle of leaflets and copies of her current correspondence. Vowing "to remain a wanderer until mankind has learned the way of peace," she walked through every state in the United States, and every Canadian province, as well as parts of Mexico, fasting until she was given food, and walking until she was given shelter, trusting at all times to the kindness of strangers.

Forsthoefel never met Peace Pilgrim. She died in 1982, long before he was born. But his first name, Andrew, is an anagram of *wander,* and from early on he felt "those were my marching orders." He was inspired too by a man called John Francis, an African American environmentalist, who went by the name of "The Planetwalker," and himself spent more than twenty-two years on the road, seventeen of them in silence. Forsthoefel heard Dr. Francis speak when he was still a teenager, and still admires him deeply. But there were more personal reasons for his project too: a hunger for deep listening and authentic conversation, which neither school nor college had been able to satisfy.

"I was never really in a class," he told me, "—other than a few writing classes—that recognized me as an individual." It was as if "truth" could only be found in the words of big-name writers, or in the news. "What about *this truth, this place?*" asked Forsthoefel. He already knew that he wanted to change the rules.

When Forsthoefel walked out of his mother's house on October 14, 2011, he had no idea where he was going, or for how long. But tucked in among his food and clothes and tent and sleeping bag, his maps and laptop, mandolin and harmonica, was an Olympus LS-10 audio recorder—the key to his new identity. As his sign made clear to everyone he met, he was *walking to listen.*

In the months that followed, Forsthoefel walked between five to eight hours a day, often as many as thirty miles or more. At times his feet hurt so much he felt as if "swarms of ant-sized rats [were] gnawing their way out." His book, *Walking to Listen,* is skillfully composed, propelled forward by the walk itself, and enriched by the interviews he conducted along the way: some condensed and summarized, embedded in the text, others bodied forth in full storytelling mode. He recorded his friend Chris on letting go of grudges, "If you hold onto unforgiveness with one person, it affects everybody else you come into contact with," and a man called Otho Rogers on taking advantage of one's youth. "So, while you got it, use it. Your mind. Your strength. Your agility. Use it." The conversations became increasingly intimate and detailed. "It was as if some of these people had been waiting to be asked these questions, holding their breath for years."

The intensity of the interviews was balanced by long stretches of solitude. Forsthoefel savored "the privilege of going dark," removing himself from the psychic bombardment of the media. The walking steadied him and slowed him down, gave him time to reflect on what he was hearing, to write in his journal, to chew the bitter cud of his parents' divorce. Above all, it allowed him to notice things: "the Buddha-fat rutabagas," or the moment when a butterfly took flight "like a flower . . . flying on its own petal wings." His book has the ardor of a youthful quest: bashful at times, self-doubting, earnest, brave. But with each step, his own interior voice is gathering strength. "You know what to do," he tells himself. "There's no need to be afraid. *Just keep walking.*"

Forsthoefel reached his final destination on September 8, 2012. His family and friends were there to welcome him, along with several members of the Navajo Nation who had fed and sheltered him along the way. His friend Chris Paisano drummed and chanted in Navajo, while Chris's brother sprinkled cornmeal under his feet. Everyone gathered round him in a great circle, and Forsthoefel walked round and embraced them one by one. Each person gave him a little pinch of cornmeal. Then they accompanied him to the edge of the Pacific Ocean, where the Navajo elder, James, greeted him, and gave him a new name. He had been "The Boy Who Walks." Now he was "The Man Who Walks for Us." And with that he waded out into the water, scattering cornmeal and blessings "to the cold blue," and whispering thanks.

In the years since, Forsthoefel has learned to share the fruits of his long walk, teaching what he calls "trustworthy listening." He describes the work as "intricate and subtle," with both spiritual and political implications. "It goes deep," he says. But the preliminary instructions are in fact quite simple. "*Just hush and listen. Turn off your gadgets, and just start trying to be here.*"

Forsthoefel understands that this can be a challenge, especially for the young people of his own generation, who are all too often edgy and distracted, multiply addicted to their various screens. Social media can teach us to disparage our own lives, he says. "Like, 'OK, this party's sweet. But the *real* party is where all the movie stars are hanging out.' Or 'the *real* suffering is in Syria, where the children are starving.'"

Forsthoefel does his best to counter this, consistently emphasizing the immediate present, *right here, right now.* The name "Forsthoefel" has a German root, meaning "little courtyard in the forest." "So, I feel like that's a mandate in my name," he tells me, "learning how to cocreate those spaces, those little *forsthoefels,* where we can be with one another and then listen."

He pictures someone "wandering through the wilderness of their lives, encountering these wild beasts and brambles, and getting lost— and every once in a while, they stumble out into a little clearing in the wilderness. And it's a courtyard! In the forest." There are rocks shaped like thrones, and a fire going in the center. The sun sets, "and someone else stumbles out into that space, and someone else. And each of us gets to take our seat and sit as the kings and queens that we are."

Consider the following quotations:

Change happens by listening, and then starting a dialogue with the people who are doing something you don't believe is right.

Jane Goodall

I invite you, in the next week, to stop and listen without expectation to another person, to their words, below their words, to the space that surrounds them, to the presence you feel once they leave.

Mark Nepo

Continue to explore:

Do you remember when you first learned how to listen—and if so, what you learned?

Make time to interview a friend or family member.

∾ 6 ∾

The Little Sounds of Every Day

You should be interviewing roses, not people.

Anne Carson

Noisy Flowers

My mother was alone in the sitting room when a strange creaking sound caught her ear. *What was it?* She paused to listen more carefully and realized that what she'd heard was the sound of a hyacinth growing: its close-packed blossoms stretching, and its glossy leaves. It made a sharp, juicy noise, she said.

In the Japanese classic, *The Book of Tea*, Okakura Kakuzō writes that such "noisy" flowers were relentlessly banished from the tea room. Tranquility was paramount. But most of us, I think, would be intrigued to hear such Lilliputian sounds. When Elisabeth Tova Bailey was laid low by a mysteriously virulent illness, a friend presented her with a white-lipped forest snail which took up residence in her pot of violets. First, "a petal started to disappear at a barely discernible rate," and then, as Bailey listened, she could hear the snail eating. "The sound was of someone very small munching celery continuously." For an hour she lay back against her pillow, transfixed by the minuscule munching of an entire purple petal.

Bailey remained bedridden for several years, too weak to hold a book, or even to sit up to watch a film. Though she longed for human visitors, she didn't have the energy for conversation. Meanwhile the snail (by then transferred to a terrarium), kept her spirit alive. She observed it at intervals throughout the day, enjoying its miniature companionship. "Watching another creature go about its life . . . somehow gave me, the watcher, purpose too." Little by little, she compiled her findings into a magical small book. *The Sound of a Wild Snail Eating* was first published in 2010, and has since won several prizes, including the John Burroughs Medal for Distinguished Natural History Writing. Bailey's prose is lucid and informative, deeply researched, and alive with richly detailed observation. It is as if in befriending the snail, she had herself come to possess the "keen vision and feeling of all ordinary human life" that George Eliot describes in *Middlemarch,* freed to hear "the grass grow and the squirrel's heart beat"—and of course to attend to the gnashing of innumerable small teeth.

Listening Out

Poets and writers, naturalists and mystics are, many of them, gifted and attentive listeners, though few have Bailey's dazzling singularity of focus. "Listen, listen, I'm forever saying," writes the poet Mary Oliver:

> Listen to the river, to the hawk, to the hoof,
> to the mockingbird, to the jack-in-the-pulpit—

William Stafford, too, draws attention to the almost inaudible sounds of every day, encouraging us to "listen out" in ever-widening circles.

> My father could hear a little animal step,
> or a moth in the dark against the screen,
> and every far sound called the listening out
> into places where the rest of us had never been.

"I wanted to be a listener," writes the blind poet Stephen Kuusisto. "And by this I meant I wanted to be a happy man."

As a boy, he would wake early every Sunday to listen to a radio program about birds, hosted by an elderly ornithologist. "The purple finch sounded more contented than any creature I knew of . . . [Its] notes were round and quick as pins dropping on a glass table." Alone in the woods, he might spend an entire hour listening to a single bird. Soon he realized that he could in fact stop anywhere—*stop and listen*—and the neighborhood would open up around him.

The ordinary street outside our suburban house was surprisingly beautiful with all its fractions of living. . . . A car slid by with its windows rolled down and a radio voice said, 'You can whip them into shape with. . . .' And then the car was out of hearing range, the voice dwindling into fuzzed vocables. . . . I stood still and a man's voice came from across the street—there was a sound of something heavy and metallic dropped on concrete. 'That's the end of that,' I heard him say. He was a man with a trash can.

Kuusisto's sense of equivalence, his refusal to privilege birdsong over the radio voice or the man with the trash can, encourages the reader to suspend such judgment too. "Pablo Neruda heard the salt singing in the shaker," he reminds us. "Franz Liszt heard apples muttering in a wicker basket. . . . Whitman . . . could reconstruct a whole day from sounds remembered in sequence."

Meanwhile Kuusisto continues to practice listening wherever he finds himself, treating each new sound encounter as a kind of music. Standing in the cavernous lobby of a hotel, he locates the escalators by their hum, followed by "the whisper of rolling metal, a feverish sound." "If you're blind," he says, "you need to make hearing as pleasurable as sightseeing . . . open all the time to lucky possibilities in the soundscape."

"Hey, Sweetie!"

For a number of years, I taught in the winter studies program at Williams College, helping students to keep a naturalist's journal. One of their favorite assignments was the so-called blind walk. Everyone worked in pairs: one whose eyes were "blinded" with a scarf or muffler, and one to act as guide. I watched them as they blundered through the snow, reaching out chilly fingers to decipher the rough bark of the trees, pausing anxiously at the edge of a three-inch curb. My heart went out to them: their courage, vulnerability, exhilaration.

But you don't have to be blind—or even pretend to be—in order to explore the act of listening. You just have to claim the time and space to stroll around for a while, focusing on the ambient sounds, stopping now and then to listen yet more closely. In the first weeks of the pandemic, Blair McLaughlin and her little daughter Eloise did exactly that. Blair had been exploring sound-walks with her students at Hampshire College, and wanted to record the campus with them gone. When Eloise's day care shut down, McLaughlin brought her along too. And immediately the experience was transformed. "Eloise will *be* the sound, you know. She'll imitate it, she'll sing with it, she'll move with it. . . . So, it turned me back into the magic of being three years old, and hearing things for the first time."

Every animal recognizes the sounds of its homeplace, and until recently, most human beings did too. "Human speech used to be part of a far wider music," writes the British mythologist Martin Shaw, all of it "intelligent, animate, filled with vitality." In introducing Eloise to the local soundscape, McLaughlin is educating her daughter's ears, teaching her to recognize the birds and bees, the chipmunks and squirrels, and how the wind moves through each of the different trees. By the time she is ten or twelve, Eloise will have a grasp of the seasonal changes, giving her a baseline against which to measure the upheavals of the future. Because she knows how things *should* sound, she will have the clarity to recognize what is lost, and what, ideally, might need to be restored.

McLaughlin also benefits from their time together. Walking with Eloise encourages her to slow down and pay attention, as she matches herself to her daughter's eager, erratic pace. Amid the challenges of the pandemic, the walk alone is soothing, boosting what some have called "soft fascination." The poet Mark Nepo describes this in terms of speech—"the speech of the sun's warmth, the speech of the water's wetness, the speech of the trees' work at turning light into leaves"—and asks his readers to "inhale slowly, letting those other forms of speech mingle with their own."

Eloise, meanwhile, is doing exactly that. "I'm pretending to be a birdie," she announces. "*Tweet, tweet, tweet!* Hey, sweetie," she sings out to the chickadee, hardly waiting for a response. "Is the recorder working?" she wants to know. "Can they hear me now?"

Alice's Kitchen

Alice Cozzolino is an extraordinary cook; one might almost call her a "food whisperer." For most of her life, she has thought of herself as "one who feeds." It is a skill that reaches back to very early childhood.

When Alice was a girl, she and her mother would make *pasta e fagiole* every week. The night before, the two of them would sit together in the kitchen sorting beans. Her mother would pour them out across the table, the pea beans and the lentils and the navy beans, all mixed up together, making one pile for Alice and another for herself. Then, taking ten or twelve at a time, they would "shush and drop" them into shiny metal bowls. The aim was to separate out the little bits of stone or grit, the less-than-ideal specimens. Her mother wanted each bean to be perfect.

"*Shush and drop, shush and drop, shush and drop,*" Alice murmurs. Even now, the sound carries her back in time, back to herself at five and six years old. "More than anything in the world," she says, "that sound transports me."

Cozzolino is in her sixties now, a sturdy, handsome woman with a mane of long grey hair and warm brown eyes. When I ask her to name her favorite sounds, she comes up with a long list, starting with "any kind of bird call," and moving on through frogs and crickets and squirrels to "the wind in the trees, and water dripping, flowing." She loves interior sounds as well, "almost any sound in the kitchen, even the clanging of pots; spoons against the rim; pouring pasta in a colander and hearing the water gush and then slowly trickle through the small holes into the sink; the sound of food sautéing in hot oil." "Come to your senses!" she tells her students. "Come to your senses in my kitchen!"

Listening to food is something Cozzolino discovered for herself. "No one ever taught it to me," she says. "I never read of it." But as she became more centered in her daily life, she found ways to translate her meditative practice into the act of cooking. As we speak, she talks me through the preparations for an imagined meal.

"Listen to the onions now," she says. "That oil is hot, so listen to the sound of the onions hitting the hot oil. If it doesn't sizzle, the oil isn't hot enough. Smell what that smells like. There's an acridness, a sharpness." And then, once some time has passed, "*Now* listen to the onions. They're juicy! It's going *shlllshh-shllssh!* It's a wet sound, where before it was dry. Smell the onions. It's a rounder aroma, it's not sharp, it's round. Look! It's reduced in volume from six cups to three."

The acids in the onions transform the sugars in response to the heat, changing the molecular structure, and the flavor too, from acrid to sweet. Soon after that, the onions will begin to stick. A less experienced chef might reach for a wooden spoon and start to stir. But from Cozzolino's point of view, that would be a mistake. Both ear and eye remind her to leave the onions to themselves. "There's a French term called the *fond*, and the fond is *treasured*," she says. "If you add any acidic ingredient—dry sherry, or a little splash of vinegar, or some lemon juice—the acid will react with the fond and it will be released from the pan, creating a richly-flavored dark brown gravy."

I ask Cozzolino how she might teach someone else to cook like this. "It's very tricky," she says, "because it has to do with actively choosing to surrender, which is an oxymoron." The challenge is to bring her students back to center, returning them to their senses, time after time. "*Touch the food,*" she tells them. "*What does it feel like? What does it look like? What do you smell?*" She might do that three times in one minute. "*Taste. Smell. Look. Listen.* Over and over and over and over."

Such concentrated focus does not come easily, even for Cozzolino. "Listening takes quiet," she says. "It takes time. You can't listen quickly." She quotes research that emphasizes the growing impatience of most western consumers, "the addiction to the instantaneous." From her point of view, "That's the antithesis of listening. Listening requires us to take a breath. It requires us to pause."

Cozzolino's partner, Amy Pulley, is especially skilled at this. The two have been together for more than forty years, but even now Cozzolino responds to her with loving wonderment. "My beloved Amy, who will allow the act of listening to supersede in importance anything else around her." She describes how Pulley's head cocks to one side as she listens, eyes wide open, gazing deeply inwards. "*Whoa, what is she looking at?*" asks Cozzolino. Watching Pulley has taught her just how crucial such listening can be.

In Mark Nepo's words, "Patience, the art of waiting, is the heart-skill that opens the world."

Listening Behind the Noise

Late at night, Allen Hirson sits in his home office, listening to forensic recordings. He plays them over and over, identifying voices, transcribing what he hears. Did someone say "bot'm" or "bomb," "3Ds" or "three of these," and if so, what might that mean? He notates background sounds with care—a ticking clock, a passing plane—using capital letters enclosed in curly brackets. Much rests on his acute, discriminating ear. "I used to boast about a case in which I was in court for six and a half days," he tells me over Zoom, "until I was in a witness box for several *weeks*. So, it can be detailed. If I think people said X, what bit of X am I certain about? Couldn't it have been something else? And the same thing with identifying a speaker."

Hirson is a professor of speech acoustics at University College, London, and a renowned forensic speech analyst, one of only a handful in the UK. He works directly for the British justice system, providing expert testimony, sometimes for the defense, sometimes for the prosecution. In the last thirty years, he has taken part in more than two thousand criminal investigations. He refuses to be told the details of the case, lest they bias him, choosing to focus only on the recordings, and reaching out for expert help as needed. Often, he will be asked to identify a specific English dialect, or to translate a few words in a foreign tongue. More interesting yet is his ability to hear behind the surface sounds, what he calls "flipping the signal and the noise," to reveal a second, partially muted conversation, or to catch, in the interstices of human talk, the roar of a plane overhead, a sudden shout, or the song of an unexpected bird.

In the right context, such details can have tremendous potency.

One of his recent cases involved a London dog-walker, who accidentally recorded twelve seconds of indistinct shouting on his phone while, twenty meters away, someone was being drowned in a small pond. Quite unwittingly, she had provided the soundtrack for the murder. "Unlike the human ear," says Hirson, "the microphone is a dumb instrument, and picks up everything in the environment."

On another occasion, Hirson heard what he took to be crickets on a recording. Or were they birds? The experts disagreed. Finally, he consulted an ornithologist at the University of Leyden in the Netherlands, who recognized the call. The bird lived along the sandy riverbanks in Iraq, which instantly pinpointed the location. Many others had listened to that recording. But no one else had picked up on the supposed cricket, or, indeed, the all-important bird. "The consequences were very significant," Hirson says. "But it was all a function of two seconds or less of birdsong."

He has also learned "to listen between the lines" of human speech. Perhaps because convicted criminals are more often male than female, surveillance recordings tend to focus on the adult male. In one such case, involving a missing drug dealer, Hirson was asked to listen to a recording which had already been transcribed, and which, as usual, foregrounded a man's voice. "Hold on a second," Hirson said. "*There's another conversation going on!*" Listening closely, behind the noise, he retrieved a conversation between a woman and her child. They were arguing over a boiled egg, which the child found too runny. In the middle of this, the child paused to ask a question: "*Where's Daddy?*" "Daddy's upstairs," the mother answered. And that, of course, was exactly what the authorities wanted to know. "Daddy" was the drug dealer at the center of the investigation, and he was, in fact, upstairs. The evidence was right there, unmistakable, but until Hirson showed up with his forensically trained ears, no one had taken the trouble to find out.

☙

Pre-Covid, Hirson would cycle to work every day, savoring the thirty-four minutes of uninterrupted calm. He is also an avid squash player. Because his work demands such concentrated focus, he is irked by ambient noise: his neighbor's loud and yappy dog, the wild green parakeets which swoop in chattering flocks from tree to tree. "My ideal office would be at the bottom of a deserted mine," he says, "and it would be totally quiet."

Meanwhile the clock ticks toward midnight, as he bends over yet another batch of recordings, alert for what he calls "the Eureka effect"—the sudden revelation of what, until then, has been unclear to other people, and even to himself, despite many, many passes over the material. "There's really only one rule in all forensic sciences," he tells me, "*When you finish, start again.*"

Teacher! Teacher!

Early one May morning, my friend Amy Pulley and I set out to look for birds. Or rather—listen. We tread softly through the long grass, pausing at intervals to look up into the branches, up into the clear dawn sky. No birds are visible, but we can hear their calls. *Chick-a-dee-dee-dee!* That one is easy. But who has that voice like a little curl of wire? Or that trill, like a rusty maraca? Amy shuts her eyes to help her focus. She knows hundreds of birds by call alone, can repeat the mnemonics, *Teacher! Teacher! Teacher!* for the ovenbird; *Witchety-witchety-whee!* for the common yellowthroat; *Sweet-sweet-sweet, I'm so sweet!* for the yellow warbler. She singles them out for me, helps me trace one bright thread through the wide mesh of overlapping sounds. I reach for my notebook, listen close. The black-and-white warbler has that wiry voice, *Wee-Zeey!* And that's the chipping sparrow, with his chestnut cap, grey-white belly, and streaky brown wings. That's the one with the maraca.

Amy steadies her binoculars, adjusts the knob. "Look!" she whispers. "It's a red-eyed vireo." I hear a wingbeat, glimpse a sudden blur.

The branch tip bounces where a small bird used to be.
Slow looking and slow listening, still so slow to learn.

The Voices Return

Janey Winter lives by herself on the borders of Provincetown, on Cape Cod in Massachusetts. A year-round resident and working artist, she has known the place for more than sixty years. But soon after the coronavirus lockdown, she heard something utterly new from her back porch—"a big long roar—a horizontal roar—that beat below everything—a cosmic sound." It was, of course, the Atlantic Ocean, always, till now, obscured by the churn of the daily traffic. "I couldn't believe it," Winter told me. The following month it was written up in the local paper. "Even people in town could hear it!" But she herself had noticed it much earlier—two full weeks ahead of the editorial— and was gleefully delighted by that fact.

Similar discoveries were made across the globe, as planes were grounded, cruises canceled, trains and buses set to run less frequently. The family car sat idle in the driveway. Motor bikes were stalled. Ordinary vibrations caused by human activity (biking, running, walking, even shopping) were reduced to almost nil. And with that came an unprecedented opportunity to listen.

"I used to think there weren't really birds in Wuhan," wrote Rebecca Franks from China, "because you rarely saw them and never heard them." In fact, they had simply been drowned out by the relentless human traffic. NPR correspondents Eleanor Beardsley and Sylvia Poggioli both had similar stories. Beardsley had heard egrets on the Seine for the first time ever, and Poggioli (based in Rome) had been taken aback by the sheer volume of the dawn chorus. That avian orchestra, proclaiming Spring, was for her "almost too loud."

With human noise on pause, seismologists, naturalists, and other professional listeners seized the chance to record how Earth sounds, uninterrupted. In the UK, seismologist Paula Koelemeijer was happy to learn that a 5.5-magnitude earthquake (usually inaudible) could now be heard in Central London. Across Europe, the Silent Cities project called forth an army of volunteers (scientists, journalists, artists and interested amateurs), eager to track "the little sounds of every day"—from bees nuzzling deep into scented blossoms to tiny beetles foraging about among the leaves.

For years, too many of us had been moving through the world in a daze of our own making. We had grown oblivious to the voices of the birds and the trees, the mountains and the rivers. But as lockdown continued, and the voices filtered back, that conversation had a chance to be repaired. Deprived of their usual workouts at the gym, people began to walk outside more regularly, enjoying the natural benefits (less stress, lowered blood-pressure, more and better sleep), whilst also responding to the ambient sounds. A friend in the Scottish Highlands reported on a pair of cuckoos calling back and forth across the glen (the male higher, the female lower, throatier). Neighbors in Vermont remarked on the shrill of the spring peepers, the creak and sway of the tall pines. Birdsong seemed notably louder, more widespread. With human traffic so drastically reduced, birds no longer had to raise their voices to compete with cars and trucks. They could focus on courtship, on providing for their nestlings. They were able, very literally, to sleep in. No surprise that 2020 turned out to be a bonanza year for them, with larger, healthier broods and more relaxed and happier parents.

With luck, that ease of being can extend to us as well. At some point as yet unknown to us, Covid's many variants will be contained, and we will revert to our unthinking human racket. Meanwhile, we can relish the opportunity to slow down and pay attention, not just to the chatter in our heads, but to all the other myriad sounds. Because if that first year taught us anything, it's that the natural world has plenty to say for itself—from the scurrying of insects to that rich, deep ocean roar—and all we have to do is stop and listen.

An Audible Gift

On Easter Sunday 2020, the Italian tenor Andrea Bocelli stood outside the Duomo in Milan, singing "Amazing Grace" to a global audience of millions. A slight man in his early sixties, with a gentle mobile face, he sang much of the hymn with his eyes closed, as if listening inwards, caressing each word or phrase as it passed his lips. The Piazza del Duomo stretched out empty in front of him. The sole applause came from a scattering of pigeons.

Bocelli's offering was a magnificent example of what one might call "an audible gift"—five minutes of delight and inspiration flowering in the heart of the pandemic. Friends toss links to such things back and forth via email: easy, free, and instantly accessible; no post or packaging required. Here is a menu of natural sounds put out by *gratefulness.org*, here a tribute to John Prine. Here is Orfeo Mandozzi playing the concerto for oboe by Alessandro Marcello, skillfully transcribed by Johann Sebastian Bach. Not since my teens and early twenties, the era of mixtapes with their carefully coded messages, has my sense of hearing been so magically beguiled.

I am delighted by this music. But at the same time, I start to wonder: What about all the *other* things that might be listened to?

The actor Peter Sarsgaard is especially fond of the Meadowport Arch at the north end of Prospect Park in Brooklyn. "Everything is amplified here," he says. "It's like an ear but made of stone and wood." Reporter Naomi Fry describes him settling on a bench inside the shallow tunnel, snapping his fingers to create an echo. "Who doesn't love a reverb?" he asks, rhetorically.

In introducing Fry to his private echo chamber, Sarsgaard is offering her an acoustic gift, the chance to luxuriate in one specific, transient sound. Such listening can be a powerful practice, educating our ear and opening our heart, braiding us into reciprocity with the larger world. The English poet Alice Oswald pays special tribute to the act of raking, both for its quality of embodiment—"a more mobile, more many-sided way of knowing a place than looking"—and for the richness of its sound. For her, it's as if those who rake were "running their fingers over the leaves, listening in, finding what's already there."

Not long ago, I met up again with Amy for an early morning walk. We spent several hours in the Windsor State Forest, looking at the spring ephemerals (skunk cabbage, trillium, the bright beads of partridge berry), and listening to the birds. Coming back, Amy was ahead of me, following the meanders of a small brook. "Very good sound right here," she told me. I made my way to the appointed spot. A frill of water was cascading over a grey boulder into a shallow sunlit pool. Such gentle, rippling music! You could see the mud and grit on the bottom and the dapples of sunlight trembling on the surface: sight and hearing, depth and clarity, beautifully entwined.

A Gift for Listening

> *The more I listened—the more I heard—the more I listened.*
>
> Gordon Hempton

Junko Oba is an assistant professor at Hampshire College, where she teaches courses in ethnomusicology, Asian studies, music theory, and popular music. She is a skilled piano player, and also plays koto and jiuta shamisen (the Japanese long zither and long-necked lute). Not long ago, she started playing viola de gamba with the Five College Early Music Ensemble. "I think I am a listener, rather than a performer or a composer," she told me. "That is my number one identity."

Oba grew up in Japan, the eldest of three children, and remembers her mother as always "very busy." When she was still small, she would be sent over to her aunt's house to play with her autistic cousin. For a long time, he refused to interact. But somehow Oba found a way to play games with him, and to connect. It wasn't until much later that she began to recognize (and value) what was, in effect, her early training as a listener. "I love music," she says now. "I play music. But music has become just one of the many things I listen to."

Oba is a graceful woman, reticent and calm, with an air of serene interiority. When she first arrived in the United States, she had a position at Wesleyan University's World Music Archives, working with archival recordings. Many of the tapes were old and frail, recently salvaged from basement storage. Oba was asked to transfer them onto digital media, keeping a detailed log meanwhile. She had to identify the instruments that were being played, the style of the music, and the number of musicians. Some of the tapes had been made in developing countries, where the power supply was erratic, and their speed would fluctuate accordingly. Oba was expected to make note of such glitches, as well as the physical quality of each tape. It was a daunting task.

It is a tribute to her diligence that she still managed to enjoy the music, and even to distinguish many of the background sounds. She remembers an epic sung by a tribal leader in the Philippines, telling the entire history of his tribe, in a language that to her was incomprehensible. The chant was maintained for days and nights together, reel after reel. "It started with the chickens running around early in the morning, and then the women came out, and started preparing breakfast. . . . So I could hear the progression of the day—the life!— and that was wonderful."

Oba left Wesleyan in 2002 and took a job at the University of the South in Tennessee. One of her students was doing an independent study with a luthier named Geoff Roehm, and Oba happened to be present when Roehm gave an impromptu performance in his workshop-garage. Because of the unique acoustics of that cluttered space, and partly too, because of her alert attentive ear, trained to pick up "tiny little strange things" in the sound archives, she was able to make out "two very distinct upper partials of harmonics" as Roehm played his guitar.

Later, after the student left, Oba approached the luthier and explained what she had heard. Roehm's face broke open in astonishment. "*What* did you hear?" The world of luthiers is largely male dominated, and at first, he found it hard to credit that "this woman from the Far East" had been able to distinguish such subtle variations in his playing. But soon it became clear that Oba did indeed possess such skill. At Roehm's invitation, she began to visit his shop regularly, watching while he worked on different projects.

Meanwhile, he put her through a series of increasingly tricky tests, exploring the reach of her extraordinary gifts. For example, he asked her to carve out a spoke using a crude spoke plane (designed to make wheel spokes and the backs of Windsor chairs). Left alone without instruction, Oba had to figure out the process for herself, finding a delicate balance between the curve of the blade, her own (relatively modest) strength, and the wood itself. The spoke-plane is in fact a simple mechanism, and "sounds right" when used correctly, with the right amount of force. Roehm had to admit he was impressed.

He also taught Oba the skill of "listening to the tone of each wood." If every instrument were to sound the same, it would be impossible to market them. So, makers of artisanal guitars strive to distinguish their own guitars from other people's, finding "the voice of the wood," by tapping on thin pieces of rosewood, spruce, or red cedar, in order to discover the special resonance of each.

Although Oba never formally apprenticed with Roehm, he taught her to identify those different voices and then to work with them, so that when he built a guitar or a ukulele, the final product was uniquely his. "It was a wonderful year," she says now. She especially loved listening while he worked. Not just tapping the wood for the tone, but shaping, sanding, shaving. "Even when he was just sanding, it was going to give a different sound."

Oba moved to western Massachusetts in 2008 and has taught at Hampshire College ever since. She enjoys her students, though she often wishes they could be a little more focused. The proliferation of cell phones, iPads, and other gadgets irks her too. She doesn't ban them outright, but she does ask that they be turned off while she is teaching. Class time, for her, is an opportunity for collaborative performance. "We are going to be creating something that can only happen here and now," she tells her students. "So, please, when you are in my class, can you just be more attentive to your immediate surroundings?"

Because Oba's ear is so especially acute, it can sometimes distract from her enjoyment. Every semester, the Hampshire music program holds a works-in-progress concert, with a talk-back the following day. One recent composition featured a drum set, a single separate cymbal, and a piano. It began with a student beating time on the cymbal, and then the piano joined in. "I don't know how to describe it," Oba told the performers in the talk-back. "But when the piano comes in, there's a very interesting acoustic clash which is disturbing to my ear." Nobody else could recall it, and she was tempted to apologize. "It could be just me." But then the student drummer, who was also the composer, began to explain. "You know," he said, "that's a very tricky cymbal. It's warped!" And another of the performers jumped in, "*Why did you use the warped cymbal?*"

No one else could have made out that slight discordance. But to Oba, with her many years of conscientious listening, it was of course quite obvious. "My ear is accustomed to hear that way," she says.

As a child, Oba lived in Kamakura, a medieval town with many temples. She remembers her feet striking the flagstones as she entered the sanctuary, edged with cedar and pine trees, and how the canopy of leaves would shift and rustle overhead. Even now, she finds it crucial to spend regular time alone: time to listen inwards, to unwind. It comes as no surprise that she wrote her senior thesis on John Cage. At the heart of her long, attentive listening is a pulsating core of silence, which she experiences each time she plays the piano. Oba of course plays many different instruments, "some very well, some not very well." But the piano feels like an extension of her body. The moment her hands touch the keys, she can shut out everything else. Every Sunday morning, she goes very early to her office. The building is empty; there are no students around. "And I just play."

Consider the following quotations:

A bulldozer starts again, moving the air like an audible corked staircase before reaching its full power. As I lean on my wooden table, my arms receive sympathetic vibrations from the lower frequencies in the bulldozer, but hearing seems to take place in my stomach. A jet passes over. Some of its sound moves through my jawbone and out the back of my neck. It is dragging the earth with it. I would like to amplify my bowl of cracking, shaking jelly . . . I would like to amplify the sound of the bulldozing.

Pauline Oliveros

The mere chink of cups and saucers tunes the mind to happy repose.

George Gissing

Continue to explore:

Get up early and write down everything you can hear for the next half an hour. Consider too, what sounds may well exist but are inaudible to you.

Norton Juster's children's book, *The Phantom Tollbooth*, features a genial character called the Soundkeeper, whose vault holds every sound that was ever made. When the boy hero and his friends are about to take off on their adventures, she hands them an audible gift—a small brown package neatly tied with string. "Here are street noises at night, train whistles a long way off, dry leaves burning, busy department stores, crunching toast, creaking bedsprings, and of course, all kinds of laughter. There's a little of each," she tells them "and in far-off lonely places I think you'll be glad to have them."

Offer a friend an acoustic gift.

∴ 7 ∴

Listening to the Wild

And all the place
there was grew out of listening.

Li-Young Lee

Island Listening

There is a knoll on the Isle of Eigg called *Cnoc na Piobaraichd,* or the Piper's Cairn. Those in need of inspiration have only to go there on a bright moonlit night, lay an ear to the ground, and listen.

Inevitably, a new tune will be given to them.

Eigg is a ragged heart-shaped island, set twelve miles off the west coast of Scotland, accessible only by ferry. I came there first in the early 2000s, and returned several times thereafter, hungry for the "new tunes" it had to offer. There was the rush and slap of the sea on the ride over from the mainland, the skirl of bagpipes down by the quay. There was the laughter and banter in the village tearoom, the steady tramp of one's own hard-working boots, the long, drawn-out *baa-aa* of the sheep as they browsed their way across the sloping fields.

Best of all was the broad swath of sand at *Traigh na Bigil*—"the strand of the whispering," as the Singing Sands of Eigg are known in Gaelic. I saw it first one bright July morning. I'd been staying with friends on the south side of the island, and we walked north-west along the one road, with brambles tousling the hedges, down through the little village of Cleadale, and over the fields to the Singing Sands. There was no one else about. For what seemed hours we shuffled and scooted and kicked along the upper reaches of the beach, while the sand chirped cheerfully underfoot.

Sand is mostly made of quartz, with smaller particles called fines. When the wind sifts it so that it is evenly milled, each grain rounded and washed clean by the salt sea, it makes a very particular kind of music, variously described as "singing," "burping," "barking," "whistling," "whispering," or "chirping." The sand "sings" at a right angle to the wind, as one layer is blown or shifted over the layer beneath. It has a distinct frequency, about 88 hertz, equivalent to the low note on a cello.

Standing on the beach, just above the tide line, you hear what the sound artist Bernie Krause has christened *geophony*—the showing forth or revelation of the earth's own natural voice, its wind and rain and tides, its changing ground, its shimmering rock and sand. These were the first sounds ever to be heard on our small round planet, preceding human habitation by some four and a half billion years, and on Eigg have remained unchanged for millennia.

Eigg's neighbor to the north, the island of Rum, is said to be the first place in Scotland to be inhabited. An archeological site there dates back 8,500 years, and Eigg too has had its share of finds, most now safely ensconced in the National Museum of Scotland in Edinburgh. Between Bronze Age hunters and fishers, proselytizing Christians, Viking marauders, and warring clans, the rocky little island has had its own complicated history, not least its recent series of capricious landlords, from the charismatic playboy Keith Schellenberg to the self-styled German artist known as Maruma, who bought the place in 1995, and sold it again, under duress, two years later. Finally, after a massive fundraising campaign, the island was bought back by its own people in April 1997, and has since been run, with great aplomb, by the Isle of Eigg Heritage Trust.

The journalist Patrick Barkham praises "the genuine fusion of Hebridean culture and mainland counterculture" that now exists on the island, with its emphasis on affordable housing, renewable energy, and land reform. In his view, a contemporary small island manifesto might start with "the realization that we need to treat other people more carefully. . . . Spend more time outside. . . . Consider animals and plants as well as people. Live more intimately with our place, for it is a complex living organism, too."

Meanwhile, the waves continue to pulse in and out as they have always done, soothing the hearts and minds of all who listen. On a recent visit, my friend Doug Gilbert and I walked over to the Singing Sands just as the sun was setting, a flare of light behind the jagged hills of Rum. The sands whispered and squeaked as before, and he showed me a dimple on the water which was an otter eating a fish, and another, larger dimple, which was a seal. Later, on the way back, he felt in the half dark for a little nugget of something which turned out to be a toad. I held it, quietly palpitating, in my hand.

The Invitation

"You are not composed of water, hills, and air," writes the Scottish poet Thomas A. Clark, "but you take your place in the conversation of water, hills, and air." Human speech, in other words, is only part of a much larger, more expansive exchange. But relatively few of us take the time to stop and listen. "We are talking to ourselves," writes Thomas Berry. "We are not talking to the river, we are not listening to the river." We do not hear the voices of the insects, birds, animals, or fish, let alone those of the plants and rocks and trees.

There are all sorts of reasons for this, ranging from simple human narcissism and distractibility to the growing racket of our post-industrial age. There's no question that modern life has helped to dull our senses. (Myopia, for example, has increased significantly in the last half century, with the rate for those born after 1960 four times that of their own parents.) We may not realize how much noise we're making as we blunder along, the tender channels of our ears plugged up with plastic, essential oblong gadget always within reach. But in most cases, our biggest distraction is the thought process itself.

One of the most helpful pieces I have read on this is a tiny five-page essay called "The Invitation," written by the naturalist Barry Lopez. As a younger man, Lopez imagined that indigenous people saw and heard more than he did, that they were simply more aware. Only gradually did he realize why this might be so. *They didn't talk.*

When an observer doesn't immediately turn what his senses convey to him into language . . . there's a much greater opportunity for the minor details, which might at first seem unimportant, to remain alive in the foreground of an impression. . . .

If, for example, he and his companions encountered a grizzly bear feasting on a caribou carcass, Lopez would tend to focus almost exclusively on the bear. His companions' attention was far more spacious and wide-ranging. They would listen for birdsong or the snap and rattle of the surrounding brush; snuff the air for recent odors. Their temporal framework was also more voluminous than his. For Lopez, "the bear was a noun, the subject of a sentence; for them it was a verb, the gerund 'bearing.'"

Over years of traveling with indigenous people, Lopez came to absorb two essential lessons: first, that whatever occasion he might enter was *still in the process of unfolding*, and second, that the core story, whatever it might be, extended far beyond its immediate physical setting. The scattered fragments of the puzzle—"a piece of speckled eggshell under a tree . . . a hole freshly dug in the ground—" might mean very little in and of themselves. But as part of a larger pattern, they could be revelatory.

Too often, Lopez was only *thinking* about the place he was in; in sensory terms, he wasn't fully present. At times he'd become so wedded to his thoughts that he'd lose touch with the impressions he was still gathering. "And so, the mind's knowledge of the place remained superficial."

What matters here is patience, presence, bodily awareness; a certain willingness to befriend the mystery. As Lopez puts it, "A grizzly bear stripping fruit from blackberry vines in a thicket is more than a bear stripping fruit from blackberry vines in a thicket. It is a point of entry into a world most of us have turned our backs on in an effort to go somewhere else, believing we'll be better off just *thinking* about a grizzly bear stripping fruit from blackberry vines in a thicket."

But in fact, that moment is an invitation, and a precious one: a chance to watch and listen, to participate, offered freely, "without prejudice," to anyone who happens to be passing by.

Mountain Truths

John Muir was born in Dunbar, Scotland, in 1838, and died in Los Angeles on Christmas Eve, 1914. His father was a strict Presbyterian and required him to learn a certain number of Bible verses every day, on peril of a whipping. By the time Muir was eleven, he had "about three-fourths of the Old Testament and all of the New by heart and sore flesh." He continued to read the Bible deep into old age. Nonetheless, the lean sinewy man with the bright blue eyes and the long reddish beard can more easily be seen as a wandering monk or nature mystic than as the reputable scion of an evangelical church.

As a young man, Muir walked from Kentucky to Florida, keeping a journal along the way. He arrived in California in 1868, and became a noted writer, botanist, and conservationist, working to create Yosemite National Park, and founding the Sierra Club. All his life he remained curious and adventurous, brimful of gusto and enthusiasm. Though he loved his wife and daughters, and was a loyal friend, he also found great pleasure in his own good company, whether taking a sled ride down a glacier, slipping behind the rushing water of Yosemite Falls, or climbing a Douglas fir in the midst of a tremendous storm. There was no such thing as solitude as far as he was concerned: even when he was tramping the Sierra on his own, the rocks and trees and waters were a shining company of friends.

"Plants are credited with but a dim and uncertain sensation," he wrote, "and minerals with positively none at all. But . . . may not even a mineral arrangement of matter be endowed with sensation of a kind?" He thought of rocks as having a certain gentle interiority or "instonation," and suggested that instead of walking on them as "unfeeling surfaces," we should instead regard them as "transparent sky." Whether rocks spoke to him with "audible voice" or "pulsed with common motion," he was eager to listen and translate, to spell out some of the "mountain truths" he had discovered.

Muir was known in human company as a nonstop talker, and it

makes sense that he'd converse with plants and flowers too. "When I discovered a new plant, I sat down beside it, for a minute or a day, to make its acquaintance and try to hear what it had to say." At times, he would conduct a regular interrogation. "I said, how came you here? How do you live through the winter? And the plants revealed their secret. . . ." Nor were his encounters always so sedate. A missionary friend in Alaska remembered Muir running from one cluster of flowers to another, falling to his knees in an ecstasy of admiration, as he greeted each new bloom in a mixture of scientific nomenclature and delighted baby talk, all in a broad Scots accent.

The Calvinists of his youth would have disdained such giddiness, seeing the glories of the natural world as fated for destruction, and Muir's exuberance as an offense against the Lord. But Muir himself had long since cast off such gloomy tenets, imagining a wild heart like his own in every cell and sparkling crystal, and addressing plants and animals as "friendly fellow mountaineers."

He brought such imaginative identification to larger species too, remembering individual trees with great precision, and well able to distinguish "the sharp hiss and rustle of the wind in the glossy leaves of the live oaks [from] the soft, sifting, hushing tones of the pines," and to orient himself, even at night, by the sounds of the wind as it played through the pine needles. There was no end to his attentive listening, or his willingness to be delighted and astonished.

"As long as I live," he wrote, "I'll hear waterfalls and birds and winds sing. I'll interpret the rocks, learn the language of flood, storm, avalanche." Or as he scrawled in the margin of one of his favorite books, not the Bible this time, but a volume of Ralph Waldo Emerson, "Between every two pine trees there is a door leading to a new way of life."

The Voices of the Trees

I was wandering the grounds of a big New England estate, following my feet along a quiet track. The trees were looming presences up ahead, their branches inclined towards each other, shifting a little with the wind. It was as if they were talking together, trading intimacies. For a moment, I could almost make out words. But when I paused beneath them, looking up, the trees turned abruptly silent. A flicker of irritation moved among the leaves. It was as if I had burst upon them unannounced—as if, somehow, they hadn't heard me coming, and my small human presence were an annoyance, an intrusion. I watched as they drew back into themselves, calm and reticent, back into their towering self-sufficiency.

Can one make friends with trees, listen in on their private conversations? Thoreau thought one could. He himself maintained steady friendships with particular trees, often tramping "eight or ten miles through the deepest snow to keep an appointment with a beech tree, or a yellow birch or an old acquaintance among the pines." In his essay, "Walking," he describes the "admirable and shining family" who had settled in the pinewood on Spaulding's Farm. When the wind died down, Thoreau could hear "the finest imaginable sweet musical hum,—as of a distant hive in May," which for him was the sound of their thinking.

As naturalists know, every species of tree has its own distinctive voice, responding differently to wind and rain and snow and shining sun. Thomas Hardy writes of this in *Under the Greenwood Tree*, allocating subtly different verbs to fir and holly, ash and beech. "At the passing of the breeze, the fir trees sob and moan no less distinctly than they rock; the holly whistles as it battles with itself: the ash hisses amid its quiverings, the beech rustles while its flat boughs rise and fall."

John Muir was alert to such distinctions too. In *The Mountains of California*, he describes a fierce windstorm in the Sierras, when he happened to be exploring one of the tributaries of the Yuba River. "Even when the grand anthem had swelled to its highest pitch, I could distinctly hear the varying tones of individual trees,—Spruce, and Fir, and Pine, and leafless Oak. . . . Each was expressing itself in its own way,—singing its own song, and making its own peculiar gestures. . . ."

It was on this occasion that Muir climbed to the top of a hundred-foot-tall Douglas fir, clinging there for several hours "like a bobolink on a reed," while the tree flapped and swished and bent and swirled, "tracing indescribable combinations of vertical and horizontal curves." Muir felt sure of its resilience, and exulted in everything he saw and heard, from the "shining foliage" to the "profound bass of the naked branches and boles booming like waterfalls; the quick tense vibrations of the pine needles . . . the rustling of the laurel groves in the dells, and the keen metallic click of leaf on leaf. . . ."

Years later, traveling in Alaska, he built himself a vast bonfire in the midst of a pelting storm. His missionary friend was baffled, as were the local villagers. But Muir made no apologies. He was sacrificing the lives of some few trees to attend more fully to the rest. He simply wanted to observe how those Alaskan trees responded to the wind and rain, "and to hear the songs they sang."

The Inside Story

"Have you ever tried to enter the long black branches of other lives?" asks Mary Oliver.

> tried to imagine what the crisp fringes, full of honey,
>   hanging
> from the branches of the young locust trees, in early morning,
>   feel like?

Until very recently, most of us would have had to say no. However much we might enjoy our daily walks, perhaps returning again and again to a particular tree, we had very little notion of how that tree itself might feel. But the publication of Peter Wohlleben's *The Hidden Life of Trees* in 2016, and David George Haskell's *The Songs of Trees* in 2017, followed swiftly by Richard Powers' bestselling novel, *The Overstory* (2018) and Suzanne Simard's *Finding the Mother Tree* (2021), has brought a welcome infusion of both scientific and imaginative understanding. Listening to trees, it turns out, involves far more than *psithurism* (the deliciously onomatopoetic word for the rustlings of their leaves and twigs and branches). There is an inside story too. Early in the spring, just before the leaves open, water pressure builds up inside the trunk, giving rise to a continuous soft murmur. "If you place a stethoscope against the tree," says Wohlleben, "you can actually hear it."

Trees too are capable of "listening," both to one another and to the world around them. Because they extend such a long way underground, the roots of neighboring trees inevitably intertwine. This allows trees to communicate through the roots themselves and through the fungal networks at their tips, "crackling quietly at a frequency of 220 hertz." Although such signals travel fairly slowly—at about a third of an inch a minute—they are nonetheless extremely effective, allowing trees to warn and protect and even feed each other. Wohlleben writes of mother trees that recognize and defend their younger kin, as well as ancient trunks still green and growing, nourished by the circle of their own great-grandchildren. In general, trees communicate mainly with their own kind. But they can reach out to other species too—Douglas firs sustaining birches, oaks helping pines—linked by a collaborative intelligence known as "the wood wide web."

One of the most lyrical tree interpreters is Robin Wall Kimmerer, a member of the Citizen Potawatomi Nation (originally from the Great Lakes), who also holds a PhD in Botany. For her people, the land itself is animate, as are fire, water, chipmunks, orioles, even a single strawberry. Trees, especially, are recognized as teachers. "In the old times, our elders say, the trees talked together. They'd stand in their own council and craft a plan."

Like Wohlleben, Kimmerer believes that the "standing people" do indeed communicate among themselves and unite in mutual defense. "We don't have to figure everything out by ourselves," she writes, "there are intelligences other than our own, teachers all around us." And to this day, she goes to them for solace.

> I come here to listen, to nestle in the curve of the roots
> in a soft hollow of pine needles, to lean my bones
> against the column of white pine, to turn off the voice
> in my head until I can hear the voices outside it: the
> *shhh* of wind in needles, water trickling over rock, nut-
> hatch tapping, chipmunks digging, beechnut falling,

mosquito in my ear, and something more—something that is not me, for which we have no language, the wordless being of others in which we are never alone.

After the drumbeat of her mother's heart, she writes, "*this* was my first language."

Stop and Listen

Robin Wall Kimmerer is approaching seventy now, a full-bodied woman with an air of wisdom and practicality. She spent her childhood in upstate New York, "raised by strawberries," as she likes to say, and taught college biology in Kentucky, where she established herself as an expert on mosses. "Learning to see mosses is more like listening than looking," she says. They "issue an invitation to dwell . . . right at the limits of ordinary perception."

To the passionate botanist, mosses are a multifaceted marvel, including some 22,000 known species. At 470 million years old, they are senior both to trees (at 385 million years old), and to flowering plants (at 130 million), as well as to our youthful human selves. Kimmerer regards them with the proper astonishment. At a recent colloquium at the Harvard Divinity School, she spoke of studying them as a form of spiritual practice: literally getting down on one's knees to look more closely.

That same curiosity and reverence shine forth in her two award-winning books, *Gathering Moss* and *Braiding Sweetgrass,* in which she honors plants as friends and neighbors, teachers and companions. At a time when the average American can identify fewer than ten plants, and treats those few with casual indifference, Kimmerer provides a model of interspecies courtesy: indigenous practice backed by scientific rigor.

Thus, when she finds a cluster of wild leeks, her first instinct is not to pull them up, but rather, to stop and ask permission, using both sides of her brain to attend to the response. The analytic left judges "whether the population is large and healthy enough to sustain a harvest," while "the intuitive right . . . is reading something else, a sense of generosity, an open-handed radiance that says *take me*," or "a tight-lipped recalcitrance" that says no.

The authority of that response is, for her, utterly convincing. Pace has a crucial part to play as well. Kimmerer does not like to rush. She prefers her shovel to be blunt, a little slow. Once again, she values the time spent on her knees, "watching the ginger poke up and listening to the oriole."

Kimmerer is not alone in her willingness to pause, whether in her own backyard, or in the larger garden of the surrounding forest. The sinologist Willard L. Johnson writes of attuning himself to his garden, linking his deep mind with its growing, so that his plants can tell him what they need to flourish. Ann Armbrecht (originally trained as an anthropologist) writes of her joy in working with herbs and making medicine. She cherishes the opportunity to sit in her garden at night, surrounded by chamomile and poppies. Like Kimmerer, she describes "messages received while sitting with plants . . . the language rising from the darkness."

In the words of the botanist George Washington Carver, "If you love it enough, anything will talk to you."

The Language of the Wild

Long ago,
In the very earliest time,
when both people and animals lived on earth,
a person could become an animal if he wanted to
and an animal could become a human being. . . .
All spoke the same language. . . .

or so, at least, claimed an Inuit woman called Nalungiaq. That dream of a common language shows up again and again in myths and poetry and children's stories, as well as in much real-life biography and ethnography. I first encountered it in "John and Barbara's Story," towards the end of *Mary Poppins*.

John and Barbara are the youngest members of the Banks household, a pair of twins, not quite one year old. Unlike their parents and their older siblings, and everyone else except for the inimitable

Mary P., they understand the language of the wild. When the sunlight stretches its golden length across the nursery, Barbara holds out both hands in admiration.

"Do you like the feel of me?" asks the sunlight.

"Dee-licious!" answers Barbara.

When the Starling perches on the railing of her cot, and begs for something to eat, she understands at once, and proffers half of her arrowroot biscuit. She and John know what the trees are saying, they can hear the voices of the wind and stars, and are confident they always will. But all too soon, their first teeth come in, and not long afterwards, they celebrate their first birthday. The Starling comes to visit, cheery and garrulous as always—and this time, the twins can't make out what he is saying. John hugs his woolly lamb, Barbara croons quietly to herself and swallows the last of her biscuit. The Starling flies off, close to tears, brushing a quick wing across his eyes. His two young friends have completely forgotten the language of the wild.

I was six or seven when I first read "John and Barbara's Story," and it anguished even then. It was as if I too had once known that marvelous inclusive language and could not quite forget it even now. *How to retrieve that oh-so-precious gift?* For long years, I scoured children's books in search of clues. I read *The Wind in the Willows*, and *The Little Grey Men*, I followed Alice through the looking-glass and back again. It was not until I was well into my thirties that I realized I'd been looking in the wrong place. Science—nature writing—was the place to start, along with almost any form of contemplative practice (poetry, music, experimental dance), so long as it was grounded in deep listening, in steady, open-hearted receptivity. Only then could you hope to hear "all the secret whisperings of the world," from the "tiny little buzzing-humming" sounds of dreams to the footsteps of a ladybird as she pattered across a leaf. Only then could you eavesdrop on the "little ants chittering" under the soil, and listen, without straining, to the far-off music of the stars.

"Do you hear the rushing of the river?" asks the monk in the Zen koan.

"Yes, master," answers his disciple.
"That is the way."

Their Listening

Awake at night, restless, out-of-sorts, I hear myself cry out: a small, raw sound. Noushka rouses almost at once. Her head lifts from the small bed on the blanket chest; she stretches, calls out briefly in response. *Yes?* she queries. *Yes?* I watch as she trots valiantly across the darkened quilt. She is a waiter taking an order, a lover hastening to the side of her beloved, a wet-nurse comforting a wailing child.

Cats are gifted listeners, with thirty-two muscles in each of their outer ears. This allows them to rotate each ear 180 degrees, distinguishing sound and distance with immense precision. A little purse-like structure known as "Henry's Pocket" is thought to enhance their ability to hear high-pitched squeaks (mice in the wainscoting, bats in the attic), while a cluster of hairy tufts inside each ear helps them to identify the finest of vibrations and track them to their source. Human beings have a hearing range of 20 to 20,000 hertz (sound waves per second), and dogs of 15 to 50,000 hertz, but cats surpass them both at 45 to 85,000 hertz.

The sense of hearing (unlike, say, taste and touch and smell), is curiously distributed across the animal kingdom. Elephants listen both through their marvelous sail-like ears, and also through their feet, which set up robust vibrations as they pound the ground, picked up by nerve endings in their ear bones and their toes. They can literally hear rain clouds as they gather overhead. They can converse with one another too, not just through their loudly resonant trumpeting, but though a much lower, deeper, "infrasound"—a kind of private whispering. This can be heard by other elephants at a distance of six miles, meaning that the leader of the herd (always the oldest female) can alert her clan to danger, or a mother elephant call out for her errant calf, without any other creature listening in.

Dolphins do not possess external ears. Instead, they emit powerful sonic pulses, audible as distinct whistles and clicks, squawks, squeals, or moans, from the cavity below their blowhole. These rapid clicks echo back into the dolphins' teeth and lower jaws, and from there to the brain, helping them locate a school of salmon or a tasty squid, informing them of the presence of an intrusive cruise ship.

There is no end to the varieties of such listening. Birds' ears are funnel shaped, set slightly behind and below the eyes, and are covered with soft feathers—the prettily-named *auriculars*—for protection. Katydids and crickets carry audio equipment on their knees. Although snakes can't hear high frequencies, they do have inner ears, and can make out vibrations through their skin, as well as some low-frequency airborne sounds. Frogs, too, possess an eardrum of sorts and an inner ear, which, in combination with their lungs, allows them to hear both above- and underwater.

But the world's best listener is the greater wax moth—for most people, a thoroughly unlikely candidate. Greater wax moths devour honeycombs and are detested by beekeepers, and, one imagines, by the bees themselves. But they can hear up to 300,000 hertz (150 times more than a human being, and 100,000 hertz more even than a bat), the highest recorded frequency of any living creature. Unlike mice (which hear less well than cats), the wax moth actually hears better than its major predator, the bat, which of course is what has allowed it to survive and even thrive.

Recent studies show that plants and animals share 70 percent of their DNA. No surprise then, that plants can also converse among themselves, sharing nutrients and recognizing kin. Some release pheromones warning of insect attacks; others seem able to "hear" or at least respond directly to the insects themselves. Researcher Lilach Hadany reports on a beneficent exchange between bees and evening primroses: within minutes of sensing the wing-vibrations of the bees, the primroses intensify the sugars in their nectar. It is as if the blossoms serve as ears, she says, their curved and rounded shapes making them "perfect for receiving and amplifying sound waves . . . while tuning out irrelevant sounds like wind."

Meanwhile, Noushka dozes comfortably at the foot of my big bed. I press my nose to hers and allow a small sound to escape. *Mmmmmmn-mmmmmmn-mmmmmmn*, a gentle rumbling hum. I murmur praise-songs to her, cat psalms, feline odes. We have been conversing like this for almost twenty years. Her ears tilt lightly forward, brush my cheek. "Noush," I say aloud, "my darling Noush." Softly, almost somnolently, she begins to purr.

A Wider Listening: Sy Montgomery

*Many young girls worship their older sisters. I was
no exception. But my older sister was a dog, and I—
standing here helplessly in the frilly dress and lacy
socks in which my mother had dressed me—wanted
to be just like her: Fierce. Feral. Unstoppable.*

Sy Montgomery

My grandmother's earliest memory was of sitting at the edge of a dried-up garden while she stroked her friend. She was perhaps three years old, the daughter of a British diplomat stationed in Japan, and this was the early 1900s. She described her friend to one of the servants—its long, sun-warmed body and dry, rustly scales—and the servant was appalled. My grandmother's special friend turned out to be a snake.

"It could have been a rat snake," said Sy Montgomery when I told her this. These are large, non-venomous snakes found on the main islands of Japan. "But there are some interesting venomous snakes there too." Unlike the servant, she was not at all perturbed. "Most venomous snakes will do anything not to bite. They'll rattle their rattles, or they'll erect their hood—there's one species of snake that will squirt blood out of its eyes to avoid biting you. They don't want to use their venom up on you. They don't want to attack you with their face."

Montgomery is a naturalist and a writer, the author of some thirty books. She's in her sixties now, a slim, poised figure with hazel eyes and curly blonde hair. The precision of her response is characteristic, as is the immediate empathy with the poisonous snake. From her point of view, we are all part of the same animal family. "We share 99 percent of our DNA with a chimpanzee, and 90 percent with a dog or goat or cat or rat. But we share 60 percent of our DNA with a banana! So, let's stop trying to separate ourselves out from everyone else."

Montgomery's father was an army general, and she had a peripatetic childhood, always moving on from one base to the next. For a budding naturalist, nature was in short supply. But she had a Scottish terrier called Molly, and a green parakeet called Jerry, with his harem of changing wives. And there were earthworms too, and bees and crickets, lizards and turtles. "I think I was optimistic," Montgomery says now. She understood that dogs could bite and bees could sting, but at the same time, she expected them to welcome her. "And each time I expected it, I was rewarded with the fact that it was fabulous. There was just so much joy."

That optimism is reflected in Montgomery's work, with its rare exuberance and lack of irony. When I asked about Christopher Hogwood, the subject of her book, *The Great Good Pig*, she broke into a litany of praise. "I loved everything about that pig. Everything! I loved his nose-disc, I loved his hooves, I loved his voice, I loved his hair, I loved his tail, I loved his ears, I loved his eyes, I loved his color, I loved his scent, I loved the way he moved, I loved his strength, I loved his kindness. I mean, just reciting it is this prayer of gratitude for having known him, and I will have that pleasure *forever*."

She remembers a day in late September, when the air smelled of ripening apples, and the yard was filled with magnificent golden light. Montgomery had resigned herself to staying inside, "reading some damn screen." But then Christopher escaped his pen, and the only way she could coax him to stay put was to sit and pet him under the apple tree, so that he would lie down and grunt with happiness. And so, they lay together in the afternoon sunshine, on what for her was the most beautiful day in the world. "I'll never forget that day," Montgomery says now. "And Christopher gave me that."

When human beings talk together, our speech and facial expressions start to mimic one another, a consequence of so-called "mirror neurons." The same thing happens with animals. In *Journey of the Pink Dolphins,* Montgomery describes a moment in Honolulu when she waved casually at the first dolphin she saw—and the dolphin waved back. "It's like a dance," she says. "If you're really receptive, if you're really listening, that's when the mirror neurons do their magic."

When Montgomery was working with Octavia, the subject of her best-selling book, *The Soul of an Octopus,* each day ended in a state of ecstasy. "I would come home singing. Being around somebody like that [she means the octopus] is so freeing, and so transformative. I just loved doing that."

At first glance, she and Octavia might appear to have little in common. "You would think somebody who could taste with all their skin, someone who's covered with 1,800 grasping suckers, someone with a beak like a parrot and venom like a snake and ink like a pen, who can change color and shape in a second and pour themselves through an opening the size of an eyeball, you would think somebody like that would have such a different mind from ours, that there would be no possibility of meeting that mind, or knowing that individual—and yet not only can you meet that mind, but that animal can come to care about you."

Again, this has much to do with mirror neurons. "When you're with somebody you care about, you really want to know *How is it with you? What's it like to be you? Is it good being you right now?* That's at the root of every real conversation that we have, except, 'How do I fix my chainsaw?' But most of our important conversations aren't really about transfer of information. They're about being present with the other. It's a more emotional exchange, like you would have with an animal. Which of course we are." Montgomery is confident that certain octopuses have been glad to see her. "They really do wear their three hearts on their sleeves: they do flush with emotion. . . . So sometimes you can really see what an octopus might be feeling and thinking."

During the "wonderful Wednesdays" she spent with Octavia, Montgomery surrendered to octopus time. "Who can flow better than an octopus? Whose body is water, and who literally pours themselves in and out of places as easily as water. To be in that kind of flow with an animal like that is—*amazing!*"

Focus has its benefits. It allows us to concentrate, and to get things done. If you really want to listen, you should put your hand up to your ear, and pull back the outer edge of the pinna into the "big ear" position. But "listening means more than just what's coming through our ears," says Montgomery. "I don't think there's a word for listening with our eyes, listening with our skin, or listening with scent. But we do that!" After all, she says, "The oldest part of us is not the intellect, it's the neurotransmitters of pleasure and pain and excitement and fear. Which is exactly the same in a human being—and a clam! So that is where you meet."

She believes that too many of us are shutting down, leading increasingly cramped, unnatural lives. "We're getting so we're just looking through a little pinhole," Montgomery says. "You can't get anything if you're all bound up," she adds. "You've got to have your heart open, your eyes open, your arms open." Only then might you begin to know what it's like to be Christopher Hogwood, lying under the apple tree on a bright fall afternoon, or Octavia, pouring herself through an opening the size of an eyeball, or my grandmother's special friend the snake, stretching his dusty length in a long ago Japanese garden.

Consider the following quotations:

I listened deeply; I also listened convivially. For the rain has a voice particular to the site it visits, and the way it touches the surface of the harbor here, and the undulations of sand, and the bayberries, is different from the lusher sounds of lowland rain or even cornfield rain. How thoroughly I have memorized the sound of that presence here, on this narrow cape, from years of rain-walk. I could lie in the dark anywhere and hear it and know whether or not I am home.

Mary Oliver

A Cherokee friend of mine told me about something he was taught as a child, part of traditional Cherokee culture, called 'opening the night.' What you do is you go out into a dark place, it could be on your back porch in the old days, and you sit, and you listen to what's around you in a very close circle, within arm's length. You concentrate on that, then you double the circle, and hear everything beyond there. And you keep doubling the circle. And he said it would reach a point where at night you could sit down and hear things a mile away.

Paul Bogard

Continue to explore:

How far can you listen? Experiment with ever greater distances.

See what you can find out about animal listening.

∴ 8 ∴

Sound Healing

Blossoms at night,
and the faces of people
moved by music.

Issa

The Earliest Music

Two million years ago, before there was language as such, or words, or music, our forebears got by with a singsong utterance known as *musilanguage*. They "spoke" through gesture and posture, through sounds and movement, now anxious and abrupt, now slow and soothing. Pitch would have been important, rhythm, tone, all of which could be imitated, replicated, passed down from one generation to the next. According to Merlin Donald, author of *Origins of the Modern Mind,* that skilled mimetic culture may have lasted for tens of thousands, perhaps hundreds of thousands of years.

No one knows the date of the first instruments, though drums and shakers are the likely candidates, created first by chance, and then with more conscious deliberation. W. A. Mathieu, who describes himself as a "life-drummer," explains how this might work in contemporary terms. "When you are a life-drummer, you learn how everything has its own surface and its own hollowness, and a voice hidden inside waiting for you." Each morning, when he practices singing, he bangs his head back against a beautiful wooden beam, and the whole room seems to reverberate in A-flat, in a rich, low octave. "Am I crazy to love this dark, round tone coming from my house?" he asks.

Just as Mathieu loves to "play his house," (and indeed his stairs and table-tops, his glasses and silverware, even the body of his dog), so our protohuman ancestors would have relished the sounds of the forest and savanna, from the reverberation of a hollow tree to the whiskery marimba of dry leaves and twigs and branches, and the shushing of the wind in the long grass. They would have explored the range of their own voices, from deep and slow and resonant to the thinnest, purest birdcall, spiraling up into the high blue sky, echoing back from a distant cliff. The world they knew was full of curious and surprising music, so much so that for a long time they barely felt the need to move beyond it, or to create actual working instruments for themselves.

The writer Martin Shaw has a story about this, drawn from his own life in Devon, England. One night, he was camping on the edge of the river Dart when he heard what he took to be a marvelous choir. The music was astonishing: layered harmonies, dazzling polyphonies, a powerful rhythmic pulse. Shaw crawled up through the bracken to catch the choristers off guard—and discovered there was no one there at all. "Deft, with intricate deviations and ruminations"—what he had been hearing was the voice of the river itself. Shaw knew the area well; he had walked those river banks a dozen times. But he had never heard music of that kind before. Naturally he felt obliged to sing along. Little by little, his "croaky, just-woken warble" found its way into that mighty tide.

The Rhythms of Nature

For most of human history, music would have been understood as an enveloping presence, guided and inspired by the rhythms of nature. Folk musicians the world over are alert to that shared soundscape, as when a flute or fiddle player is able to imitate the cry of the wind or the fall of running water, a squirrel chittering or a flock of geese. Music is communal and collective, casual, unceasing, unselfconsciously braided into daily life.

One of my favorite stories about this is told by the sound artist Bernie Krause. Back in the 1960s and early 1970s, he worked with the

Nez Percé in the western United States, recording music, oral history, and natural sounds. One icy morning early in October, the tribal elder Angus Wilson led him out to Lake Wallowa in northeast Oregon. For what seemed a long time, they sat huddled at the edge of a small stream, hearing nothing but the call of a few ravens. At last, a slight breeze came up, and began to stir the aspens and the firs. And then, as Krause describes it, "Suddenly the whole forest burst into a cathedral of sound!"

"Do you know what makes that sound?" Wilson asked. Krause shook his head. Without a word, the old man walked to the water's edge, and pointed to the reeds broken into different lengths by the wind and ice. Slipping a knife from his leather sheath, he cut off one of the reeds, whittled a few holes, and, not even stopping to tune the instrument, began to play. "This," he said, "is how we learned our music."

Classical music, too, draws much of its inspiration from the natural world. The Finnish composer Jean Sibelius lay down in the grass to catch the overtones in a neighboring rye field. Both Vivaldi, in his *Goldfinch* Concerto, and Messiaen, in his *Quartet for the End of Time*, were strongly influenced by birdsong, as were Respighi in *Pines of Rome*, John Cage in *Song Books*, and of course Beethoven in his *Pastoral* Symphony. The twentieth-century composer Morton Feldman made notes for his percussion piece, *The King of Denmark*, while sitting on a beach on Long Island.

"I wrote it in a few hours, just sitting comfortably on the beach. And I can actually conjure up the memory of doing it—that kind of muffled sound of kids in the distance and transistor radios and drifts of conversation from other pockets of inhabitants on blankets and I remember that it all came into the piece, these kinds of wisps."

Attention to such "wisps" remains a core creative practice, in which even human-generated sound can prove inspiring. Music, after all, is in the ear of the listener. Or as Gertrude Stein once said, "After all anybody is as their land and air is. Anybody is as the sky is low or high, the air heavy or clear and anybody is as there is wind or no wind there. That is what makes a people, makes their kind of looks, their kind of thinking, their subtlety and their stupidity, and their eating and their drinking and their language."

Each of us is composed, in large part, by our local soundscape.

Panpipes

Henry David Thoreau is best remembered as a naturalist and writer. But he was a skilled flautist too, as well as a delighted and surprising listener. He describes striking a paddle against his boat on Walden Pond, till he had filled "the surrounding woods with circling and dilating sound," and he exulted in the music of the brand new telegraph, pressing his ear to one of the posts to hear every changing inflection. "Of what significance is any sound," he asked, "if Nature does not echo it?"

More than half a century later, Edward Emerson sketched his memories of the Thoreau he had known as a young boy: how he made use of a "low continuous humming sound" to draw wild creatures to him, and taught his students to make flutes for themselves out of grass or leaf stalks, squash or pumpkin, or the thin shoots of golden willow. "This youthful, cheery figure was a familiar one in our house," he reports. When Thoreau, "like the 'Pied Piper of Hamelin,' sounded his note in the hall," all the children would run to him and hug his knees, till he had been persuaded to sit down by the fire and tell them stories or perform magic tricks (making knives and pencils disappear), or best of all, perhaps, shake the heavy copper warming pan over the flames till "a white-blossoming explosion of popcorn" fell down over their heads.

In the sorrowful months after Thoreau died, Louisa May Alcott wrote a poem in his honor, entitled "Thoreau's Flute." Even as she grieved, she imagined Thoreau's flute playing on by itself, reminding her he would remain:

> A potent presence, though unseen,—
> Steadfast, sagacious, and serene. . . .

"For such as he," she wrote, "there is no death."

Breath Becoming Sound

I spoke with Steve Gorn one summer morning, in the garden of his house in upstate New York. A kindly man with grizzled curls and long, elegant hands, he is also a master bamboo flautist and saxophone player, shifting effortlessly between classical Indian, jazz, and contemporary world music. Among his recordings are the best-selling *Asian Journal, Wings & Shadows, Luminous Ragas, Rasika,* and *Pranam.*

Gorn grew up in New York City, the son of a professional concert pianist. But from early on, he resisted his father's expertise. "When I was small, like six or seven, I was really kind of intentionally stupid," he told me. "I did *not* want to learn music from my father." Nonetheless, he soon learned clarinet and saxophone, and by ten or eleven, had become passionately fond of jazz. One day he was in a music store, poring over a record by Sonny Rollins, when another customer glanced up. "You need to listen to Coltrane," he said. John Coltrane, Charles Lloyd, and Yusef Lateef had all begun to weave aspects of Indian music into their own playing.

"So, the horn in the hands of a jazz musician bridged the link to Indian music."

By 1969, Gorn was en route to India, traveling overland via Greece and Turkey. He spent the following winter in Benares, before journeying on to Kolkata, where he met with the bansuri master, Sri Gour Goswami. The maestro kept him waiting for a long time. Finally, he was asked to play. Then Sri Gour Goswami took out his own flute and played a raga. Even now, Gorn remembers the wonder of that moment. "The tone was deep, warm, and velvety, utterly weightless. The raga unfolded and time stopped. It was breathtaking. . . ."

Gorn just sat there, stunned.

"May I come back?" he asked.

On returning to the United States, Gorn devoted himself to the study of Indian music. He had planned to do a PhD in ethnomusicology. Instead, he simply moved out into the larger world, recording with Paul Simon, Richie Havens, Paul Winter, Glen Velez, and many others. Little by little, he acquired what he calls a vocabulary, a way of moving: "*Breath becomes sound, sound settles into form, which then is recognizable as music.*"

He describes how it feels to rest at the center of that growing sound, the sense of inevitability, of entrancement. "You start playing, and you put on this drone. . . . And then maybe twenty minutes later, forty minutes later, in the nature of a piece, you're 'in tune.' And then, capital I, capital T. *In Tune.* There's the sense of the whole body being 'in tune.' Time and space merge: leading and following become effortless." He particularly enjoys playing back and forth with yoga practitioners. "Their movements or their breath will inspire how I play. A bird flying by will inform a phrase. . . ." Music, for him, has become a healing art.

Meanwhile, he finds himself letting go of a certain dazzling virtuoso quality, taking things more slowly, savoring the moment. The Covid lockdown gave him a welcome opportunity to reflect. "Very often when I'm listening back to something I've played," he says, "I think I played too much. That more space, more silence, would be just fine."

Sound Healing

Almost every adult knows how to comfort a young child, rocking and crooning over the small, unhappy body, and drawing it into alignment with their own. But there are times when the opposite is true, and the nurse or caretaker, therapist or social worker must choose to set aside their own internal preferences in order to match rhythms with the one they're trying to help.

Oliver Sacks tells the story of an elderly Jewish man afflicted with dementia. David had led a highly Orthodox life. But in old age, instead of chanting the traditional Hebrew prayers, he would rock and chant, "*Oy, vey. Oy vey, vey,*" exploring the phrase in all its variants, and repeating it ad infinitum. "*Vey ist mir, mir ist vey, oy ist vey, vey ist mir.*" His clinical social worker had been asked to bring him breakfast, and wanted to know what food he would prefer. But all inquiries were greeted with the same "*Oy vey. Oy vey, vey.*" Only when the social worker sat down next to him and began to rock in tandem, addressing him in his own familiar rhythmic cadence, was David finally able to respond, returned to welcome clarity, at least for that short time.

Sacks has a number of such stories, in which music and rhythm permit daily life to continue, often against almost intolerable odds. "The man who mistook his wife for a hat" (the central figure in Sacks' book of that name) was in fact a musician by profession. By the time Sacks met him, he was unable to recognize objects, or even to distinguish them from human beings. But his musical skills were unimpaired. If he sang while he took a bath or dressed himself, sang while he ate or took a walk, he was able to do all these things quite well.

Such music need not be given voice. It can also be imaginary, internal. Another of Sacks' patients, also a musician, suffered from an extreme case of Parkinsonism, and described herself as "unmusicked." For minutes at a time, she would be frozen into brutal immobility. But as soon as she was able to recall a tune, however humble, she would be freed, instantly, by the power of those remembered harmonies.

One does not have to suffer from insomnia or dementia or Parkinsonism to experience this. We all know what it is to be stressed and anxious, our attention splintered, calm and focus lost. "Urban civilization cuts us off from our own inner lives," writes the psychoanalyst Anthony Storr. "We easily lose touch with the well-springs of creative phantasy which make life worth living." At such times, music, whether real or imagined, can help return us to ourselves again, as we surrender to its restorative flow.

One of my favorite examples of this is taken from William Styron's *Darkness at Noon*. Like many writers, Styron suffered from mood swings and depression, and for a while was thinking seriously about suicide. But first he made himself watch the tape of a movie in which someone he knew had been cast in a small part. One scene took place in a music conservatory, and when Brahms's *Alto Rhapsody* burst from behind the walls, the music pierced him. Suddenly Styron was overcome by all the joys his house had known—"the children . . . the festivals, the love and work," and realized he could not possibly kill himself.

Restorative Chant

In the early 1960s, the ear specialist Alfred Tomatis was invited to visit the Benedictine monastery of Saint-Benoît d'En Calcat, in the French Pyrenees. The Second Vatican Council had recommended that the Latin Mass be replaced by the local vernacular, and a zealous young abbot had banished all Gregorian chant. The monks were not responding well to the new regimen. In the past, they had managed easily on three or four hours of sleep, but now they were always tired, "slumping in their cells like wet dishrags." Extra sleep didn't seem to help. Nor did adding meat or vitamins to their diet. Even after Tomatis urged that the chant be reinstated, many remained too depressed to sing. Only when he had them sing into an "Electronic Ear" (allowing them to hear their own voices played back through a special filter) did the monks finally begin to recover. Within nine months, they had returned to their centuries-old schedule: chanting six to eight hours a day, sleeping three to four hours a night, and spending the rest of their time in hard physical work and prayer.

Gregorian chant is especially rich in high-frequency sounds, which themselves are highly energizing. Its rhythm matches the steady pulsations of the human heart. No wonder the monks had missed it so viscerally. They were hungry not for meat or sleep or vitamins, but for the robust nourishment of their own enveloping music.

Half a world away in San Francisco, the Beat poet Allen Ginsberg was helping to organize a peace march with several friends. This involved them in direct negotiations with the local chapter of Hell's Angels, most of whom saw the march as a protest against freedom. Tempers began to fray, and the talks became increasingly hostile, until Ginsberg, inspired, brought out his harmonium, and began to chant the Prajnaparamita ("Highest Perfect Wisdom") sutra, in a voice from the abdomen, "a monosyllabic, deep-voiced monochordal chant."

For a few moments, no one spoke.

Then one of the Angels joined in, making up his own words as he went along. "*Om, om, zoom, zoom!*" This was Tiny, who'd been especially combative at an earlier march, but was now caught up in the chant. "*Om, om, zoom, zoom, zoom, om!*" he persisted. Soon everyone was chanting together—Allen Ginsberg, Neil Cassady, Ken Kesey, and the Angels—the potential rage completely quelled.

The chant "settled everybody's breath in a neutral territory where there was neither attack nor defense," Ginsberg explained later. As with the Benedictines, a sturdy grounded energy had been restored.

O Rare Delight!

Mariel Kinsey was born in China where her parents were missionaries. On Sunday evenings, the entire congregation would go down to the ocean for a picnic. The children would play together in the tidal pools, while the grown-ups sang hymns. Kinsey remembered the sun going down, the crash of the waves, and the tingling salt-sea air. "And the sound of those wonderful voices just singing, 'And day is dying in the west.' Oh, my God!"

Kinsey was well into old age by the time she described this to me. But as she spoke, it was as if she were transported back to early childhood: a little harum-scarum girl of six or seven, wading in the tide pools as the sun went down. "You're hearing me into speech," she cried delightedly, quoting Nelle Morton. "You're listening me into memories!"

Music can be found in every country on earth, and for millennia has been a deep source of human pleasure. But only in the last two or three decades has neuroscience developed to the point where experts can observe its effects on the human brain, as people listen to music, imagine listening, and even compose it for themselves. It turns out that imagining music is (neurologically) almost entirely identical to actually hearing it played. Strange as it sounds, we can be refreshed by music that is inaudible.

In his classic book, *Musicophilia*, Oliver Sacks remembers his own father, who "seemed to have an entire orchestra in his head." The older Sacks was a practicing physician, and always kept two or three miniature orchestra scores in his pockets, which he would pull out between patients, enjoying a little impromptu concert. "He did not need to put a record on the gramophone," writes Sacks, "for he could play a score almost as vividly in his mind."

Sacks himself had similar skills, which may well have been inherited. As a student pianist, he was able to rehearse his pieces in his mind. Years later, with music he knew well, such as Chopin's mazurkas, he only had to glance at the score, and the mazurka would start to play internally. "I not only 'hear' the music," he wrote, "but I 'see' my hands on the keyboard before me, and 'feel' them playing the piano—a virtual performance which, once started, seems to unfold or proceed by itself."

Such skills are confirmed by the cognitive neuroscientist Robert Zatorre and others, using sophisticated brain-imaging techniques, which show that "imagining music can indeed activate the auditory cortex almost as strongly as listening to it."

Sacks' friend, the psychologist Jerome Bruner, lived to a great age, dying at more than one hundred. But he was born with congenital cataracts, and until he had surgery at the age of two, was able to see nothing but light and shadow. Perhaps because of this, his auditory sensitivity was unusually acute. He told Sacks that on calm days, sailing solo across the Atlantic, he would sometimes hear classical music "stealing across the water." On at least one occasion, he listened with great pleasure to a favorite Mozart record, only to discover, when he went to turn it over, that he had never actually plugged in the record player. The entire concert had taken place in his imagination.

Not surprisingly, the brains of experienced musicians differ notably from those of other people. Indeed, most anatomists can identify a musician's brain on sight: the *corpus callosum,* which connects the two hemispheres of the brain, is much enlarged (asymmetrically so, in those with perfect pitch). The volume of grey matter is also much increased, compared to non-musicians, both in the motor, auditory, and visuospatial areas of the cortex, as well as in the cerebellum.

Such findings are of more than casual interest. As Sacks says, it is clear that exposure to music (especially singing or playing an instrument) stimulates development in different parts of the brain, and indeed enhances the connections between them. Because we live in a world of almost constant noise, our auditory systems are under considerable strain. All the more reason then, to nourish them with music, whether real or imagined, and to allow ourselves to be transformed. As the poet Philip Whalen put it jokingly in a letter to a friend, "I got J. S. Bach into both ears at once and my brains are now growing a long curly wig and a lace jabot and velvet waistcoat. . . . O rare delight! All sentient beans should know such sublimities!"

Song of the Union

I sat on a folding chair inside the small temple of the Burns Monument in Edinburgh, as twenty-eight recorded voices sang "Auld Lang Syne," each in their mother tongue. Speakers were placed at intervals against the walls, so that you could listen along to just one voice if you so chose, or, from a different vantage point, to all at once. The recording was set on a continuously changing loop, first one voice and then another rising to the fore, in a rich weave of ever-changing sound.

The piece had been conceived by the Nigerian sound-artist Emeka Ogboh in response to Britain's departure from the European Union. "Auld Lang Syne," a plaintive appeal to memory and friendship, constancy and kindness, itself long attributed to Robert Burns, was by no means a casual choice. Eighteen months earlier in Brussels, after the last votes had been cast and the last speeches made and Britain, finally, withdrawn from the European Union, all 751 members of the "EU–UK friendship group" had risen to their feet, stretched out their hands, and sung that same song together, "some tearful, some stoic, others visibly uncomfortable."

For auld lang syne, my dear
For auld lang syne
We'll tak a cup o' kindness yet
For days of auld lang syne

Now it was being sung again, by EU citizens living in Scotland, only three of whom (citizens of Ireland, Cyprus, and Malta) had had the right to vote in the 2016 Brexit referendum. In recording their individual voices (working through lockdown, with sound studios in Edinburgh and Glasgow) and offering them a shimmering place in the chorale, Ogboh was able to give each of them, however belatedly, the chance to be heard.

I arrived at the Monument around lunchtime on a mild, white-skied day, and settled in for the duration. Twelve pale columns surrounded a floor made of small hexagonal tiles: yellow and garnet red, clear blue and chocolate brown, with a floral motif. Visitors came and went: some local residents, some tourists. Often, they would burst in, rushed and anxious, keen to get to grips with yet another new experience, and then pause, as if enchanted, on the threshold, as they realized just how little was required. *Take a moment and listen.* Time and change, breaking and mending; the great beauty of the mingled voices, burnished and warm, followed by a stretch of silence, and then another voice, a new beginning.

Standing in the doorway of the little temple, with the music washing through and over me, I spoke with the young Frenchwoman who was employed as guard. Unlike other events she'd been responsible for, she told me, this one made everybody welcome.

"Everyone can understand it," she said quietly. "They just need to open."

Sound Fishing

It was May 1953, and Pauline Oliveros had just turned twenty-one. She picked up her brand-new Eico tape recorder (a birthday present from her mother) and set it in the window of her San Francisco apartment. *What would she hear?* The crash and rattle of the trolleys on the street outside, the *click-tick* of her own alarm clock, the boom of someone practicing trombone? Later that day, when she played back the tape, Oliveros was astonished by how many sounds she'd missed.

As an ardent musician (and committed listener) she'd expected to hear more. "Listen to everything all the time," she told herself, "and remind yourself when you're not listening."

More than half a century later, that practice remained central to her work as a composer, improvisor, and teacher of what she came to call Deep Listening. "Deep listening is listening in every possible way to everything possible to hear, no matter what you are doing." Next-to-impossible, perhaps. But for Oliveros it became a mantra for herself and others, guiding her on through a long and dazzling career.

Pauline Oliveros was born in Houston, Texas, in what was then a surprisingly rural neighborhood, surrounded by pine woods, berry patches, and a pecan orchard. All her life, she remembered the audible bounty of those early years, the bird song and the choruses of frogs and insects: "very, very dense sound that varied according to the time of day or night."

Despite the "disembodied music" emanating from radio and gramophone, Oliveros grew up listening to live music every day. Both her mother and grandmother taught the piano professionally, and she herself started playing accordion at nine, later mastering violin, piano, tuba, and French horn. She was able to attend numerous concerts by the Houston Symphony Orchestra, as well as recitals by soloists and chamber groups, and by the age of sixteen had already decided that she wanted to be a composer.

"How we listen creates our life," she said. "Listening is the basis of all culture."

In 1967, Oliveros began to teach a course called "The Nature of Music" at the University of California, San Diego. Most of her students were non-music majors, so she composed pieces that would allow anyone to participate, whatever their level of technical skill. This grew into a body of work called *Sonic Meditations*—"recipes for ways of listening and sounding, transmitted orally without conventional musical notation." Or as Oliveros put it, "pieces based on the structure of human attention."

These were violent times. Martin Luther King Jr. was assassinated in April 1968; Robert Kennedy, two months later. The Vietnam war would continue for another seven years. Oliveros felt that people needed to come together not just to play music, but "to be together well" as human beings. She was "trying to facilitate inward experience," she said years later. "I don't think one can create change just with words. One has to have a full body response..."

In 1981, Oliveros resigned her professorship, and moved to upstate New York, living in a simple A-frame at the back of the Zen Mountain Monastery in Mount Tremper. Over time, she founded her own non-profit organization, the Pauline Oliveros Foundation (later renamed the Deep Listening Institute) for the creation of new work, ceremonies, and retreats. Among her projects was a piece called "Deep Listening" recorded in a disused cistern in Port Townsend, Washington, with her good friends Stuart Dempster (trombonist, didgeridoo player, and composer) and the vocalist and composer Panaiotis. The cistern was fourteen feet underground, so the title was very literal. But "Deep Listening" came to have a more expansive meaning too, implying that one listened not just to the musical performance per se (rhythm, melody, intonation, etc.), but to more random sounds as well: the roar of a passing truck, the echo and resonance of a particular space.

Oliveros had been fascinated by such things from early on. For her, listening could be "focal" or one-pointed (when you listen to one sound above all else), or what she called "global," when you are equally receptive to everything you hear, both internal and external.

In her 1992 piece "Sound Fishes," Oliveros invites her students to listen for what has not yet sounded, "like a fisherman waiting for a nibble or a bite." Just as there are sounds in the air, she writes, so, too, there are sounds in the water.

When the water is clear you might see the fish.
When the air is clear you might hear the sounds.

Another assignment, "Native," from *Sonic Meditations,* reads simply, "Take a walk at night. Walk so silently that the bottoms of your feet become ears."

A third, "Global Listening," asks everyone to listen to their bodies and to the sound of their own breathing, gradually expanding their listening outwards, first to those sitting close by, then to the outer reaches of the studio, the hallway and adjacent rooms, and finally outside the building, to the street, the next town or city, the other side of the world. . . .

Such assignments made it possible for Oliveros to draw attention to the natural soundscape, and then to enliven it through playful interaction. At a Sound Symposium in Newfoundland, in the 1990s, she asked everyone to say or sing their name in a way that pleased them, calling it out loud to the larger group, and then listening as the sound echoed back to them. The response, she said, carried more meaning than just uttering one's name. "It seemed to suggest an emotional message, one that translated something like, "You spoke and we were here to listen; you spoke and you were heard.""

Listen with Everything

> *The softer the sound, the more important it is that we perceive it.*
>
> Yehudi Menuhin

Some years ago, the Klezmatics were playing a concert in Warsaw, Poland. After it was over, the trumpeter, Frank London, went on to a kosher restaurant with a friend. There were some Mizrahi musicians there, singing *piyutim,* and when London took out his trumpet, everybody turned to look at him. *Piyutim* are Jewish praise-songs, but the rhythms and melodies are Arabic, and the trumpet is not part of that tradition. "*Very good!*" thought London. For a while he just listened, playing very softly, what he calls "ghosting along." But every so often, there were songs he actually recognized, and then he could play a little more forcefully.

"*How do you know those songs?*" his friend asked him afterwards. "I don't even know," London told him. "Somewhere along the way I just learned—"

London is in his sixties now, lively and energetic, with sparkling eyes and tousled dark brown hair. We have known each other for more than thirty years. When I told him I was working on this book, he said he had to talk to me. He's a composer and bandleader, a well-known trumpeter, the cofounder of the Klezmatics. But even as a teenager, he was recognized as a skilled listener. Somehow, he could hear music in his head and understand how it was put together. "It's an acuity," he told me, as we sat together in his Lower East Side apartment. "It's like a chef tasting stock. You learn to focus your hearing."

London started to play trumpet when he was in fourth grade, and by the time he graduated from high school, he'd begun to listen seriously to world music and jazz. At the New York Conservatory, he listened to everything from Charlie Parker and Max Roach to klezmer recordings from the 1920s and 1930s. Since then, he has become what he calls "a naive native speaker in thirty or forty different musical languages." Whether he is playing trumpet in a Brazilian jazz orchestra, or "ghosting along" with a group of Arab-Israeli singers, he knows "how to match timbres with the musicians, match the style, match the rhythm, blend in and sound like them." The crucial skills are always the same. "So, *listening listening, listening, listening, and being able to imitate.*"

What London is listening for depends on what is being played. He tries to remain open and receptive, alternating "total Zen blank mind" with a more thoughtful, analytical approach. A classical violinist and a Blue Grass fiddler will play the same notes differently, just as a stockbroker and a psychiatrist will "listen differently" to the same person. "So, I'm evaluating . . . what is the timbre, what is the nature of the sound? What are the melodic elements, the rhythmic elements, the formal elements? The structure, the system of intonation?"

When London hears something he has never heard before, he may not know if it is "good or bad." But for him such total novelty is rare. He almost always has some frame of reference and can find a way to enjoy what he is hearing, and ideally, play along. A friend of his commented that London could be set down at a party anywhere in the world. By the first tune, he'd be sitting with the band, and by the third, he'd be calling out the tune that was to follow. "It's about learning in repertoires," says London. "I know songs in hundreds of different repertoires."

❧

One of London's favorite projects was a collaboration with Boban Marković and his Serbian Gypsy band. When they first met up in a small town in Hungary, they had no common language, and their manager-translator was occupied elsewhere. Somehow eight Americans and fifteen Serbians had to come up with a playlist, give a concert, and then record together the following week. Miraculously, they pulled it off. The Klezmatics would play a tune they thought the Serbians might enjoy, and they'd see the Serbians' eyes light up. And then the Serbs would start playing what was obviously the same song. The Klezmatics might play it in four-four time, and the Serbs in seven-eight. They might have three sections, the Serbians only two. But "We created a concert, and then an album, and it worked very well. It went on for years!"

London's skill is obviously innate. But it is also based on what musicians call "ear training." For most of his twenties, he belonged to a group called the Garuda Ensemble. They met four hours a day for "free improvisation," and together came up with hundreds of different exercises. They alternated foreground and background, they explored counterpoint and instant imitation, they experimented with static and active textures, blending sound, or not. They taught themselves to recognize "real time," playing for two and a half minutes without looking at a clock, or coming up with an improvisation in four parts, each of which had to last precisely thirty seconds. Sometimes, they'd begin a session with the lights off, then close their eyes, and ask everyone to start playing at once. When London realized that the horn and wind players made a little *hhhoaa* of breath as they inhaled, he had the group start over. "OK, let's try it without breath."

"It was always about listening," London says now. In order to walk out on stage and perform for two hours at a stretch, the ensemble needed all those weeks and months of practice. "You have to hear the other people," says London. "You have to balance with them. You have to be aware of when you are dominating, and when you are following. *You have to listen.*"

When audience members use their phones to video the Klezmatics during a show, he sees them as losing out, choosing to mediate what ought to be a fully engaged experience. "When you listen to someone play," he says, "it's an act of love, it's an act of gratitude." Listening requires a certain self-surrender. It is the decision to be fully present.

European audiences are famously more skilled at this than most Americans. London remembers a festival of sacred music in Bremen, Germany, featuring two Iraqi Sufi drummers. The men played more or less in unison for an hour and a half. "It was as if you had two people, who had both memorized all of Dante's *Inferno* . . . reciting it—together!"

The audience listened, motionless, as the intensity built. Suddenly, the drummers paused—and one collapsed. There was huge applause. When it stopped, the man was still lying on the stage. It later turned out that he'd gone into a trance. But even at that moment, no one moved. No one panicked, or jumped up, or asked, "*Is he OK?*" Then somebody brought water, and the drummer began to stir. He got to his feet, and the men played one last piece. London is still haunted by those long, attentive minutes, the purity of the silence, the willingness to wait. It astonishes him, even now.

To this day, if he is working with an ensemble, he likes to start with listening. He might ask everyone to sit in a circle and play a note together, then look round at each of the other players, to make sure that they can hear. "If you can't hear the other person, you're too loud," says London. "And if you can't hear yourself, you're too soft." Once the group has found their balance, he has them raise the volume from soft to loud and back to soft, keeping the sound steady at every level. "'Cause we listen with our eyes," he says. "We listen with our nose, we listen with our hands. That's what we learned from our experiments. So—listen with your heart, listen with your spirit. Listen to what someone's saying. Listen with *everything*."

Consider the following quotations:

From the most unlikely sources come the sweetest sounds. Some of them may have been waiting centuries for their freedom. . . . Remember, one honors a thing by vibrating it. Garbage cans. Buckets, jars, bottles. Boxes. Cases. Barrels. Stop signs. Mailboxes. Toothbrushes on your teeth. Screens. Rakes. Posts. Awnings. Umbrellas. Lampshades. Walls. Air. This list should be endless. Life-drummers never rest.

W. A. Mathieu

In the evening, the Amadeus [Quartet] played opus 132, and I danced to the last movement, I rose up and danced, among the cats and their saucers, and only when I was too far carried away to stop did I realize that I was behaving very oddly for my age—and that perhaps it was the last time I would dance for joy.

Sylvia Townsend Warner

Continue to explore:

Can you remember a time when you loved to make mouth noises? For the next five minutes, whistle and squawk and hum, puff out your cheeks and make popping noises with your lips. How does that feel?

Experts concur that listening to your own chosen music can enhance creativity, strengthening connections between different parts of the brain, and heightening introspection and self-awareness. Return to some music you particularly love and explore your own version of sound healing.

∴ 9 ∾

Writers Listening

Imagination, inspiration, and intuition are all arts of the ear.

Paulus Berensohn

Moments of Being

When W. S. Merwin was a little boy, he was perfectly happy playing by himself. His mother remembered him sitting on the kitchen floor with two copper bowls and a box of dried peas, pouring the peas from one bowl to another, "listening to the sound of rain."

Almost every writer has some memory like this, some sound that calls them back across the years. Here, for example, is Virginia Woolf, in her half-finished memoir, *Moments of Being*:

> If life has a base that it stands upon, if it is a bowl that
> one fills and fills and fills—then my bowl without a
> doubt stands upon this memory. It is of lying half
> asleep, half awake, in bed in the nursery at St. Ives. It
> is of hearing the waves breaking, one, two, one, two,
> and sending a splash of water over the beach; and then
> breaking one, two, one, two, behind a yellow blind. It
> is of hearing the blind draw its little acorn across the
> floor as the wind blew the blind out. It is of lying and
> hearing this splash and seeing this light, and feeling,
> it is almost impossible that I should be here; of feeling
> the purest ecstasy I can conceive.

Woolf was not satisfied with the words she found for this. "I could spend hours trying to write it as it should be written." If she were an artist, she said, she'd paint those first impressions in pale yellow, green, and silver, a strange, globular image that included the yellow of the blind, the green of the sea, and the silver of the passionflowers outside the window, as well as "the caw of rooks falling from a great height." The sounds and the colors were all intermingled, all equally resonant, as she lay there in her bed, still half asleep, filled with a rapture that even she could not describe.

Woolf's near contemporary, the poet Edwin Muir, grew up on the tiny island of Wyre, in the Orkney Isles, and had a parallel memory of his own, in which sight and sound were miraculously entwined. He was lying in some room, "watching a beam of slanting light in which dusty, bright motes slowly danced and turned, while a lower murmuring went on somewhere, possibly the humming of flies." He could not date the memory, which for him was both "clear and yet indefinite," and which he thought might well go back to earliest infancy.

It was as if, while he lay watching that beam of light, time had not yet begun.

Listening to the Radio, Listening to the Page

The poet Seamus Heaney grew up in rural Ireland in the 1940s, the eldest of nine children. In his Nobel Prize acceptance speech, he remembered the "intimate . . . creaturely existence" of those early days, in which the night sounds of the horse shifting in its stable mingled with the adult voices from the kitchen.

> We took in everything that was going on, of course—
> rain in the trees, mice on the ceiling, a steam train
> rumbling along the railway line one field back from the
> house . . . we were as susceptible and impressionable as
> the drinking water that stood in a bucket in our scul-
> lery: every time a passing train made the earth shake,
> the surface of that water used to ripple delicately, con-
> centrically, and in utter silence."

Into that cozy, crowded "den-life" came the voice of the BBC, booming from the wireless with news of bombers and of cities bombed, of planes lost, and of prisoners taken. At first Heaney was too small to understand how much was at stake, though he was stirred even then by the exotic listings on the radio dial, and by "the beautiful sprung rhythms of the old weather forecast: Dogger, Rockall, Malin, Shetland, Faroes, Finisterre."

But as the years went by, and his "listening became more deliberate," he would climb onto the arm of the big family sofa and press his ear to the speaker, thrilling to stories about Dick Barton, special agent, or the RAF flying ace known as Biggles. Even as a schoolboy, he loved Keats's ode "To Autumn," with its luscious freight of language and sensation. By adolescence, he was enthralled by the intensities of Gerard Manley Hopkins, while at the same time drawn to Robert Frost and Chaucer for their "wily down-to-earthness." Later he found his way to Wilfred Owen, Patrick Kavanagh, Elizabeth Bishop, and Robert Lowell, and later still to Wallace Stevens, Emily Dickinson, and Rainer Maria Rilke. What had begun as an unselfconscious act of listening had become a journey into the universe of literature itself.

The Writer's Voice

Most of us nowadays read to ourselves, which is to say we do not sound the writer's words aloud, or even murmur them quietly under our breath. Our eyes speed ahead of us across the page. We read much faster than we could hope to speak. And yet there is a subtle osmosis taking place, what the Canadian poet Robert Bringhurst calls a transfusion. It is not form or phrase or image that is at issue here, not story or plot or characterization. Instead, it is the half-heard, half-imagined timbre of the writer's voice, exhilaratingly specific and unique. "You come voice to voice with the voice you hear," writes Bringhurst, "as if you were face to face with the speaker. The voice becomes part of your mind."

Those quiet insistent cadences draw the reader back again and again, with an answering hunger, an almost sexual pull: the desire to be inhabited by that one particular voice, to accept the breath of that particular breathing body, reaching back across the decades and the centuries. If the eager reader is also an apprentice writer, chances are good that the text will serve as catalyst to his or her own work. When Stanley Kunitz read Gerard Manley Hopkins aloud, he felt as if he were "actually occupying his selfhood and speaking out of it . . . somehow merging into his bloodstream and nervous system." Heaney too found the Jesuit priest inspiring, and when he first put pen to paper "what flowed out was what had flowed in, the bumpy alliterating music, the reporting sounds and ricocheting consonants typical of Hopkins' verse."

Years later, he saw the parallels between his own Northern Irish accent and the "heavily accented consonantal noise" of Hopkins' work. But what mattered at the time was that Hopkins helped him, in a very literal way, to find his voice, so that the words he wrote were his, had his own feel about them. First came the thrill of encountering those marvelous new poems. And then, slowly, and often clumsily, came the craftwork, the technique. As Heaney puts it, "You hear something in another writer's sounds that . . . delights your whole nervous system. . . . 'Ah,' you tell yourself, '*I wish I had said that in that particular way.*'"

And then if you are lucky—lucky and diligent—you settle down to write.

Double-Tongued

The poet Alastair Reid was born in Galloway, in southwest Scotland, and described himself as "a longtime listener, an eager receiver of the speaking voice in all its tones, forms and variations." Like many writers, he grew up "double-tongued," speaking the local dialect with his friends at school, while at home and in the classroom he spoke standard English. His father was "soft-spoken, gentle . . . edging on shy," but he was also a Church of Scotland minister, and as a child, Reid was enthralled by the cadence of his voice, "mesmerized by the sudden incandescences of a phrase, fascinated by the convoluted metrics of certain hymns . . . aware of language as a kind of spell."

All his life he savored particularly apt and evocative Scottish words (*flist,* for a spark of wit, a flash of lightning; *clishmaclaver,* for lively gossip or incessant chatter; *swither,* being unable to make up one's mind), whilst himself writing a very pure, graceful, cosmopolitan prose. Nevertheless (and the swerve of the word is itself quintessentially Scots), everything he wrote retained a certain native emphasis and rhythm, what Robert Louis Stevenson once called "a strong Scots accent of the mind."

Whether Reid's own Scottishness was audible to the average reader, casually browsing one of the many pieces he wrote for *The New Yorker,* I have no idea. But he was certainly capable of wrapping himself in his ancestral plaid, the better to lambast his fellow countrymen. In "Letter from Edinburgh" (first published in 1964, when he was not yet thirty), he describes them with gleeful pleasure as "girning over their lot" (bewailing their fate), with a "rocky, heathery chip on their bowed shoulders." "Tartan blood runs sluggishly in their veins . . ." he writes, "and a mixture of whiskey and sentimentality starts the tears in their bloodshot eyes."

Such verbal high jinks were completely absent from Reid's poems, and from his Spanish translations too, which were clearly, in Charles Simic's terms, "an act of love" and of "supreme empathy." But here too he was double-tongued, or what one might call "ambidextrous," able to give voice both to Jorge Luis Borges and to Pablo Neruda, "about as different from each other as writers and as human souls, as it is possible to be."

> Borges' work is as spare as Neruda's is ebullient, as dubious and ironic as Neruda's is passionately affirmative, as reticent as Neruda's is voluble. Where Neruda is open, even naïve, Borges is oblique and skeptical; where Neruda is a sensualist, a poet of physical love, a man of appetites, Borges is an ascetic; where Neruda is rooted in what he has experienced, Borges seems to have lived almost entirely in literature, in the mind-travel of his reading.

Translating someone's work, especially poetry, was for Reid akin to being haunted or possessed. Soon he found he could no longer read a poem of Neruda's "without hearing behind it that languid, caressing voice," and began to learn the words by heart, so as to be able to repeat them to himself at odd moments—"on buses, at wakeful times in the night"—until, at a certain point, the English translation began to gel. "The voice was the clue," said Reid. "I felt that all Neruda's poems were fundamentally vocative—spoken poems, poems of direct address—and that Neruda's voice was in a sense the instrument for which he wrote." While he worked on the translations, he spent hours listening to Neruda's voice on tape, until he could hear it in his mind at will. In Borges' case, too, he never stopped rereading him, "finding that mischievous, elusive wavelength, hearing that soft, ironic voice in my head."

Neruda died in 1973, and Borges in 1986. By the first decade of the new millennium, when Reid was in his seventies and eighties, many of his friends were already dead. He wrote explicitly about this, noting how the death of friends "shocks one into mourning through a ferocity of remembering," and then starts up a conversation in the memory, if only to hear the dead one's voice again. Borges said once that when writers die, they become books. But for Reid, their voices were what mattered. "If I can recover a voice . . . the atmospherics of place swim back with the sound, and the lost wavelengths reconnect themselves, across time, across absence, across loss." When he was translating Neruda and Borges, their voices were "the crucial, guiding element" in the work. Long after they died, Reid went on listening to them both. "I hear them often in my head," he wrote, "always with awe, and with enduring affection."

The Musical Wave

My friend Maia (she prefers the monomial) lives in Southern California, not far from the Pacific Ocean. A gifted poet, she describes the act of listening as essential to her practice, "listening into the sounds that are out there, and also to the spaces in between . . . hearing sounds freshly, as we did when we were children." Some of this is prayerful and attentive, some more playful: singing back to the frogs or the crickets or the wind in the trees, experimenting with call and response.

Occasionally Maia listens and hears only silence. But such silence, for her, is never absolute. There is always some little whisper, some little tendril of surprise. It is as if underneath everything there were a musical wave, "out of which words can be shaken loose, and thrown all over," and those words might reveal themselves at any time. Attending closely to the entire range, from near silence to the loudest and most joyful noise, remains the source of her creative life, "as elementary as water, and as necessary."

Just as linguistic rhythms are rooted in physiological ones (the steady pounding of the heart, the soft susurrus of the breath), those bodily rhythms are themselves informed by the larger rhythms of the natural world, as well as by the clatter and throb of our omnipresent gadgets and machines. The English poet Alice Oswald worked for many years as a gardener, and writes with delighted authority about exactly that. "I don't know anything lovelier than those free shocks of sound happening against the backsound of your heartbeat. Machinery, spade-scrapes, birdsong, gravel, rain on polythene . . . high small leaves or large head-height leaves being shaken, frost on grass, strimmers, hoses. . . ." Her poems, she says, are "all about listening to things outside the self . . . a kind of complex onomatopoeia, or naming through listening."

For example, the language of the spade is very real to her. "You smell it, you feel its strength under your boot, you move alongside it for maybe eight hours and your spade's language (it speaks in short lines of trochees and dactyls: *sscrunch turn slot slot, sscrunch turn slot slot*) creeps and changes at the same pace as the soil."

Oswald distinguishes two distinct levels, the sound itself, "out of which the poet's melody emerges," and a second, almost inaudible range, where hearing and speaking come together. At that level, she can make out "sentences, distinct grammatical waves coming off things like waves of energy."

Calm, receptivity, a willingness to pause, to make oneself *not central*. I think of James Joyce in *Ulysses*, transcribing the rasping irritable hiss of the family cat—"*Mkgnao! Mrkgnao!* and *Mrkrgnao!*"—each time with a slightly different spelling, or of Tolstoy in *Anna Karenina* entering the body of Levin's hunting dog, Laska, and exploring the marsh through her keen nose and supple legs, her eager, anxious eyes. I think too of the writer Susan Griffin, as she pulls back out of sleep one Berkeley morning.

> Waking, my hand meets the cotton sheets on my bed .
> . . my eyes meet the morning light . . . my ears meet the
> sounds of a car two blocks east. Everything I encounter
> permeates me, washes in and out, leaving a tracery,
> placing me in that beautiful paradox of being by which
> I am both a solitary creature and everyone, everything.

This is what it means to listen, as Mary Oliver once said, *convivially*—reaching out beyond human self-absorption to greet the spacious, generous rhythms of the larger world.

Early Morning

Every summer morning, well before dawn, Aldo Leopold used to settle on the bench outside his cabin with a mug and a notebook and a pot of coffee along with his sturdy pocket watch. Three-thirty a.m. As each bird joined the early morning chorus—the field sparrow from the jack pine copse north of the river, followed by the robin in the big elm, the oriole, the indigo bunting, and the tiny wren (whose home was the knothole in the cabin eaves)—he would make note of the time, along with the bird's name, shorthand. He wanted to know how often he could hear each species singing, and for how long. But what interested him most was the sequence itself. *Why did each bird join the chorus when it did?* He thought perhaps it had to do with light intensity, a theory that was later proved correct. Grosbeaks, thrashers, yellow warblers, bluebirds, vireos, towhees, cardinals—as the light strengthened, all the birds began to sing at once, until his ear could no longer distinguish them. By then it would be almost sunrise, and the coffee pot long empty. Time to go for a wander with the dog, he would tell himself, time to go back inside for breakfast, to transcribe his notes.

Leopold died in 1948, aged only sixty-one. The manuscript he'd been working on, based on more than a decade's observations of the dawn chorus, remains unpublished to this day. But *A Sand County Almanac*, pieced together by his son Luna after his father's death, became a classic of the new environmental movement. It has been translated into at least fourteen languages, and still sells some forty thousand copies every year.

Learning to Wait

The burn was scarcely more than two feet wide, dark water glittering over sleek round stones, cutting between tall and grassy banks. As a child I went there most afternoons, wading upstream against the current, a fizz of midges hovering overhead. I was guddling, catching fish with my hands.

Sometimes my sister Kate came with me, or a younger cousin. But for the most part, I was on my own, crouching in the water in my father's outsize waders, following my chilled fingers underneath the bank, where the slim trout lurked in darkness. They liked the hollow places under the bridge, the jutting crevices between two stones. If you were lucky, you could trap them there, haul them out onto the grass for nursery tea.

Guddling taught me to be quiet as nothing else could do, all attention in those reaching hands. Writing, I came to realize, felt very much the same. You explored the sunken rocks, the craggy edges; did your best to catch the bright quicksilver thoughts before they sped away. There was a posture too, which was common to them both: a steady watchfulness, a dogged willingness to wait.

I was not the first to make this analogy. Robert Bly wrote of fishing as "a kind of daydreaming in daylight, a longing for what is below." He saw novelists as fisher-people, and poets and psychologists as well. Ted Hughes described his own apprentice work in similar terms.

> At school . . . I became very interested in those
> thoughts of mine that I could never catch. Sometimes
> they are hardly what you could call a thought—they

> were a dim sort of feeling about something . . . [and]
> for the most part they were useless to me because I
> could never get hold of them. . . .

Many beginning writers have the same trouble. Either our thoughts are too fleeting—a sudden flash, then gone—or they remain hidden, skulking somewhere out of reach. At such times, said Hughes, "our minds lie in us like fish in the pond of a man who cannot fish." The situation baffled and intrigued him. *What best to do?* "I am talking," he said, "about whatever kind of trick or skill it is that enables us to catch these elusive or shadowy thoughts, and collect them together, and hold them still so we can get a really good look at them."

Hughes had his own sense of what that "trick or skill" might be. Years later, when he was working with Peter Brook on the experimental play, *Orghast,* he explained to him how he went about it. "I listen," he said, "to the patterns that arise in the deep levels of the brain, when impulses become sounds and syllables—and before they shape themselves into recognizable words." It was as if he identified not with the searching hands, but with the cool dark water, himself become the pool in which the fish might congregate.

But what if, as for so many of us, there is no hum, no musical wave, no shapely pattern emerging from the depths? The trout slips out from under its protruding rock and scoots off upstream. The net comes up empty, and the hands as well. *Ah, what then?* You can still continue to listen. "*Listen to what?*" everyone wants to know. But as W. S. Merwin explained in the course of an interview, "That's what you have to find out. Only you can tell you what to listen for. But listen. If you hear the silence in the room, that's something. If you hear your own breath, that's something. If you hear the empty stream bed. If you hear the birds waking up in the morning. If you hear the car shrieking to a stop at the red light. Whatever it may be. You're listening to it. You belong. *Listening, listening, listening.*"

Soft, Imagined Voices

In the fall of 2016, I began to read—and sometimes, reread—the novels of Charles Dickens. There are fourteen in all, including his last unfinished novel, *Edwin Drood*, and I rummaged delightedly through every one of them, reading them eagerly, "to find out what came next," as I imagined his first readers would have done. As the months passed, they became my sanctuary, my private bolt-hole, a retreat from the growing miseries of present day America to the (not so very) different miseries of nineteenth-century England, with an occasional foray to the United States, or across the Channel to Italy and France.

Dickens started life as a journalist, and I marveled at his ability to set a scene, whether it was the fog rolling in over London, "dark yellow, and a little within it brown, and then browner, and then browner, until at the heart of the City—which call St Mary Axe—it was rusty black," or David Copperfield's little bedroom, tucked in the stern of the Peggotys' boathouse, with its whitewashed walls and patchwork quilt, its mirror framed with oyster shells, and the nosegay of seaweed set in a blue mug on the table.

But what moved me most was his skill as a listener. Like Sloppy, in *Our Mutual Friend*, who was "a beautiful reader of a newspaper," Dickens could "do the Police in different voices." Whether he was describing the tender hesitations of David's "child wife" Dora, the wry antics of the Artful Dodger, or the kindly soldier's wife in *Bleak House,* with her battered umbrella and stalwart heart, his characters were inimitably, consistently, *audibly* themselves. Dickens was an ardent theatergoer as a young man and would have loved to be an actor. In later life he took great pleasure in arranging amateur theatricals. His books came out in monthly serials and were designed to be read aloud around the family hearth. No wonder he worked so hard to distinguish the different characters, playing each one over in his mind, and at times even giving voice to them himself.

We know this to be true, because on one occasion his little daughter Mamie was taken ill and spent the day in Dickens' study while he worked. He may have forgotten she was there or thought perhaps that she was fast asleep. But all of a sudden, he leapt up from his chair and rushed to a mirror which hung nearby. Mamie could see the reflection of some extraordinary faces he was making. She watched as he returned to his desk, scribbled furiously for a few minutes, and then went back to the mirror. Once again, he resumed the facial pantomime, and turning towards her, began to mutter softly to himself.

Mamie couldn't make out what her father was saying. But she immediately realized that the strange faces, muttered words, and speedy scribbling were all in the service of his work. Dickens heard every word his characters uttered, as he told his friend John Forster. There in his study, he was rehearsing their various expressions, attending to the flavor of their speech, tasting their words on his own tongue.

Dickens is not alone in this. Marilynne Robinson is the author of five marvelous novels, including the Pulitzer Prize-winning *Gilead*. "I don't revise," she says. "The scene is written in the order in which it comes to the page. In a way, it's as if there are different voices in my head." Whether or not she says the words aloud, the sense of hearing them is very strong. *Gilead* began with the voice of a Congregationalist minister writing a letter to his young son. "It came easily, like he was telling me the story, and all I had to do was listen." As she told her students at the University of Iowa, "Language is music . . . It is essential to remember that characters have a music as well as a pitch and tempo, just as real people do."

Anyone who has read even one of her books will be able to vouch for Robinson's peerless listening. Whether she is indulging the genial metaphysics of the Reverend John Ames or retrieving the fraught memories of his much younger wife, Lila, her tone, vocabulary, and syntax ring true. You never wonder who is speaking, or how to pace their speech, or where the stresses should or should not fall.

Dickens and Robinson are, of course, unusually skilled at this. A surprising number of writers—often expert in other aspects of their trade—find themselves stymied when it comes to writing dialogue. Some never do succeed. Their characters remain flat and unconvincing. Others come up with their own innovative ways to solve the problem.

Ursula K. Le Guin was a prolific writer, fluent, original, wide ranging. She is best known for her science fiction, though she also wrote
novels, criticism, and children's books, as well as several volumes of
poetry. She understood patience and knew what it was to wait. She
taught herself to "listen for the tune, the vision, the story. Not grab-
bing, not pushing, just waiting, listening. Being ready for it when it
comes." But even for Le Guin, that wait could sometimes be excruciating. Her novella, *Hermes,* set on the coast of Oregon, took her many
months. She was listening for the voices of four different women, each
of whom had to speak in her own characteristic cadence, and yet
somehow combine into a rhythmic whole. Le Guin described herself
as feeling "diffident and often foolish," as she walked the beach, or sat
alone in a silent house. She was listening for those "soft, imagined
voices," trying to track them and transcribe them, and for a long time
she heard nothing at all.

When James Baldwin began work on his first novel he faced similar difficulties, which for him were exacerbated by race and class. He
wanted his characters to speak as he himself had done. But he was
ashamed of the voices of his Harlem childhood, ashamed of his father
and of the church that he'd grown up in, ashamed of blues and jazz. In
order to survive in the white world, he'd had to teach himself to lie and
to disguise his speech, adopting affectations he now wanted to reject.

Baldwin moved to Switzerland to focus on his book, and lived on
his own for several months, surrounded by "white snow . . . white
mountains and white faces." The isolation was tremendous. But he'd
brought with him two Bessie Smith records, and through that long,
cold, foreign winter, he listened to them every day. Slowly, he began to retrieve his own lost childhood voices, testing their pace and
rhythm against Bessie's songs. It was not a matter of dropping s's or
n's or g's, he realized, not a matter of "dialect" at all, but rather of the
tone, the timbre, the elusive beat.

By spring, he had completed the first draft of *Another Country.*
And as he told Studs Terkel, it was all thanks to Bessie Smith—all
because "Bessie had the beat."

Listening to the Work

Writing takes time and silence, diligence, commitment: what Elizabeth Bishop once described as "a self-forgetful, perfectly useless concentration."

There can be great terror in that concentrated focus, that prolonged self-forgetting. For Adrienne Rich, the impulse to create often began "in a tunnel of silence." She struggled to find words for what it meant to her, "a sensation that feels sometimes buoyant and sometimes earthbound, sometimes like lighting fires in snow, sometimes like untying knots in which you have been bound." If, as she said, "poems are made of words and the breathing between them," for a long time, breath alone was all she heard.

For the Russian poet Osip Mandelstam, and for his friend Anna Akhmatova, a poem began with a musical phrase ringing insistently in the ears: at first random and opaque, then gradually more focused and precise. Such intrusive music wasn't always comfortable. In her memoirs, Nadezhda Mandelstam describes her husband trying to exorcise this kind of hum. "He would toss his head as though it could be shaken out like a drop of water. . . But it was always louder than any noise, radio, or conversation in the same room."

Gary Snyder is more welcoming. "I listen to my own interior mind-music closely," he says. Most of the time, he hears nothing of great interest. But once in a while, there will be something he recognizes as "belonging to the sphere of poetry." And then he listens with enormous care, giving the poems plenty of time to ripen before he actually writes them down.

It was Robert Frost who came up with the phrase, "the audile imagination," or what he sometimes called "the imagination of the ear." By this, he meant the act of listening to a work-in-progress, attending to what the work is trying to say. If a handful of phrases feels alive and energizing, the writer may be able to build out from them, hearing his way forward, following the linked meanings and associations, and weaving in yet more rhymes and echoes.

There is a kind of magic in this, touching in on the place that seems most vivid, and revising accordingly. Critical intelligence is involved, but there is a tactile quality too, a sense of physical rightness. "A good shovel fits the hand and foot," writes Robert Bringhurst, "and a good sentence fits the voice. . . . A sentence or a paragraph that pays no attention to the reach and rhythm of the voice is uncomfortable or painful, like a shoe that doesn't fit the human foot or a glove on the wrong hand. But a sentence that *does* fit the anatomy of voice and breath will touch, through them, some other rhythms of the body: those of the heart and hands and feet, and of the memory and mind. The limbs—the arms and legs—in Greek, are *meloi*."

And that, he tells us, "is the root of the word *melody* in English."

> *I put the shell down and wait for the snail*
> *to emerge. I have much to learn of patience.*
> *I no longer wonder where did love go,*
> *or why the nights are so long. Issa says*
> *the words will find a way across the page,*
> *they will make a path into morning.*

Joseph Stroud

Listening Across Time

> *Poetry is . . . a way of eavesdropping on other times*
> *and places, different regions of society, and the work-*
> *ings of other people's minds.*

Robert Bringhurst

My mother's mother was an actress, with a forty-year career in the British theater. In the 1930s, she played Gertrude to Alec Guinness' Hamlet in a modern-dress production at the Old Vic. She had a particular affection for Shakespeare, whom she always referred to casually as "William." Joseph Stroud addresses several of his favorite poets in the same way, using only their first names. In the months before his father's death, despite his "tawdry" Spanish, he translated thirty odes by Pablo Neruda.

> *Forgive me, Pablo, but my father was dying.*
> *I needed something—anything—to hold to.*

I know you have many translators,
but none of them, and this I swear to you,
none of them, compadre, *lived in your poems*
the way I lived, holding onto the little artichoke,
a pair of socks, the smell of firewood at night.

Stroud is a rangy man with keen eyes, grey-white hair, and beautiful mobile hands. He is also the author of six books of poetry, most recently *Everything That Rises*, published by Copper Canyon Press. It includes a series of six-line poems written in homage to those he most admires, from the eighth-century Chinese poet Wang Wei to such twentieth-century masters as George Mackay Brown and Wallace Stevens. There is room in his galaxy of admirations for his old mentor, the poet and translator Kenneth Rexroth, and for "the Quiet Masters" of long ago.

> *. . . poets whose poems disappear*
> *as soon as you read them. . . .*

"If you live a while alone," he told an interviewer, "where your only companionship is through the poems of poets who might be long dead, then they become a living presence." The words of Cavafy or Emily Dickinson are, for him, "voiceprints of consciousness," brought back into existence though the act of reading. "So, I welcome the shades into my life," says Stroud. "I bring something of them into my own poems. It's conversation of sorts, a communion with the living past."

Stroud was born in Glendale, California, in 1943, when the surrounding hills were still fragrant with orange groves. He had a complicated, charismatic father, and a gentle, introverted, poetry-loving mother. She read aloud to him: Keats, Shakespeare, Edna St. Vincent Millay. When she bought him the early recordings of Dylan Thomas, Stroud had barely turned thirteen, but he listened to them over and over. "So, I grew up hearing poetry," he says. "It got into my blood."

Stroud studied Latin and Spanish in high school, and had a fine

English teacher, who took the class line by line through Matthew Arnold's "Dover Beach," and T. S. Eliot's "The Waste Land." Later, he enrolled at San Francisco State, which at the time was "seething with poets." There he read the high modernists—Yeats, Eliot, Stevens, William Carlos Williams—whilst also exploring Lorca and Rilke on his own. His reading in those days was mostly horizontal, he says, reading a wide range of different poets, whereas in the decades since, it has grown more vertical—plunging deep into Chaucer or Shakespeare, the Greeks or the Chinese. "Taking my time, no hurry, living awhile with the work."

That vertical reading has given rise to some of Stroud's most playful and surprising poems, in which he conjures up beloved poets from the past and describes their imaginary encounters. In one, he finds himself in the little village of Baeza in southern Spain, and notices a house marked with a plaque in honor of Antonio Machado. Soon after, he passes a hall where a woman is dancing flamenco, and watches her, enthralled. When it is over, he carries the dance to Machado's house, calling out to him to join him. And they dance—

> *Machado danced*
> *the color of light on the mountains—*
> *I danced the silver of leaves—together*
> *we danced the sun on the river—*
> *just the two of us—two men*
> *dancing alone in the shimmering*
> *fields of Baeza.*

In another such poem, Stroud walks out into the meadow near his cabin, accompanied by the Sung poet Yang Wan-li. They look down into the flowing water of the creek, and Stroud wishes that his life were as translucent. Yang would prefer to escape his personal story altogether. He begs Stroud to release him from his own time and place and set him down in the Imperial City.

> *or better, yet, let me drink and be happy*
> *like Li Po, drifting in a boat with only*
> *the moon for company.*

Stroud shuts his eyes for a moment. He is the writer, after all, the composer of this poem. And by the time he opens them, Yang's wish has been fulfilled.

Stroud lives part of each year in the city of Santa Cruz, part in his cabin high in the Sierra Nevada. Despite teaching for more than thirty years at Cabrillo College, he has traveled widely (Southeast Asia and India, Bhutan, Afghanistan, Iran, Turkey, Greece and Europe), and knows what it is to live alone. In one of my favorite poems, he pictures himself sitting up late with the poet, Tu Fu, moonlight scattering opals on the river. The two of them drink cup after cup of warm rice wine. It's time to take out the ledger and do the year's accounts. "If I subtract my grief from joy, what is left?" asks Stroud. "How does it balance?" He addresses Tu Fu directly,

> *In one of your last poems you talk about*
> *the stars outside your hut, how impossible*
> *to count them. There are no numbers,*
> *you say, for this life.*

Tu Fu is right, Stroud tells himself. "Who cares if we're / in the red? Or the black?" What matters is their friendship, the living bridge between the worlds.

> *Rich or poor, the night*
> *each night burgeons within us. The mornings*
> *open with sunlight. Why count them?*
> *Instead of numbers, let me enter words*
> *into the ledger, the account of our friendship,*
> *this little poem from me to you, across*
> *the glimmering, innumerable years.*

Consider the following quotations:

When one says somebody else's poem aloud, one speaks in *that person's* breath.   If I say, "Tomorrow, and tomorrow, and to-morrow, / Creeps in this petty pace from day to day / To the last syllable of recorded time, / And all our yesterdays have lighted fools / The way to dusty death," everything that's happening in my physiology Shakespeare quite literally put there. It's a very mysterious process. Probably he's writing in silence, but he's *hearing* all these vocalizations, *hearing* these rhythms, and when you take them in, you take in the physiology of the phrases.

Robert Hass

When I first begin a poem, I don't know what form it's going to take; I'm listening to sound, feeling a cadence or rhythm, surf-ing a wave. Every poem has its own unique terrain, and part of the skill or craft of writing is learning to adjust to that. It can be a kind of dance, where sometimes the poem is leading and sometimes I am, but through it all I'm listening to the music, that's what's determining the shape and where it's going.

Joseph Stroud

Continue to explore:

Choose a poem that intrigues you, and try reading it aloud to yourself, noticing how it feels as the words move through you. As Philip Pullman writes, "A whisper will do; you don't have to bellow it and annoy the neighbors; but air has to pass across your tongue and through your lips. Your body has to be in-volved."

Listen closely to your friends and family members and see if you can write a story or a poem that includes the particular flavor of their conversation.

~ 10 ~

Communing with the Dead

...If
the air could empty, you would be there
as a listening
that would move with the rooms.

Tess Gallagher

Communing with the Dead

I have lived in Massachusetts for almost thirty years. But every summer, when I go back to Scotland, I visit Polwarth Kirk, a small, white-painted church just down the road from my mother's house. I make my way to the worn gravestones honoring my father, Robin McEwen, my sister Katie, and my brother James, lay a little posy of wildflowers at the foot of the graves, and stand there for a while, remembering. My father has been dead for more than half my life, and my siblings too. But in some essential way, the conversation continues.

Nor am I alone in this. Each culture has its own particular way of communing with the dead. Jews bring pebbles to lay on the grave each time they come to visit. Mexicans celebrate the Day of the Dead (*Dia de los Muertos*) with brightly colored skulls and vibrant costumes, as do the people of Ecuador, Guatemala, El Salvador, and Brazil. Contemporary Russians bring baskets of food to the cemetery—rolls, eggs, something to drink—and picnic on the grass around their family graves. A woman called Zinaida Yevdokimovna Kovalenko goes to the graveyard often, to visit her mother, her husband, and her little daughter, all now dead. "I sit with them all," she says. "I sigh a little. You can talk to the dead just like you can to the living." Somehow it still feels possible for her to hear what they have to say. "When you're alone . . . and when you're sad. When you're very sad."

But such conversations are not always sorrowful. In *The Seasons at Quincey: Four Portraits of John Berger*, two leggy teenagers are shown idling in the garden, eating raspberries from an immense bowl. A jug of cream rests on a tray nearby, along with a bowl of sugar, beyond which stands a half-circle of empty chairs, with a smiling photograph propped up on every seat. The film was made by the actress Tilda Swinton, and the young people are her children, Honor and Xavier Swinton-Byrne. They are there to honor their friend Beverly, John Berger's wife, who has recently died. It was she who planted the raspberries, it is her face that smiles down from every chair. And though Berger himself was unable to join them, he was the one who suggested the memorial, instructing the twins to gather the fruit and feast on it, because he said, "your pleasure would give her pleasure." Beverly was dead, yes. But somehow, he felt confident their enjoyment would percolate to her.

One of my favorite examples of such imaginative outreach comes from the Mexican writer Miguel Serrano, who maintained close friendships with both Carl Jung and Herman Hesse. After Hesse died, Serrano held a private ritual, focusing on music Hesse had loved. He lit several sticks of sandalwood incense, placed Bach's Mass in B Minor on his record player, and lay back on the sofa, giving himself over to a state of total receptivity, so that Hesse could listen through him, "lending him his senses" for the duration of the piece.

The experience, for Serrano, was profound. He felt certain Hesse was there, he said, and felt his gratitude. When the Mass ended, Serrano listened to two more pieces, the Passion of St. Matthew and the Passion of St. John. Then he prepared a ceremonial meal for all the friends—now dead—whom he had known and loved, leading them into the dining room, and seating them at the table, while the music continued. Finally, he raised a toast to Hesse to ease his journey, promising to remember him. He also drank to each of his lost friends, and to the enveloping world of dreams.

The Wind Telephone

Several months before the tsunami struck Japan in 2011, one man was already grieving. This was Itaru Sasaki, whose much-loved cousin had died the previous year. In an effort to continue the conversation, if only in his mind, Sasaki acquired an old-fashioned British phone box, and set it up in his garden overlooking the Pacific. Most such phone booths are bright red, but Sasaki's had been painted white—in Japan, the color of mourning. He fitted it with an old black rotary phone, resting on a wooden shelf. The phone itself was broken. It connected to nothing and nowhere, which is to say to everywhere one could imagine.

Sasaki is a garden designer, a kind-looking man with thick white hair. He lives in a technologically savvy country. But unlike most of his peers, it was not enough for him to reread old emails when his cousin died, or to click through smiling photos on his tablet or iPhone. Nor was he drawn to traditional Buddhist practice: setting out rice and fresh fruit on the family altar, lighting incense and ringing a bell in honor of the dead. Instead, he set up the old, glass-fronted phone box, with its sturdy black phone (a model dating back to his own youth), intending to use it as a place to talk, a place where he and his cousin could commune at leisure. He called it "the wind telephone." Just as prayer flags ("wind horses") are said to scatter their blessings on the wind, so Sasaki felt his own good wishes would be carried on the wind phone to his cousin.

He began work on the booth in November 2010, and completed it some six months later. In between, came the tsunami.

The tsunami struck the coast of Japan on March 11, 2011, followed swiftly by a ferocious earthquake. Almost 20,000 people lost their lives. Sasaki's town was one of the hardest hit. 1,285 people were missing or declared dead, and the town itself was flattened. Forty percent of the houses were washed away; 98 percent of the businesses destroyed. Sasaki himself was lucky to survive.

But the true miracle is what happened afterwards. Sasaki had not advertised his use of the wind phone; no one had posted a link or written it up on Facebook. But word got out nonetheless, and soon after the catastrophe, friends and strangers began to show up outside Sasaki's house, eager to pay a visit to the tall white phone box. Like him, they wanted a chance to talk to their beloved dead.

A widow in her early seventies, whose husband had died in the tsunami, arrived at the phone box with her two young grandsons. "Grandpa, I've finished all my homework," boasted the younger boy. "Everyone is doing fine," he added. And then, as they all three left the booth, "Maybe Grandpa will say he heard us."

An old man spoke to his son, who'd been killed in the tsunami, and asked him to look after his wife, now also dead. "Sorry to ask you this, but take care of her, and your grandpa and grandma too," he said.

Not everybody felt the need to speak. A woman in her mid-sixties came to the phone box on her own. Her husband had been killed in the tsunami, and her house had also been destroyed. But she dialed the familiar number of the home they'd shared together, and stood for a long time just listening, holding the phone to her ear, and quietly weeping.

We know these things because NHK Sendai (Japan's largest news station) filmed many of the people from a distance, and, with their permission, also placed an audio recorder inside the booth. Excerpts from that program were played on American radio and were later made into a book.

What struck me, listening, was the courage and openness of the survivors, their willingness to set aside their skeptical, ironic, modern selves, and simply reach into the void. The wind telephone could not bring the dead back to life. But it could offer a space where truth could be told, love could be made manifest; honoring the grief of those who were left behind, and giving them a sense, however tentative, of being heard. Among the visitors to Sasaki's booth was a young man in heavy glasses and a long black jacket. He had lost both his parents, as well as his wife and their one-year-old son. When he spoke, he named them each in turn. "*If this voice reaches you, please listen. . . .*"

The Voices of the Dead

"He's dead, really, but it doesn't show," said my little sister, airily. She'd been watching 1940s movies with the rest of us and was particularly drawn to Humphrey Bogart. He had died in 1957, aged only fifty-six. But as she rightly said, it didn't show. His face gazed back at us with wry authority, his voice still husky and seductive, still inimitably alive.

It is an eerie power, like something out of fairytales, to be able to see the dead alive again, to hear again the dear familiar voice. Not long after Nadine Gordimer's husband died, a journalist sent her an audiotape of an interview he'd conducted with him. Gordimer was astonished, deeply moved. She had photographs, of course, and letters. But as it happened, there was no other recording of her husband's voice. Nothing else could have evoked his presence (or his absence) with such power.

The first sound recording was made in 1860, more than 150 years ago. Since then, our ability to "listen to the dead" has only continued to expand. We can watch Cary Grant sparring with Kathleen Hepburn on late night television, turn the dial to catch the stately cadences of Martin Luther King Jr. or JFK. We can replay the laughing voices of our long-lost uncles, listen to Caruso crooning on a scratchy old LP, or to a gleaming remix via YouTube or Alexa.

Our ancestors would have been amazed to know such things were possible. For most of them, as for those visitors to Sasaki's booth, "listening to the dead" would have been an act of imagination—a willed (if entirely willing) suspension of disbelief. At times, they might have reached out to the ghostly presences of those they'd loved: hoping, yearning, for some last shred of communication. More often, they would have encountered previous generations through their songs and music, catching in the arc of their own voices the shadowy echoes of those who'd sung them first, tracking them through letters or manuscripts or fragments of poetry, or the few precious volumes of their private library.

For the Renaissance scholar Niccolo Machiavelli, such reading was also a method of conversing with the dead. Each evening, he would pause on the threshold of his study, take off his ordinary clothes, and dress himself in "royal and courtly garments." Only then did he feel ready to approach his literary elders, discoursing with them freely, and (through their books) listening attentively to what they had to say. In the hours that followed, he claimed to fear neither poverty nor death. He was, after all, communing with the ancient ones, while they, in their great kindness, made him welcome.

Listening to the Ancestors

The novelist Leslie Marmon Silko grew up in New Mexico among the Laguna Pueblo people, listening to her aunts tell the traditional stories. Even when Aunt Susie or Aunt Alice were cooking or cleaning or chopping wood, they were never too busy to answer her questions. Each rock and mesa had its story, likewise each dry streambed and jutting promontory. In Silko's telling, "Everything became a story."

More than anything, she loved to listen to one of her aunts' tales and realize that she already knew the particular cave or mesa in which it had been set. That was when the stories moved her most powerfully, because then she was able to picture herself "*within* the story being told, within the landscape."

From the Pueblo point of view, that landscape is composed not just of land and sky and rock and tree, but of human beings too, both the living and the dead. Storytelling is a way of drawing everyone together: ancestral spirits from the deep past and those yet to be born, as well as the people of the present day. "We are still *all* in *this* place," writes Silko, "and language—the storytelling—is our way of passing through or being with them, of being together again."

A century earlier, when Aunt Susie's grandmother told her stories, she would instruct one of the younger children to run and open the door. "Go open the door," the old woman would say, "so that our esteemed ancestors may bring us the precious gift of their stories." It was as if those long ago elders were truly present and needed only to be called upon. Aunt Susie followed the same practice when she herself became the storyteller. "They are out there," she would say. "Let them come in. They're here, they're here with us *within* the stories."

Presences, Visible and Invisible

Growing up in Scotland in the early twentieth century, my great-aunt Katharine was especially sensitive to ghosts, or what she called "unexplainable people." She took it for granted there would always be invisible presences in the room and learned never to stand in doorways "because of all the people coming in and out." Once, at a hunt ball, she drew my grandfather aside. "Look," she told him. "Look! There's someone there." My grandfather stared doubtfully at the empty chair, and immediately sat down on it.

"Now what's happened?" he demanded.

But of course, the ghostly visitor had disappeared.

In the weeks and months after the Japanese tsunami, the desolate survivors were besieged by ghosts. Some were former friends and family members, some casual acquaintances, others total strangers. They were seen at home, at work, in public places, strolling the devastated beaches and the ruined towns. Experts debated over what the sightings meant.

"I don't get into it," said the Reverend Taio Kaneta, chief priest at the Zen Temple in Kurihara, thirty miles from the coast. "What matters is that people are seeing them, and in these circumstances, after this disaster, it is perfectly natural. So many died, and all at once. . . . The dead had no time to prepare themselves. The people left behind had no time to say goodbye."

He thought it was inevitable there should be ghosts.

In the first month after the disaster, Kaneta alone conducted more than two hundred funerals. Local services were completely overwhelmed. 18,500 people had been drowned or burned or crushed to death. Four out of ten survivors complained of insomnia, one out of five of depression. "And yet they didn't cry," Kaneta said. The silence and numbness were pervasive.

As the weeks went by, he came up with a modest and unusual strategy: a traveling event called Café de Monku. "Monku" is the Japanese pronunciation of the word "monk"; it also means complaint or lamentation.

"We think it will take a long time to get back to a calm, quiet, ordinary life," read Kaneta's flyer. "Why don't you come and join us, take a break, and have a little moan? The monks will listen to your complaint—and have a *monku* of their own too."

Café de Monku was set up like a mobile library, traveling from place to place, hosted by different temples and community centers along the way. Because Reverend Kaneta loves jazz (Thelonious Monk especially) Monk's music would be playing in the background. At each new venue, the monks would offer tea and coffee, cakes and biscuits, a shoulder rub, a friendly chat. They would set out trays of glass beads and colored cords, so that those who wanted could string Buddhist rosaries. They were also ready to inscribe and bless new memorial tablets, since so many had been lost in the flood. Most important of all, they listened sympathetically, and didn't ask too many questions.

Little by little, the survivors began to speak, first awkwardly, apologetically, and then with increasing fluency. They spoke of the terror of the tsunami, the agony of bereavement, their fears for what was still to come. They also described their encounters with the supernatural. In *Ghosts of the Tsunami,* Richard Lloyd Parry summarizes some of the more startling stories.

A civil servant in Soma caught sight of a lone woman in a red dress, far from any house or means of transport. When he looked back at her a moment later, she had disappeared.

A fire station in Tagajo had its services repeatedly requested, although all the calls came in from places that were now in ruins. The crews drove out anyway and prayed for the spirits of those who had died—whereupon the calls abruptly ceased.

An unhappy-looking man hailed a taxi in the city of Sendai and asked to be taken to an address that no longer existed. Halfway there, the driver glanced up at his mirror, and realized that the back seat was now empty. He drove on as requested, stopped in front of the piled-up rubble, and politely opened the door to let out his invisible passenger.

There was no end to the proliferation of such stories. In Celtic terms, the veil between the worlds was very thin.

A Handful of Words

"Where *is* she?" my cousin asked, the morning her mother died in a hospice in South London. One moment she was there, this warm, courteous older woman, sitting up in bed, smiling, cracking jokes. And then, abruptly, she was somewhere else entirely. That tall, graceful body was empty, uninhabited.

Most of us face death with the same visceral bewilderment, though as many as 80 percent of those who have lost a loved one describe seeing, hearing, or feeling them in the months that follow. The invisible person speaks once, or maybe twice. Their words are potent, sparse. "*I will always be with you.*" "*I love you.*" "*Yes.*"

And then there are the gifted listeners who somehow hear far more.

There is, for example, an intuitive called Sarah, who lives with her husband in the Santa Cruz mountains, and works full-time as a nurse. Sarah is able to see the souls of her dead patients as they leave their bodies; at times she also hears what they are saying. Some give her messages for those they've left behind. But mostly, she just helps them to let go—to recognize that they have actually died. A few stay around for as much as an hour, though all eventually dissolve, back into the surrounding air.

Sarah herself is a rarity: grounded, calm, comfortably accepting of her special skills. Another such listener is a man called Hajji, who volunteers at a North London mosque, washing the bodies of the Muslim faithful. Hajji is in his sixties now: a bald man with a curly white beard and small brown eyes. He washes two or three bodies a week, singing to them in Arabic as he works. Mostly he washes old men, whom he describes as "very peaceful." But there are others too, who didn't want to die, and then the body is very stiff, and the skin "all grey."

Worst of all are those who commit suicide on the London Underground. Hajji faints each time he unzips the bag. But his hands are practiced as he turns the bodies, crooning a lullaby, caressing them gently with the soapy water. "Sometimes the body talks to me," he says. "That moment when I see the person's eyes. Then I feel the situation. How bad it was. . . . It is like looking into the negative of a photo printed on the eyes." Sometimes, the man has come from Pakistan, and has had to submit to an arranged marriage.

> The bodies, they are telling me they were fighting
> . . . and that he was mentally upset always, and his
> head put in the wall, that he was living saying, 'I have
> done a mistake . . . I have to go back.' They are say-
> ing . . . sometimes their work problem, sometimes
> their finance problem, sometimes he make some little
> mistake . . . and the police catch him. A lot of different
> things they tell me in the washing time.

Later, once the work is finished, Hajji asks the family about the dead man. *Who was this person?* he wants to know. Almost always, he finds his sense of them confirmed. "90 percent of the time I am completely satisfied what this person is telling me in the washing time was true."

Hajji himself is getting older now and would like to retire. But the mosque authorities want him to continue. He has an obligation, they tell him. He is the only one who knows how to listen, the only one the families can trust "to wash with love."

The Conversation Continues

In May 1980, sometime in the week after my father died, I took a walk in the rough grass beyond our house. And there, half hidden among the dark green reeds, the bristly thistles, and the stinging nettles, I found a nest. It had originally contained eight eggs. But one of the eggs had rolled out beyond the rim, leaving the other seven clustered together at the center.

There had been six children in our family, two parents. It was impossible not to see the nest in terms of metaphor. "*Like us,*" I told myself. "*Like us.*"

My father's death reverberated through the years that followed.

His voice persisted just beyond earshot: gruff, admonitory, impatient, kind. Often, on his birthday, or the anniversary of his death, I would "go for walks with him" around my neighborhood in New York City, strolling the streets of the Lower East Side, where he had never been, pointing out the ornate stonework on an old house, or the tugboats thrusting their bright way up the East River. I had no precedent for what I was doing, no private explanations. But like Tilda Swinton's teenaged twins, like Miguel Serrano or Itaru Sasaki, in some instinctive way I was communing with the dead.

The Christian mystic Cynthia Bourgeault writes of her experience after the death of her close friend, the Trappist monk and hermit Brother Raphael Robin. At first, she was overcome by what they'd lost: a mutual wholeness, the chance to grow together into "those unknown but amazing people" their friendship had seemed to promise. But as the months went by, she began to realize that his death was not necessarily so final—that, as she puts it, "death is permeable by love from both sides"—meaning their relationship could actually continue.

Just as Serrano had sat listening to Bach, lending his senses to his old friend Herman Hesse, so Bourgeault, watching light flicker on the surface of the river, transferred that seeing to her beloved Rafe. For a brief moment, she even seemed to hear his voice. "I love to see the water through you," he told her. Traditional Christianity has no language for such things. But Bourgeault remains unperturbed. As she carries on with her life, "spreading roots in the good soil of here-below," Brother Raphael continues to flourish, "stretching his leaves and branches skyward in the kingdom above."

Strange Radio

> *I've been trying to listen to my great-grandmother.*
> *What is she saying?*
>
> Karen Werner

Karen Werner was born in Pittsburgh, Pennsylvania, and grew up in what she calls "a phantom Vienna," with a Jewish mother and a professional academic father. She remembers herself as a small child, sitting in a high chair in the gathering dusk, listening to the broken static of the radio. It is an apt image for her recent work, which has focused on war, displacement, and Holocaust post-memory, "a mix of the inaudible past with the audible mundane."

A warm, vibrant woman with a ready smile, Werner teaches at Goddard College's non-residential program, and defines herself as a radio artist and sociologist. Her first radio program was "Laws of Lost and Found Objects," for which she won the Grand Prix Marulić in 2016. It was planned as a tribute to her great-grandmother Sheva, who had been a Talmud scholar (rare for a woman in the 1930s) and who was killed in Auschwitz.

The piece opens with the sounds of birds. "*Why look back?*" comes her mother's voice. But Werner feels compelled to do just that. She lies on the crumbling cement near the tower at Birkenau (itself part of Auschwitz), and stares at Sheva's photograph. She stands in the gas chamber, hoping to sense her presence, but finds nothing. At the start of the piece, she is afraid of the place, afraid of the ground underfoot, the very dust. By the end that dust is in her hair, her clothes, in every fiber of her bright pink scarf. But something has been recovered—call it clarity, call it truth—and Werner's lengthy quest is underway.

Her next project, "Strange Radio," "mixed radio waves and memory" in a series of seven linked pieces. Werner had been granted an artist's residency in Vienna, and as soon as she arrived, she was flooded with sensation. "It wasn't just listening to sounds," she says. "It was feeling—or 'feeling-listening'—*listening to other people's memories* . . . to my own experience of other people's memories that I feel I was raised with."

In "Dispatches from Vienna," she describes strolling through her father's old neighborhood, glimpsing the market near where he'd grown up, then finding her way to his front door. Somehow, she knew exactly where she was going. "*I touched my daddy's door,*" she says in a soft voice, still caught by the astonishment of it all.

Werner's mother arrived in Vienna shortly afterwards, and the two of them walked the streets together, searching for the original family house. "I think this is it!" her mother tells Werner, as they stand outside the door at Novaragasse 40. Again, it is as if the place, the past, is speaking. *"That's it. Yeah!"*

The building is substantial, almost half a block long. Werner's grandparents left it in 1934, just before her mother's birth, and set out on a long trek to Holland, Brazil, Israel, Austria again, and Canada, before finally settling in the United States. The house was taken over by the Nazis, who evicted all the original inhabitants, and used it as a deportation center, or *Judenhaus*. Some 220 Jews were transported from there to Theresienstadt, and later killed.

What is it to listen to the dead? Werner asked herself, as she tried to finish "Strange Radio." *Is it possible to heal and restore the past?* Before she returned to Vienna the following year, she consulted with a medium, who told her that the family house was still haunted by all those who'd suffered there. Their spirits were "stuck," and needed help to be released. *"How do you undo a haunting?"* Werner wondered.

One of her final pieces, "Covenant of the Tongue," is intended as an answer to that question, "a space of receiving, transmitting . . . connecting, and I hope *mending, mending. . ."* It was inspired in part by a book called *Ghostly Matters,* by the sociologist Avery Gordon. If Gordon is right, and haunting is "the price paid for violence, for genocide," then it can only be resolved by "arduous bodily transformation" on the part of the living.

For Werner, that "arduous bodily transformation" took two forms, both rooted in Kabbalistic tradition. The first had to do with a practice called "soul letters," in which one repeats psalms linked with the names of the deceased, to free and bless them. Because so many people had been held, however briefly, at the house on Novaragasse, it was necessary to recite psalms that included every letter of the Hebrew alphabet. Werner recorded a local community leader and his mother as they recited Psalms 34 and 121, intercut with lengthy stretches of her own chanting.

"I let myself be rearranged through the vocalizations," she writes, "often chanting them at two in the morning at top volume."

Werner herself was not reciting psalms. Rather she was chanting the three "mother letters"—*aleph, mem,* and *shin*—along with a rotating series of vowels. She had learned this from the thirteenth-century mystic, Abraham Abulafia, who drew on an ancient text called *Sefer Yetzirah* to create his own vocalized meditations. "*Sefer Yetzirah* ["Book of Creation"] is about the power of the breath, letter, and word to form the world," writes Werner. In assuaging the hungry ghosts, she was also soothing and nourishing herself. The long hours of "chanting through the throat, through the teeth, by the lips, the palette, by the tongue . . ." became a prayer, an exorcism, a form of service, a surrender of her living voice to meet the needs of those who had died.

It seems clear to her that the time for this is now. Germany has done its best to acknowledge the ravages of its Nazi past; Austria is still learning to claim responsibility. Werner sees her work as "a resonating space" for that difficult history: first listening to the dead, then finding ways to respond to them and heal. "I want a whisper," she writes, "two tongues at once. The articulated and the barely audible at the same time. . . . I am this body, and I am all of us at once." She is in western Massachusetts in the twenty-first century, and in Vienna, Austria, in 1945. "I am living and alive, and I am dying, dead. I am here and there."

Consider the following quotations:

The dead are still there in the dark. They are only waiting to be acknowledged. Their voices speak in the language of dreams.

Clark Strand

The intangible that is invisible as well as untouchable can still be audible.

Theodore Reik

Continue to explore:

How might you begin to listen to the past?

How might you evoke—and even transcribe—the voices of your ancestors?

∾ 11 ∾

The Sounds of Silence

May my silences become more accurate.

Theodore Roethke

The Not-So-Silent Night

At night I lie in bed listening to the sound of my own ears. At times I find it delicate, mellifluous: a sequined cloak swept wide across a polished floor. But tinnitus is not so charming, not so delicate. Not at all.

What for me is a thin, tinselly sound, only moderately intrusive, has been described by other sufferers using words like *ringing, hissing, chirping, cheeping, buzzing, humming, whistling,* even *roaring.* Some 32 percent of American adults are affected, with symptoms ranging from "slight" to "catastrophic." Diet can help alleviate the worst of these (more fresh fruit and vegetables, seaweed, beans and tofu; less acid-producing food, such as yogurt). Acupuncture can help too, as can sound therapy (masking that inner orchestra with the thrum of an air conditioner, or the throaty purr of a domestic cat). Some find relief in small movements of the face and neck, others through humming or focused toning. *Ah* or *Ou* seem especially efficacious.

But at present, there is no known cure.

Most people get tinnitus as a result of noise-induced hearing loss, and I am no exception. One winter morning, the fire-alarm began to shriek in the empty apartment below mine—and continued shrieking for the next ten hours. When I rang the landlady, she asked me to wait until someone from the local oil company came with the key, and then to call her back, to confirm that the alarm had been turned off. It was a bitterly cold day, the library was closed, and I had a project I needed to complete. Foolishly, I agreed to stay put, buckling down to work at the computer, doing my best to ignore the constant high-pitched shriek, and persuading myself I could endure it. I rang the oil company at intervals, begging them to hurry, but relief did not arrive until late that afternoon. By then my ears were raw and tingling, and it was painful even to talk on the phone.

The definition of tinnitus is "hearing sound when none is actually present," most often because of damage to the cilia, the delicate hair cells in the inner ear. In my own case, an audiogram showed a notch or "dent" in my hearing, making it impossible to hear high-pitched sounds. When the ear is deprived of input in this way, auditory neurons in the brainstem start to fire, amplifying whatever signals they encounter. It's as if the brain took off on a private quest—*searching, searching*—until it found some ersatz satisfaction in its own internal workings. We can cover our ears, of course, but there is no way to soothe that poor beleaguered eardrum, or to silence the tiny ossicles in the middle ear. So, the eardrum continues to vibrate, along with the hammer, the anvil, and the stirrup, and the cilia too, and the noise, in whatever form, continues to torment.

Tinnitus is known to interfere with memory and concentration. Even at a lesser intensity, it has been linked with sleeplessness, anxiety, and depression. One to 3 percent of sufferers find it extremely traumatizing. Some have even been driven to suicide. But most people, myself included, reach a wary sort of truce with their own ailment. We lie awake reciting half-forgotten poems. We make a cup of steaming herbal tea. We reread old *New Yorkers*, scribble in our journals. We listen to the not-so-silent night.

> *Winter solitude—*
> *in a world of one color*
> *the sound of wind.*

wrote Basho long ago.

> *The temple bell stops—*
> *but the sound keeps coming*
> *out of the flowers.*

The (Many) Sounds of Silence

How many kinds of silence can you name? For the writer Paul Goodman, there were at least nine, among them, "the dumb silence of slumber or apathy," "the fertile silence of awareness," "the noisy silence of resentment and self-recrimination," and (perhaps the most welcome and harmonious), "the silence of peaceful accord with other people, or communion with the cosmos."

Any one of us could come up with a similar catalogue.

My own list would include the looming silence of an empty house, the corrosive silence of anger and betrayal, the hollow rush of extremely bad news. But it would make space too for astonishment and awe, and for the genial silences of relief or gratitude or shared companionship, lying in bed together, more than half asleep, looking up through a darkened skylight at the far-off stars.

So many silences, so many different sounds!

❧

I
TACET
II
TACET
III
TACET

reads the score for John Cage's famous piece, *4'3"*—which is to say, three stretches of (orchestrated) silence, instructing the audience to "Stop for a moment and look around you and listen; stop and look; stop and listen."

More than half a century after its first performance, the novelty of that imperative has perhaps worn thin. But for Cage himself, the piece remained marvelously invigorating. "I listen to it every day," he said. "More than anything else, it's the source of my enjoyment of life." When he came to write a new piece, he tried to write it so that it wouldn't interrupt "this other piece which is already going on."

This is Cage's enduring lesson: that greeted with curiosity and affectionate attention, any ambient sound can be a source of pleasure—can, indeed, be understood as music. What matters here is making time to listen—not to Goodman's sounds and silences, or to mine (most of which are human, psychological)—but to the perpetual small shifts of the surrounding world. This can be challenging. But as Cage explains, "In Zen they say: If something is boring after two minutes, try it for four. If it is still boring, try it for eight, sixteen, thirty-two and so on. Eventually one discovers that it's not boring at all, but very interesting."

Not long ago, officials at St. Peter's Church in Seaford, England, recorded thirty minutes of "total silence" from inside the sanctuary, first as a local fundraising project, and later for sale to the general public in the form of a CD. Very little could be heard, just the occasional creak of footsteps on the wooden floorboards, and the hum of a distant car. But requests for copies came in from as far away as Ghana. No one seems to have raised the name John Cage, but I can't help thinking he'd have been delighted.

The Silent Brain

In her annual Deep Listening retreats, the composer Pauline Oliveros required her students to maintain silence from ten o'clock each night until one o'clock the following afternoon. She wanted to help them rebalance the two sides of the brain, restoring potency to the right or "nonverbal" hemisphere. In her view, such a lengthy stretch of silence allowed "for the detection of new constellations of awareness and sensation, for vulnerability, for respect . . . for kindness, for listening."

Monastics have long made time to practice silence, as have numerous contemplatives and healers. "Go and sit in thy cell," said the fourth-century Desert Father, Abba Moses, "and thy cell shall teach thee all things." Contemporary scientists would agree. Recent studies have confirmed the power of silence to clarify our thoughts, calm our bodies, and draw us into harmony with the larger world.

One such project was conducted back in 2006 by Luciano Bernardi, then studying the effects of music on the human body. He and his colleagues played a range of music to two dozen test subjects, tracking their responses through changes in blood pressure, heart rate, and blood circulation in the brain. They weren't planning to study silence. But it turned out that the two minutes of "downtime" between tracks were in fact far more relaxing than the so-called "relaxing" music, or than the longer silent pause before the experiment began.

Bernardi's findings were supported by other researchers, among them neuroscientist Michael Wehr. Studying the brains of mice in 2010, Wehr found that just as short bursts of noise caused auditory neurons to light up, so too did a sudden stretch of silence. "When a sound suddenly stops," he wrote, "that's an event just as surely as when a sound starts." And if that silence continues, the brain will settle into a calm, relaxed state.

In daily life, many of us face nonstop demands on our attention. These exhaust the brain's prefrontal cortex (which directs higher-order thinking, problem-solving and decision-making), and all too often leave us cranky and distracted, unable to concentrate or focus. Maintaining silence, even while we continue with our daily chores—watering the garden, cutting up vegetables for soup—can help tremendously. In a recent book, psychologist Robert Sardello suggests that each day, at an appointed time, we make our way to the same quiet, secluded place. "Sit down in a comfortable chair," he tells us, "with both feet firmly on the floor, body perfectly relaxed, and as far as possible, do not think of anything." *Learn to be silent. Let your quiet mind listen and absorb more silence.* Over time, he says, that silence will accompany us in everything we do.

The Charm of Quiet

Every morning, as soon as she wakes up, my friend Meg Fisher steps out onto her little balcony, and stands there, listening. "There are so many melodies," she says, "and I try to learn some of them. I just love to hear what comes."

Fisher is tall and slender, with a narrow face and thoughtful brown eyes. She valued silence, even as a child. Her parents trusted her and left her to herself. "I had a pretty undisturbed rich inner life," she tells me now. "*Thank God!*"

Fisher provided that same calm ambience for her two sons. While the boys were growing up, their house was fairly quiet. They could hear the sounds from outside: children playing, trucks passing up and down the street. But there was no radio, no television, no adult voices filling the air with their own thoughts and opinions. And because of this, she feels "like the house was a listening for them."

When her sons were six and eight, Fisher began teaching at the local Waldorf School. Here too, the children are given room to hear themselves think, so that any words of theirs can bubble up in their own slow time, and not get plowed under by adult conversation. "From the moment the children walk in the door, I'm sitting outside the classroom, and right away, there's a quietness. There I am in my teacher clothes, my big teacher apron with the pockets in it, and they come in babbling with their parents—their parents are talking to them, in a busy way—and then right inside that little coatroom, there's a kind of a hushed quality. I'm just there, being present to them coming. And often, if you're quiet, just like an animal, a child will come right up and tell you something. Whatever's on their mind. There's this sense of joy in each one—just the joy of each one being on earth for whatever purpose! Yeah!"

The day that follows is very carefully orchestrated. Weather permitting, the children spend much of their time out-of-doors, playing with simple blocks or plain-faced dolls. Meanwhile, Fisher and her assistant do what she calls "meaningful work"—kneading bread, chopping vegetables, gardening, or sewing—something that makes sense to the children, something they can imitate if they so choose. Fisher continues "to hold the classroom etherically," even while she kneads or chops or sews. And often there comes "a sort of a hum" in the children's play, confirming just how deeply they're absorbed.

The day is also structured musically, with songs or soft humming sounds by way of transition. "Instead of saying, 'OK, time to wash our hands!' or 'Line up for the bathroom!' we just sing," says Fisher. "'Wash hands, wash, the folk have come to plow! Now's the time to wash our hands, wash our hands now!'" Or later on, she hums softly,

"'*Hmm—hmm—hmm.*' And the children just sort of dreamily go."

Silence too is an accepted part of the curriculum. For example, each time the eurythmy teacher visits Fisher's classroom, she brings a toy gnome with her called Tippy-toes. While the children are waiting, eager and excited, Fisher asks them to sit very still. "Let's see if we can hear Tippy-toes!" she says. Meanwhile the eurythmy teacher makes it a point to jingle her bells in the hall, "just ever so faintly," so everyone knows the little gnome is on his way.

Fisher gives a daily puppet show as well. But her story basket never appears until everyone is quiet and ready, waiting. "It's like this spell comes over them, excitement that the basket is about to come, and *who knows what's going to come out of it!* So, the charm of quiet is part of the classroom every day."

Private, Secret, and Anonymous

Not everyone is comfortable with silence, which they associate with powerlessness, the enforced quietude of school and church and work. When silence means repression and control, casual cruelty or indifference, or what Martin Luther King Jr. once called "the appalling silence of the good people," it makes sense that one should try to break it. But for writers and artists, scholars and seekers, as for monks, mystics, and musicians, silence is more usually a cherished thing, the crucial prerequisite to creative work. The sustaining silence of a kitchen or spare bedroom, a renovated garage or tiny attic studio, is part of what allows the mind to sink down into itself, slowing and deepening each passing moment, gathering courage for the road ahead. "Silence can be fertilizing," writes Adrienne Rich. "It can bathe the imagination, it can, as in great open spaces—I think of those plains stretching far below the Hopi mesas in Arizona—be the nimbus of a way of life, a condition of vision."

Many others agree, from St. John of the Cross ("Whereas speaking distracts, silence and work collect the thoughts and strengthen the spirit") to Virginia Woolf ("I must be private, secret, as anonymous and submerged as possible in order to write"), to the great contemporary writer, Pico Iyer:

> In silence, we often say, we can hear ourselves think,
> but what is truer to say, is that we can hear ourselves
> not think, and so sink beneath our daily selves, into a
> place deeper than mere thought allows. . . . Silence is
> a way of clearing space and staying time; of opening
> out, so that the horizon itself expands, and the air is
> transparent as glass.

Silence, then, and solitude and calm, a sufficiency of time, an inner spaciousness. Annie Dillard says it best, perhaps, in *Teaching a Stone to Talk.*

> At a certain point you say to the woods, to the sea, to
> the mountains, the world, 'Now I am ready. Now I will
> stop and be wholly attentive.' You empty yourself and
> wait, listening. After a time, you hear it: there is noth-
> ing there. . . . You feel the world's word as a tension, a
> hum, a single chorused note everywhere the same. This
> is it: this hum is the silence.

The Quiet Activist

It was the fall of 1980, and Gordon Hempton was twenty-seven years old. He was on his way to graduate school in Madison, Wisconsin. But it was a sultry afternoon, and Hempton was exhausted. Perhaps he could sleep for a while, he thought, save himself the cost of a motel. He pulled his car to the side of the road and lay down between two rows of stubby cornstalks. When the thunder began, booming out across the far horizon, he went on lying there between the rows, as the clouds darkened and the lightning flashed, and the storm broke open overhead. By the time it ended, he was completely soaked. "The thunder rolled up the valley and rolled through me, and for the first time I truly listened."

Hempton had grown up in a military family, moving from Southern California to Hawaii and back again to California, before going on to Washington, DC, Seattle, and at least a dozen other places. He'd spent a lot of time attending to other human beings, and almost none at all to the ground underfoot or the sky overhead. Those moments in the cornfield were a revelation. When he pulled himself to his feet, and got back on the road, he had only one goal: to become a better listener. As he explained in a TED talk years later, "The more I listened, the more I heard, the more I listened."

For more than a decade afterwards, Hempton got by hand-to-mouth. He dropped out of graduate school, bought himself a superb binaural microphone, and began recording everything he could. From the start, he was especially drawn to vanishing landscapes— places of natural silence, natural sound. But his projects were pricey and time-consuming, and support was hard to find. So, he'd make as much as he could as a bike messenger—earning a single dollar for each delivery—and then take off on long treks with his recorder. It took years, but finally his persistence was rewarded. These days, he is widely known as an acoustic ecologist and sound recordist, and also as what one might call "a quiet activist." In 1992, he won an Emmy for his documentary, *Vanishing Dawn Chorus,* and in 2009, he published his first book, *One Square Inch of Silence: One Man's Search for Natural Silence in a Noisy World.*

Hempton believes in silence the way an artist believes in light and color, the way an arborist believes in trees. For him, "silence is not the absence of something, but the presence of everything"—above all, "the experience of place." His favorite place is what he calls "the cathedral of the Hoh Rain Forest" at Olympic National Park in Washington, not far from where he lives. During an interview with radio host Krista Tippett, he conjured up an imaginary walk through that cherished territory, naming each of its remembered sounds. These included the high-pitched twittering of a winter wren, the gentle wash of the Hoh River, and the far-off bugling of a Roosevelt elk, for a total of some 25 to 35 decibels.

But as Hempton understands all too keenly, such quiet is increasingly under siege. "Silence is so endangered now, we even need another word for it," he says. "The modern measure of silence is the noise-free interval."

In April 2005, he created the "One Square Inch of Silence Foundation," aiming to establish a twenty-mile radius no-fly zone over Olympic National Park and hoping to inspire by example. But in 2018, the US Navy increased the number of training flights over the western corner of the park. The racket was tremendous. One passing jet, 36,000 feet in the air, can destroy one thousand square miles of silence down below. And the navy jets were exceptionally loud, often exceeding 70 decibels. Hempton was appalled. His response was to expand his mission globally, replacing "One Square Inch" by a more ambitious project, "Quiet Parks International" or QPI. "It wasn't enough to talk about one place," he says. "We needed to talk about all places."

QPI aims to protect the natural quiet that already exists, first by identifying exceptionally tranquil places around the world and certifying them as "quiet parks," and then by certifying smaller places too: quiet neighborhoods, hotels, and urban parks. Two hundred and sixty wilderness areas have currently been selected. Meanwhile Hempton's work has already had a profound influence, in particular on the UK's Quiet Garden Movement and a new organization, Silent Space, both of which offer visitors a chance to switch off their phones and cameras, and simply stop talking for a while, whether in a private garden or retreat center, or a protected corner of a public park. Research confirms that such quiet is highly beneficial—especially quiet time outside. It reduces stress, lowers our heart rate and blood pressure, and helps us to relax and even to be more generous.

Hempton doesn't doubt this for a minute. "Go to a quiet place in nature," he says, "and after a few hours you will notice that your thoughts have slowed; you are no longer thinking in words, but in feelings." As our hearts calm, and our ears return to stillness, we become better listeners, not just to the good green world, but to each other.

A Breath of Life

Strolling through London's National Gallery with my uncle Johnnie, I notice as we pause together, look again, remark on some shared moment of surprise: the tender blue-green distances behind the shoulder of the

Virgin, the man in Piero's "Baptism" caught in the moment of undress, his naked legs, the coarse white shirt pulled high over his head.

We don't talk much. There is no need to talk. I savor his steady kindness and affection, the long years of knowing him and being known.

"Perhaps the most important thing we bring to another person is the silence in us," writes Rachel Naomi Remen, "the sort of silence that is a place of refuge, of rest, of acceptance. . . ."

Soon after the blind writer Jacques Lusseyran arrived at Buchenwald, in January 1944, he met a man called Jeremy Regard. They knew each other for less than a month, but Lusseyran always remembered him. One went towards him "as toward a spring," he wrote. "One didn't ask oneself why."

Regard (from *regarder*, "to look at closely," or "consider"), had been a welder in the west of France. He told ordinary stories about his life, the kind that any working man might tell. He was not stern or frightening or especially eloquent. But his presence was somehow tangible, a source of strength. When he walked through the barracks, the other prisoners would press in close around him, while at the same time giving him "a little halo of space."

"Each time he appeared, the air became breathable," wrote Lusseyran. "Jeremy's walk across the quad was that: a breathing." Years later, he would picture "the path of light and clarity he made through the crowd." In that sea of misery and rage, there was this one small, elderly man, this serene and joyous being, whose silence was "truer, more exact, than any words."

Room Sound

Each space has its own distinctive resonance, its own unmistakable "room sound." If you interview a painter in her big echoey loft overlooking the Bowery in Manhattan, you had better record a stretch of room sound, too. That way, if you need to insert pauses later on, you'll have the wherewithal to do so. A stretch of "silence" from the local editing studio simply wouldn't match—any more than one could splice a piece of rough white blotting paper into a sheet of handmade vellum.

But such precious emptiness is increasingly hard to come by. Our buildings are noisy, our days riven by distraction, splintered into phone calls, errands, chores. As Philip Roth once said, half in jest and wholly in earnest, "Literature takes a habit of mind that has disappeared. It requires silence, some form of isolation, and sustained concentration in the presence of an enigmatic thing."

The writer Doris Grumbach saw this all too clearly. When her partner took off for the city in search of new books for their store, she seized the opportunity to be alone. In the long days that followed, "The house expanded. It now seemed to have more rooms than before. . . . I found that the silence I maintained also increased until it filled every space, pushed out the walls, invaded closets, drawers, and cupboards. Eventually it seeped out through the house's seams and surrounded the whole property with a blessed, protective wall of quiet."

For the right person—perhaps composers especially—that quiet can itself become a source of inspiration. In 1975, Brian Eno lay in his room, listening to seventeenth-century harp music. Outside it was raining hard, and he could barely hear the record, "just the loudest notes, like little crystals, sonic icebergs rising out of the storm." Confined to bed, immobilized by a recent accident, he was unable to get up and raise the volume. But as the record continued to play, he found himself entranced by what he heard. "I realized that this was what I wanted music to be—a place, a feeling, an all-around tint to my sonic environment."

Later that year, he made a thirty-one-minute piece called *Discreet Music*, "evenly textured, calm, and sonically warm," leading in turn to a series of records called Ambient Music, for which he is still known.

Playing What You Don't Know

Forgetting oneself is opening oneself.

Dōgen

When Gary Peacock was a little boy, growing up in the Pacific Northwest, he used to lie awake at night and listen to the rain. "I could hear the rain hitting the roof," he remembered. "And it wasn't steady! You know, it actually seemed to have a rhythm to it. It would be heavy, and then it would be light, and then it would be heavy, and then it would be gone. And then it would start up again—"

Gary Peacock died in 2020, at the age of eighty-five. A lean man with a handsome craggy face and bushy white eyebrows, he was also an astonishing bassist, who had been playing world-class jazz for most of the last half century. From early on, he learned trumpet and piano, and later took up drums. At high school graduation, drumming for his fellow students, he first saw with utter clarity that he was indeed a musician, and that his life would be spent making music. "I didn't even question it," he said. "It was just going to be, and it was."

Peacock went on to music school in Los Angeles, and then was drafted and stationed in Germany, where he joined a piano trio. In the years that followed, he played on both coasts with a dazzling array of musicians, including Art Pepper, Bill Evans, and Miles Davis, who remained for him a guiding spirit.

"He was always listening to what was going on," Peacock said. "Always listening to '*What's next? What's next?*'" On one occasion, Miles was doing a recording with a well-known saxophone player. "They did a take," said Peacock, "and Miles said (here he imitated his mentor's grainy voice), 'I know what you're playing, man. I hear what you know. What I want to hear is what you don't know.'"

"You do have to be accurate," Peacock added, "You do have to respond. But beyond that, "You just simply—*trust!*"

Peacock had a precise practice regimen, which he followed for decades. First, he made sure that his bass was in tune, after which he might just play a note, and spend a moment, listening. Meanwhile, he was paying close attention to his posture, and to the contents of his mind, consciously relaxing, letting go. If something came to him,—an arpeggio, for example—he might try that. All the while, he was becoming more fully present, alert to his fingers touching the strings or the fingerboard, or to the movements of his arm.

At times, Peacock's practice became entirely silent and internal. He would take a shower, put on some loose clothing, and lie down on a firm bed. Then he would focus his awareness on his toes, feet, ankles, and calves, each in turn, releasing any tension he might find. By the time he'd reached the top of his head, he often felt as if his entire body had dissolved. At that point, he'd begin to give himself instructions. "OK, play a major scale." For the next little while, he imagined himself playing a major scale. "OK, now do it in thirds." He did it in thirds. "OK, now play it faster." Soon he would reach a threshold where he could imagine what he was doing internally, but as he imagined it, he'd feel a crick in his neck, or a pain in his wrist or elbow. Or perhaps he experienced himself as playing out of tune. Then he'd stop and repeat the sequence until the problem was resolved.

"You can do anything in your mind," he told me. "You can imagine anything. So, it's a question of paying attention—paying attention to what is going on, particularly with the body. *Particularly with the body!*"

Peacock had never aspired to be a soloist, or even a composer. From early on, his desire was "simply to serve the music." But once he realized just how noisy the brain can be—"*Yak-yak-yak!*"—he devoted himself to an altogether conscious letting go. "So, although you're in the midst of a performance, the drums are playing, and the bass—in your mind, you're silent. And in that silence, you somehow become informed of what will happen next. Your ears and hands simply move to the appropriate place."

Peacock studied Buddhism for more than fifty years and was a long-time lay practitioner at the Zen Mountain Monastery in upstate New York. Most of his time was spent out in the world, he said. "And it's insane out there. It's like I've finally found a place where people are actually striving for sanity."

That sanity infused his music, in the same way that meditative practice infused his daily life. It just has different expressions. "If I'm chanting, I'm chanting. If I'm playing the bass, I'm playing the bass. If

I'm washing dishes, I'm washing dishes." He laughed out loud. "I can't practice yet while I'm asleep, but I'm working on it!"

As a boy, Peacock took great pleasure in the little sounds of every day: dogs barking, cats meowing, trucks speeding past. Deep into old age, he loved listening to the sound of the rain, to water running in a brook, to passing birds. He enjoyed human-made sounds as well. "The furnace going on. Water coming out of the faucet. . . ." As for music, his preferences were always changing. Some days, he wanted to listen to Shostakovich's Fifth Symphony, or to *Wozzeck* by Alban Berg. Even musicians he did not especially admire, he came to see as teachers. "They were teaching me—*don't go this way!*" There was nothing that didn't influence him, he told me, and all of it was good. "Just gratitude for the diversity of everything."

Consider the following quotations:

Isn't that lovely," she sighed. "It's my favorite program—fifteen minutes of silence—and after that there's a half hour of quiet and then an interlude of lull. Why, did you know that there are almost as many kinds of stillness as there are sounds?

Norton Juster

The youth walks up to the white horse, to put its halter on
and the horse looks at him in silence.
They are so silent, they are in another world.

D. H. Lawrence

Continue to explore:

What happens when you listen to the pauses between words as well as to the words themselves? Can you actually do this?

Make your own list of the many kinds of silence. What do you notice? How does one silence differ from another—when you are alone, in familiar company, with strangers, walking out under the trees?

～ 12 ～

Listening to the Spirit

Coolness—
the sound of the bell
as it leaves the bell.

Buson

Only Listen

As I picked up my pencil to draft this section of the book, a bell sounded, slow and sonorous, from a nearby church. It was early in November, the maples still ablaze against a cloudless sky. Such rusty reds and flaming golds, such a delicate pale bright blue! It was as if the chimes swirled out around each separate tree, burnished and released each leaf, caressed the grass, entranced my watching eye. Such listening is at the heart of spiritual practice, opening (if one is fortunate) into a new clarity and serenity, a deeper knowing. "When you listen with your soul, you come into rhythm and unity with the music of the universe," says the Irish writer John O'Donohue.

In *A Listening Heart*, Brother David Steindl-Rast writes with graceful lucidity about the act of listening, which is central to his own monastic practice. "The very first word of the rule of St. Benedict is 'Listen!' '*Ausculta!*'" he says, and everything follows from that initial instruction, "as a sunflower grows from its seed." Even the word "obedient" derives from the Latin *ob-audiens*, which is to say, "thoroughly listening." For Steindl-Rast, such obedience is by no means a dry, unthinking submission, but rather "the heart's willing reply to the call of a given moment," an openness, an attunement, or as he puts it elsewhere, an "alertness to the secret signs pointing the way towards true joy."

In one of my favorite Bible stories, the boy Samuel is woken by a voice calling him, "Samuel, Samuel!" Thinking it's the high priest, Eli, he runs to answer him. But Eli says firmly that he did not call. Samuel goes back to bed, and the voice calls him again, a second time, a third. Each time he runs to Eli. Finally, Eli tells him simply to be still and listen. When the voice calls for the fourth time, Samuel is ready. "Speak Lord," he says, "for thy servant heareth."

The God of the Old Testament may not be visible, but is widely conceived as audible, with a voice like thunder or a mighty trumpet, the sound of many wings or crashing waters. The prophet Elijah encounters him on Mount Horeb, first in the form of a whirlwind, then an earthquake, a fire, and finally, miraculously, as "a still small voice." That last phrase, translated from the Hebrew as "the sound of a slender silence," pierces the enveloping clouds of human self-absorption like a shaft of sunlight, a fine-tuned clarity, both physical and metaphysical. This is the voice that reaches Mary's ears through the mediation of the Angel Gabriel, and that instantly causes her to conceive. That same voice speaks from the heavens at the moment of Christ's baptism: "This is my beloved Son, in whom I am well pleased."

It is a voice that continues to be heard in the centuries that follow, whether by St. Augustine, St. Joan of Arc, or the fifteenth-century English mystic, Margery Kempe. According to her autobiography (thought to have been dictated to her son, since Kempe herself was illiterate), she had numerous conversations with God, as well as with Jesus, Mary, and other religious figures. Christ spoke to her "in a sweet and gentle voice," advising her, among other things, to take Communion every Sunday, and to be still and speak to him in thought. She was visited by more ordinary voices too, ranging from the leathery wheeze of a pair of bellows to the *roo-coo* of a dove, and the cheerful twitterings of a robin redbreast. She also heard a celestial melody that made her weep.

Such tales are not restricted to the distant past. God's voice is still heard even now, by those who listen. In *The Music of What Happens,*

Father John J. O'Riordain reports on a number of older women who commune with the deity on a daily basis. One such woman, from the Scottish island of Eriskay, spends almost all day in cheerful converse with the Lord, "chatting and mumbling, arguing and gently chiding." Another woman, from the Irish town of Drogheda, has such a sense of invisible companionship that she is outraged when the priest describes her as living on her own. "'Alone!' said she, in astonishment. 'Not at all!' And raising her hand to a variety of religious pictures hanging on the wall, she continued, 'Haven't I himself?' (the Sacred Heart), 'and herself,' (the Mother of Perpetual Help), 'and all of these?' (her favorite saints)." The woman is neither lonely nor alone. On the contrary. Her days are spent in harmony and contentment, absorbed in conversation with her heavenly friends.

Listening Angels

When the director Wim Wenders returned to Berlin, Germany, in the mid-1980s after a long sojourn in the United States, he was struck by the stone angels looking down over the city—in particular, the Friedensengel monument. He saw them as witnesses, listeners, ancient presences, like the angels in Rilke's *Duino Elegies*, or the winged figures in the paintings of Paul Klee. His film, *Wings of Desire,* appeared in 1987, starring Bruno Ganz as the guardian angel Damiel; Otto Sander as his fellow angel, Cassiel; and Solveig Dummartin as the beautiful trapeze artist with whom Damiel falls in love. I saw it first soon after it came out, and have returned to it several times since, haunted by the presence of the listening angels, and by Wenders' power to reach for the ineffable and somehow make it visible on screen.

Damiel and Cassiel have been companions since the beginning, far back before human time began. For countless eons, they simply watch and wait. Then, very gradually the land below them starts to be transformed. A glacier calves. Icebergs sail up north. A tree trunk drifts by, still green, an empty nest caught in its branches. Fish leap from the water. Two deer fight each other on the grassy shore. And finally, one day, a man steps out onto the savannah—someone who looks like them. Neither Damiel nor Cassiel can recall precisely what he says. "Was it *ah* or *ohh*? Or was it just a moan?" But already they are listening, listening hard.

In the millennia that follow, the two friends see generations come and go. They bear witness to everything that takes place in the city that is now Berlin—however large and newsworthy, however small. Early in the movie, they sit together, trading observations.

> Twenty years ago today
> a Soviet jet fighter crashed
> into the lakes at Spandau.
>
> Fifty years ago there were . . .
> —*The Olympic Games!*
>
> Two hundred years ago,
> Blanchard flew over the city in a hot air balloon.
> —*Like those refugees the other day.*
>
> And today
> on the Lilienthaler Chausée,
> a man slowed down
> and looked over his shoulder into empty space.

The two angels listen to everything both audible and inaudible, miraculously able to eavesdrop on human thoughts and ruminations, anxieties, revelations, hopes and dreams. At one point, a young girl peers up out of the window of the bus and catches sight of Damiel (still winged) perched on a monument. "Look!" she says. A blind woman senses his presence, and gropes for her watch. But for the most part, the angels remain wingless, invisible, anonymous. They stroll through Berlin side by side, dressed in matching trench coats, their long hair drawn back into simple ponytails. Damiel moves through the subway, as an older woman frets about her tiny pension. "How can I pay for everything?" A little further down the train, a middle-aged man broods over his losses: the parents who have disowned him, the wife who has betrayed him, the good friend who has moved to another city. Damiel puts an arm around his shoulders, and the man brightens, sits up straighter, begins to gather his resolve. "I'm still here . . . I just have to set my mind to it, and then I can get out of there. I got myself in, I can get myself out again. Yes, of course, mother was right. . . ."

That sense of the angels as an enveloping presence, deeply kind, focused, and attentive, comes to a crescendo in the big modern library, with its individual desks and reading lamps, its long tables shining under tall glass windows. The two friends drift unhurriedly from room to room, surrounded by a tapestry of voices—excerpts from poems, newspapers, and textbooks read at random by a choir of male and female singers—some whispered, some shouted, some read at normal range, combined with further phrases sung to match "the angel chord." When Cassiel pauses for a moment, and closes his eyes, it is as if he were drawing all those myriad strands of sound into himself: listening become embodiment, become prayer.

That deep compassionate listening is put to the test towards the end of the film, when a young man is flung from his motorbike, and lies dying in the road. His first thoughts are broken and scattered. "I saw it all so clearly, the Mercedes, the pool of oil. Karin, I should have told you. . . . I've still so much to do." But then Damiel places his invisible hands on the young man's head, and he too begins to speak—an inaudible flow of beautiful soothing images. Little by little, the dying man joins in, until his mind and spirit merge with Damiel's own, and his bafflement and panic fall away. By the time Damiel walks on, the man is able to continue on his own, his last words a tender reckoning of all that he has loved. "The veins of the leaves. The blowing grass. . . . My father. My mother. My wife. My child."

The Ones Who Listen to the Cries of the World

Like Christianity, Buddhism has numerous teachings centered on the act of listening. It is said that when the Buddha first taught, two deer stepped softly up, knelt down beside him, and pricked up their ears. Their image can still be found in almost every Buddhist temple. "The Buddha is always teaching," writes the Zen master Thich Nhat Hanh. "Times are teaching, living beings are teaching. If you have an attentive ear, you can hear the authentic Dharma all the time."

One of the most beloved texts in the Buddhist canon is the Lotus

Sutra, composed in India in the first century AD. It describes a bodhisattva known as Wondrous Sound or Avalokiteshvara, who is dedicated to the liberation of all beings. He is said to have been born from a ray of light sprung from Buddha's right eye, and is thus a manifestation of compassion, with the miraculous ability to address each person in his or her own language: movement or music, art or song. Like Wim Wenders' listening angels, Wondrous Sound has the power to bestow the gifts of fearlessness and transformation. His name, in the original Sanskrit, translates as "He Who Listens to the Cries of the World."

The original Avalokiteshvara was always shown as male. But starting in China, around the eighth century AD, the figure began to be seen as female too, in the form of the goddess, Kwan Yin, or "She Who Listens to the Cries of the World." Kwan Yin is often shown resting on a lotus, holding a willow sprig or vase of "sweet dew"—the vase symbolizing the nectar of compassion, the willow sprig her flexibility and strength. Other accoutrements include an arrow, to draw friends towards her; a precious mirror, signifying wisdom; and a vajra-topped bell, with which to play the most mellifluous music. She has also been depicted with a thousand arms and hands, and as an armed warrior, laden with crossbow, thunderbolt, sword, and shield. But in all her manifestations, she remains "The One Who Listens," attentive to the sorrows of the whole lamenting world.

A Hundred Thousand Voices

Christianity tends to anthropomorphize the voice of God, even when it thunders from the heavens, or seethes and crashes "like the sound of many waters." But every so often, especially in the Celtic nature poets, we glimpse a more lyrical and capacious understanding of the sacred, and so, in turn, of what's worth listening to. The cosmos itself becomes audible. This, of course, is true of most indigenous traditions. Once someone listens closely to the natural world, a hundred thousand voices will begin to speak.

Legend has it there was once an Irish monk named Phoenix. One day he was reading his breviary, alone in the monastery garden, when all of a sudden, a bird began to sing. Phoenix became utterly absorbed.

When at last the song was finished, he picked up his book and went back to the monastery—only to discover he knew no one there. Centuries had passed while he sat listening in the garden. His original community was long gone, and the new monks had no idea who he was. But when they searched their annals, they discovered yes, indeed: many years before, a Brother Phoenix had mysteriously disappeared.

In the passage that follows, Maidu writer Marie Potts, who grew up in a cedar bark house in northern California, remembers the sounds of her girlhood with affectionate precision:

"How wonderful it was lying awake at night . . . to hear the coyotes bark and the hoot owls uttering their calls among the trees. Sometimes there would be the running clatter of squirrels on the bark slabs above us; and in spring and summer, just as it grew light . . . there came the enchantment of the bird chorus, the orchestra of the Great Spirit all around us."

A Wintu woman of the same generation harkens back to her own childhood, describing her grandfather at his prayers. Every morning, he would get up early, splash his face with water, and begin to pray. "He prayed to Olelbes, He-Who-Is-Above, the Wintu world creator. He also prayed directly and intimately to the things around him—to the rocks, trees, salmon, acorns, sugar pine, water, and wood." And, "At the end of his life, he talked to the world—sharing his sadness and regret—as one might talk to an old and very trusted friend."

That sense of equivalence, of mutuality, shows up again and again among tribal peoples, from the Chukchi reindeer herders of Siberia to the Maori of New Zealand. A member of the Pawtucket tribe put it this way, speaking to the writer John Hansen Mitchell, "The Indian people, we're all this, you see," and here he lifted his head, indicating the marshes and the dark line of the pines. "We're made of this, the marshes here, the trees. No different, see what I mean? You don't understand because you look on this world as something that is not you. But Indian people believe that we are no different from a squirrel or a bear, just a different form. We're all the same, squirrel, bear, me."

Or, in the words of the poet Linda Hogan, "We don't have to do anything special to have contact with the spirit world. It's just natural if you stop and listen. Just there, always. Like your own heartbeat."

✿

Take a moment. Listen. Catch your breath. One of the strange gifts of the pandemic was that people had more time for this, more time to listen to both inner and outer worlds. The musician Anoushka Shankar is a case in point. Caught in London during lockdown, she was allowed to leave the house for exercise just once a day. Each time, she took pretty much the same route. But as the months went by, she developed what she calls "an intimate loving relationship" with the trees along the way. "It got to the point where in my heart I was saying hello, and I felt like they were saying hello back."

After a time, she started leaning against the trees, pressing her back against their trunks. As she explained in a radio interview, "I figured if I was hugging them behind my back, I didn't look like a weirdo." But from her point of view, it was still a hug. "I'm just kind of leaning and my heart's still poking through my back rib cage, so this is still a hug, you know." And for her, the solace was immense.

Such practices help us to slow down and pay attention, to remember, viscerally, that we are interdependent, intertwined. One of my models for this is the Buddhist teacher Milarepa, who sits calmly on his cushion, one hand curved around the arch of his right ear. Milarepa was an eleventh-century poet and musician, the first ordinary Tibetan to attain enlightenment. He could hear a snail as it oozed over the stony ground, a couple quarreling in a distant village, the most thwarted, muffled sob. Nothing was foreign to him. In the course of his long life, he became "Someone Who Listens," alert to all the many voices of the surrounding world.

Tibetan Medicine

In their classic book, *How Can I Help?*, Ram Dass and Paul Gorman give an account of the Dalai Lama's physician, Yeshe Dhonden, and his long listening to a particular woman patient. Her doctors, of course, already knew what was the matter with her, but Yeshe Dhonden had not been told the diagnosis. When he was introduced to the patient, he simply stood gazing at her for a long time. Then he took her hand in both of his, closed his eyes, and began to take her pulse. And for the next half hour, he remained bowed over the woman, "cradling her hand in his . . . like some exotic golden bird with folded wings." It was as if the two of them had withdrawn into some place all their own, sacred and inviolable.

At last, Yeshe Dhonden released the woman's hand. He took a portion of her urine specimen, poured it into a wooden bowl, whipped it with two sticks until a foam was raised, and then inhaled, three times. Finally, he gave his diagnosis. He spoke of winds coursing through the woman's body, currents eddying against barriers. Those vortices were in her blood, he said. "Between the chambers of the heart, long, long before she was born, a wind had come and blown open a deep gate that must never be opened."

As the western doctors testified, he was right. Burning through the metaphoric language of Tibet was a precise rendering of the woman's illness: *congenital heart disease, interventricular septal defect, with resultant heart failure.*

"A gateway in the heart," writes the narrator, "that must not be opened. Through it charge the full waters that flood her breath. So! Here then is the doctor listening to the sounds of the body to which the rest of us are deaf. He is more than doctor. He is priest."

A Double Listening

Mariel Kinsey was in her eighties by the time I knew her, a bright-eyed woman with a head of snow white hair. She had worked as a psychotherapist and a hospital chaplain, and as a birth coach too. Long after her retirement, she made herself available as an unofficial "spiritual guide," and it was in this capacity I knew her best. The Benedictines speak of listening with the ear of the heart. Kinsey was one of the best such listeners I have ever known.

She spent her early years in China, where her parents were missionaries, and had clear memories of the songs they sang together. But neither one was a good listener. "I think because being listened to was kind of sparse," she told me, "*being a listener* filled a huge need in me. I could listen! And I could have the connection."

She described a memorable session with one of her patients. The woman was so frozen, so awkward and defended, that it had become really hard for her to talk. "Let's pretend," said Kinsey. "Let's put our chairs over here by the window and pretend we're sitting together on the porch. We don't have to say anything." She didn't want to force the woman to talk, or to have her suffer in embarrassed silence. "'Cause she *would* suffer." So, the two of them sat together "on the porch."

Later, she reported on the session to her supervisor, and he was horrified. He felt she had been indulging the woman, pandering to her neurosis. But Kinsey disagreed. She had wanted to make things easy for her client, and she felt that she'd succeeded. She quoted a Jungian teacher, "You know, a client and a therapist come together once a week, and they spend an hour, and they talk. They think that what's important is the content of their listening and speaking. But that's not really it. What matters is that they sit together for an hour. That's where the healing takes place."

As she sat with her patient, Kinsey took the time to listen inwards, attending to minute shifts in her own body, to passing thoughts, and to her own response too. "When we're going really deeper," she said, "we're in a process that has its own pattern and its own flow: *Surface, surface, surface, drop down, drop down, drop down, Euuurghhh!* and then come up, *come up, come up, come up. . . .*" The listening made a bridge, stretching out between her client and her self—*a double listening*—"a listening that is so interested and so slow that you hear even what isn't being said."

Staying Open

> *Even a practice as simple as noticing our breath as we breathe in and out can remind us of the impermanence of life and the inevitability of death. . . . Being with people who are dying is living on the edge of awakening.*

Ram Dass

Soon before he turned thirty, Charles Atkinson traveled around the world to India and Nepal. En route home, the plane passed over the immense darkness of Iran, illuminated, just then, by one brilliant point of light. Was that what life was like, he wondered, "a little flare that would just wink out?" Or was it somehow possible to live more fully, so as to arrive at death without regret? Atkinson pulled out a notebook and began to write. In the question he had recognized his own vocation.

Charles Atkinson is a poet and a longtime Zen practitioner, a thoughtful man with a full head of white hair and clear brown eyes. He taught for more than thirty years at the University of California, Santa Cruz, and has now retired, though he still volunteers regularly at a local hospice. "I think my main life work consists of trying to stay open to experience as it happens," he says, "without closing off in fear or judgment or ignorance. Just to inhabit those moments as fully as I can."

Had he not established a spiritual practice early on, Atkinson doubts he would have been able to stay open in that way. He's been what he calls "a pretty steady meditator" in Vipassana, Zen, and other mindfulness traditions, sitting in formal retreats, some for as long as a month. "I believe in the dailiness of practice," he says, "where you set aside a little time to allow things to settle in the body-mind, and to listen to what's there."

That "listening" shines forth in a recent publication, *Skeleton, Skin and Joy*, much of it drawn from his hospice work. At first, he felt awkward and uncomfortable, "stepping into a stranger's life at this momentous transition into the unknown." But over time, his fear and aversion were replaced by compassion. "This is what we do for each other," he explains, "the personae and the projections, the things that we cloak ourselves with, begin to fall away, and eventually we're simply human beings." He tracks that journey in a poem called "Angel Manor, Lynn,"

> *Here's the one you came to visit—fetal*
> *curl in a recliner, spittle thread, chin*
> *to knee.*
>
> *. . . oily hair pulled*
> *back, sunken temples, bottomless silence.*

The narrator wonders what he can possibly say to such a person, and answers:

Anything.
It's the tone that counts; a steady cadence
draws her in.

The patient lies there, hunched in that fetal curl, and the narrator reaches out, pushing past his own resistance and distaste.

Reach out slowly, stroke her
forehead first, the pointy shoulder, wrist.

. . .

Take her tremor, hold it, bone on bone,
pulse that shudders back and forth, shared
heartbeat. How long can you hold on?

"The question at the end is personal for me," says Atkinson. "How long can I stay in the presence of this body-mind who's so very near to death?" He admits to his own discomfort, and does his best to befriend it, "listening into" the liminal space, and letting silence lead the way.

When Atkinson first began hospice work, he was carrying a considerable amount of fear. He chose to volunteer in part to heal that aversion, to soften and explore it. Ten years in, he feels calmer and more grounded. "I may bring a little less self-hood, a little less ego, to the encounter," he says. "It doesn't take as long as it did at first to be present with my patients." It has helped him, too, in facing his own death. "You know," he says, "I fiercely want to keep on living. But I've seen a lot of people move beyond me—into the mystery we all travel through—and most of them seem to leave in peace."

In another poem, "Visitor, Carol," the narrator steps into the patient's room, his eyes "down, braced as if something were/coiled beneath her bed." After weeks of visits, folding her thin hand in both of his, he smells what's really "huddled under/that bed"—his "poorest, frightened self."

It is not Carol's panic he has come to soothe; it is his own.

I lifted it, shaking almost weightless,
into my lap and stroke its cool—
There now, dying looks like this.

By the end, he stands at the patient's shoulder, following her jagged breaths,

surprised—not that I can love her,
but that I might love myself.

Such transformations are not easily come by. But Atkinson recognizes that they are entirely possible. He tells a couple of stories about being on the threshold, "listening in" to the need or fear of the one who is about to die.

> One of my first patients was apparently a lapsed Catholic, overwhelmed by guilt as she felt herself dying. She was distraught, flinging herself about like a caged wild thing while she clutched her rosary and begged forgiveness from God and from all those she felt she'd wronged over the years. She couldn't hear me, so I sat on the bed next to her and held her as she rocked like a child. Immediately she calmed herself, until the next wave of guilt gathered and spent itself. It was as if her frail body-mind needed assurance in that hour, and sought it out over and over until she felt safe.

> Another actively dying patient, a large and powerful man—a professional bike racer—hadn't wanted to be touched for all the weeks I visited him. He prided himself on his toughness and independence, and kept me at a little distance. But one day, he sat up in bed and looked directly at me. I asked him what was on his mind. He said, "Kiss me, kiss me here—" rubbing his shaved head and upturned face—"a shower of kisses." So, I did. He said nothing after that—and gestured that I could leave. He knew exactly how he wanted closure.

Both people died peacefully the next day. Atkinson would be hard-pressed, he says, to draw more general conclusions. "But many patients seem to register the active listening that can happen in silence. Some of them come to trust it more than words."

"I think there's something like a silent spirit at the center of each sentient being," he adds. "Maybe within non-sentient beings, too . . . And here's the mystery: within the silence that remains, we can begin to hear those sentient beings speak to us. We can hear what the hospice patient is saying, and what she hasn't yet said. In those rare moments it feels like there's no boundary between the self and the world—which may be what we're yearning for all along."

Consider the following quotations:

God made everything out of nothing, but the nothingness shows through.

Paul Valéry

Everything in life is speaking, is audible, is communicating, in spite of its apparent silence. . . . It is not just a tale . . . that the saints spoke with trees and plants in the wilderness, that a voice from the sea rose and the saints heard it, that masters talked with the sun, moon, and stars.

Hazrat Inayat Khan

Continue to explore:

"Prayer," says David Abram, "in its most ancient and elemental sense, consists simply in speaking *to* things—to a maple grove, to a flock of crows, to the rising wind—rather than merely about things. As such, prayer is an everyday practice common to oral, indigenous peoples the world over." Who or what might you choose to pray to?

Rippling out

When you throw a stone into a pond there is a lively *splash!*—followed by a series of calm, concentric circles, rippling out and out.

That image is the basis for the following meditation. I learned it first from Michelle Francl, professor of chemistry at Bryn Mawr College, found it again in a book by the German writer Joachim-Ernst Berendt, and have since used it many times with my own students. The instructions are simple: *pause a moment, come to center, then "listen out" in ever-widening circles.*

Or, to offer it in greater detail—

Settle yourself in your chair, with your feet flat on the floor and your shoulders relaxed. Straighten your spine, lower your gaze, and lay your hands in your lap. Bring your focus to your breath, noticing not just the act of breathing, but the little huff of sound as you draw in the air, and the soft whoosh as you exhale. If there are other people in the room, listen to their breathing presence too: the modest cough as someone clears their throat, the way their chair creaks as they shift position.

Keep breathing.

Then send your attention out into the room, and its own distinctive sound. What can you hear? The spurt and hiss of an old-fashioned radiator. The purr of an air conditioner. Someone laughing with a neighbor down the hall. Don't make any special effort to identify these sounds. Just greet them and release them, let them go.

Then, as you keep breathing, allow your focus to ripple out yet further, out through the walls of your building and into the surrounding world. What sounds can you hear now? A boy tossing a basketball at the hoop across the way. A passing car. A sudden flock of chattering birds in the little tree outside your window. Welcome those sounds, let them resonate. If thoughts show up—or complicated feelings—don't try to engage with them, just smile at them, release them, let them go. . . .

There is a point in this meditation where actual listening can be replaced by what one might call "auditory imagination"—where you send your ears *out, out,* beyond the boundaries of your house or town or village, and simply imagine what you then might hear. You picture long lines of cars and trucks and "hear" the roar of the freeway. You picture the jagged shoreline of the distant coast, and "hear" the waves breaking on the sand. You swoop high into the air, and gaze down on the whole long continent, the diminishing globe, on clouds and planets, sun and moon and stars.

You meditate like the wind—like the sea—rippling out and out—until finally you arrive at the enveloping silence, a place of calm and ease and deep serenity. You continue to breathe, continue to listen—

What do I hear now? you ask yourself. *What do I hear?*

∴ 13 ∾

All Our Relations

*I want to hear what the world is thinking—not the
human world so much as the world of rocks and trees
and rivers.*

Robert Bringhurst

Lost Sounds

These days I live in western Massachusetts, on the top floor of
a big, white-painted farmhouse, at the edge of a small village.
The farmhouse was built in the 1880s, and recently renovated. But
its beautiful curved banister remains, along with its high glazed windows and hospitably spacious rooms. One of the previous inhabitants was a woman called Ruth Hemenway, who worked as a doctor in China in the 1920s and 1930s, and then returned home to the
United States to set up a local practice. I've been told that her con-
sulting room was on the ground floor, along with her bedroom and
living quarters. Apparently, she rented out the floor above, the one
that is now mine. Often, I find myself thinking about her as I sit at
my desk, glancing up at the little hilly graveyard across the street, or
into the tall maples she'd have known. I wonder what memories of
her the house still holds, what sounds—now lost—were once heard
under its roof.

Williamsburg was officially incorporated in 1771; the first house
was built in 1735. For millennia before that, the twenty-five square
miles of sloping hills and river-valley that compose my local village
would have been inhabited seasonally by native tribes, most likely the

215

people known as Nonotuck. They lived in rounded wickiups made of springy saplings, covered with bark or animal skins; fished along the banks of what is now the Mill River. Men cut points and arrowheads, fashioned hoes from clamshells or the shoulder blades of deer, carved sturdy fish hooks out of stone or bone. They hunted duck and pigeon, rabbit, beaver, porcupine, and deer. Women (always the gardeners) made clearings in the woods, where they grew small plots of corn and beans and squash. They gathered wild greens: fiddlehead ferns, marsh marigold, Canada lily, Indian cucumber, to be eaten raw or steamed, or stirred into a pot of robust stew. Children helped pick nuts and berries in season, plants and roots.

Each of these activities had its accompanying sounds.

When a woman prepared a basket of dried acorns, you would hear the peeling click of their thin skins as the nuts were shelled, the swash of water as they were set out to leach, the rhythmic thump as they were ground into flour. As meat or fish was stewed or roasted, there would be the spit and crackle of flames, the comfortable roil of water over heated stones. When a point was carved, a needle smoothed, you'd hear the tap of the sharpened stone as the flakes of bone or antler fell away. Each morning there'd be the *sssshhh*-ing sound of grass against bare legs, as the elders left the shelter of their wickiups and walked out to pray and greet the dawn. You'd hear the children playing, someone laughing, singing. At times too, there'd be the sounds of ceremony, whether sorrowful or joyous: keening, weeping, chanting, drumming, the slap of hands on thighs, the thump of feet.

There were no sheep or goats before the settlers came, no cattle or pigs, no horses; even the purr of the domestic cat was missing. But the barred owl that croons "Who-cooks-for-you?" called out the same low notes (though not those words) for the native peoples of five hundred years ago. Bohemian waxwings arrived in chattering flocks to feast on dogwood and chokecherries just as they do today. Long before the shrill of the first telephone, the roar of the first car, the rush of the river in its spring melt still possessed the same authority and beauty.

All Our Relations

There are thought to have been over 112 million native people in the continental United States when the Europeans arrived. By 1650, that number had shrunk to six million, and has now been reduced even further, making Native Americans about half of one percent of the total population. The word "genocide" is too rarely used in this context, but that of course is what it was: a deliberate ousting and eradication of the original inhabitants, along with a brutal seizure of their land.

> *They have come, they have come,*
> *Out of the unknown they have come;*
> *Out of the great sea they have come:*
> *Dazzling and conquering the white man has come*
> *To make this land his home.*

wrote the Cherokee poet Ruth Margaret Muskrat Bronson in her poem "Sentenced."

> *They have gone, they have gone,*
> *Our sky-blue waters, they have gone,*
> *Our wild free prairies they have gone,*
> *To be the white man's own.*

Where the native peoples understood themselves as part of the natural world, with plants and trees, birds and animals all members of the same extended family—*all our relations*—the newcomers conceived of life as a pyramid, with themselves on top, and all the rest in diminishing ranks below. What mattered was ownership and extraction, and above all, revenue.

"The white people never cared for land or deer or bear," said Wintu tribal member Katie Luckie. "When we Indians kill meat, we eat it all up. . . . We don't chop down the trees. We only use dead wood. But the white people plow up the ground, pull up the trees, kill everything. The tree says, 'Don't. I am sore. Don't hurt me.' But they chop it down and cut it up. The spirit of the land hates them. . . . Everywhere the white man has touched it, it is sore."

Five hundred years of human-centered greed have brought us to the brink of self-annihilation. "We can't save humanity unless we save all the other species too," says plant ecologist Robin Wall Kimmerer. "Our flourishing is mutual. We have to engage humbly with all our relatives. We have to listen."

For Kimmerer, such listening has a lot to do with language. She delights in Potawatomi, which she describes as having "a grammar of animacy" as well as a rich treasure-trove of verbs. "You hear a blue jay with a different verb than you hear an airplane," she explains, "distinguishing that which possesses the quality of life from that which is merely an object. . . . There is no *it* for nature . . . personhood is extended to all who breathe and some who don't."

Potawatomi is famously difficult—hard to pronounce and harder yet to spell—and came perilously close to being eradicated by the colonists. But Kimmerer has now acquired some fluency in her native tongue. She draws on it to model personhood for her students, replacing "it" by *ki,* from the Potawatomi word *Aakibmaadiziiwin,* meaning "a being of the earth," and using the familiar *kin* as plural. "So, when the robin warbles on a summer morning, we can say, 'Ki is singing up the sun.'"

In doing this, Kimmerer is practicing *re-story-ation*—the reclaiming or reshaping of the old stories to meet the urgencies of today. Other likeminded activists work to extend legal personhood to plants and trees and rocks and rivers, protecting their rights as most of us protect our own (or, indeed, the rights of corporations). Simple as this sounds, such revisioning can have far-reaching consequences, not least by providing a legal tool with which to prosecute polluters.

"We see ourselves not as an owner of wild rice, but a symbiotic partner and a parallel entity," says Frank Bibeau, a member of the White Earth Nation, who designed legislation granting wild rice (or *manoomin*) its own rights under tribal law, "including the right to pure water and freshwater habitat, a healthy climate and a natural environment free from human-caused global warming."

Manoomin was the first plant ever to be honored in this way. But an increasing number of rivers, forests, and natural qualities have now been granted such protection. In New Zealand, the Whanganui River has been named a person in its own right, as have the Ganges and Jumna Rivers in India, and all the many rivers in Bangladesh. In 2019, the Yurok tribe declared rights of personhood for the Klamath River, the first in the United States to be so designated. Ecuador has enshrined the rights of nature—personified as Pachamama, the Andean Earth Mother—in its constitution. Bolivia and Uganda have done the same, and Sweden, too, is keen to follow suit.

Robin Wall Kimmerer exults in all of this. Land, for her, is not just capital or property, but "the healer, the sustainer, the ancestor, the sacred, the home of our relatives," and we need to attend to it. "As we work to save the world," she says, "the world saves us."

A Mutual Listening

There are many ways of engaging with a tree, as the philosopher Martin Buber understood:

> I can accept it as a picture: a rigid pillar in a flood of light, or splashes of green traversed by the gentleness of the blue silver ground.

> I can feel it as movement: the flowing veins round the sturdy thriving core, the sucking of the roots, the breathing of the leaves, the infinite commerce with earth and air—and the growing itself in its darkness. . . .

> I can assign it a species and observe it as an instance, with an eye to its construction and its way of life. . . .

And finally, writes Buber, "if will and grace are joined," it may happen that one is *drawn into relation* with the tree, so that (as in Potawatomi) it "ceases to be an It," and becomes a Thou.

In a recent book, Terry Tempest Williams tells a story about the ecologist Sue Beatty, who worked for many years at Yosemite National Park. Two or three times a week, Beatty would stroll through the Mariposa

Grove, among the towering pillars of the Giant Sequoias, many of them two to three thousand years old. Like Buber, she would relate to them as "Thou." And on at least one occasion, they spoke to her quite clearly. "We are suffering," they told her. "We are dying. Can you hear us?"

The Mariposa Grove had been part of the Yosemite Land Grant, created by President Lincoln in 1864. In the years since, their roots had been trampled and their soil compacted, both by human traffic and by cars. The Sequoias were suffocating; they could not breathe. Beatty went back to her colleagues, charged with what she'd heard, and together they decided on a plan of action, including a complete inventory of the trees, wetland and wildlife surveys, and an evaluation of current visitor use. Sue Beatty had a vision of restoration and renewal. And her colleagues listened.

In the years that followed, forty million dollars was raised, much of it from citizen donations. Roads were rerouted, asphalt paving torn up. Cars and trucks and buses were banned from the immediate area. The parking lot was replaced by walking paths and trails. And for three long years, the trees themselves were allowed to rest. Sue Beatty and her team had listened to them, both as scientists and as empathetic human beings. The Giant Sequoias weren't just a popular tourist attraction or an impressive stand of timber, they were also "venerable members of the Yosemite community," who deserved to be treated with respect. And if Sue Beatty and her team were hearing them, it seemed entirely possible that the trees were listening back.

For, as Gary Snyder put it in his perfect three-line poem,

> *As the crickets' soft autumn hum is to us,*
> *so are we to the trees.*
> *As are they to the rocks and the hills.*

Zen Master Ikkyu

In *The World is Sound: Nada Brahma*, first published in 1987, Joachim-Ernst Berendt quotes a little teaching story about Zen Master Ikkyu, which could have been written especially for our time:

A disciple comes to Ikkyu, asking for some wise advice.

Ikkyu takes his brush and writes, "Attention."

"Is that all?" asks the disciple.

Ikkyu writes the same word twice. "Attention. Attention."

The man is disappointed; he had hoped for something more. "I can't see much depth or subtlety in that."

Ikkyu returns to his scroll and writes the word three times. *"Attention. Attention. Attention."*

"What does that mean anyway?" the disciple wants to know.

Ikkyu smiles and looks up from the scroll. "Attention means attention," he says gently.

Thus Spoke the Plant

Plants appear to be entirely silent, something most human beings take for granted. But Monica Gagliano disagrees. From her point of view, the vegetal world has never stopped talking, reaching out to us through visions and through dreams. Meditating in California, she heard an oak instruct her, "You are here to tell our stories."

Gagliano grew up in northern Italy, but these days she lives in Sydney, Australia, where she is a pioneer in the field of plant bioacoustics. In 2018, she published *Thus Spoke the Plant,* told by and on behalf of the plants themselves, in which she describes a series of experiments on plant learning, memory, and decision making. One of her subjects was *Mimosa pudica,* also known as the "sensitive plant." When it is touched or dropped or shaken, its leaves immediately spring closed, protecting the plant from danger, but also depriving it of crucial sunlight. Gagliano subjected her mimosas to a series of gentle drops, and at first, they closed their leaves. But as the drops continued, the plants learned not to react. If they were shaken, their usual reflexes returned. But the lesson of the drop remained.

Another such experiment focused on young peas. Just as Pavlov taught his dog to salivate at the sound of a bell (which it associated with the reward of a meal), so Gagliano taught her peas to associate the light breeze of a fan with the promise of sunlight. Placed in individual Y-shaped mazes (constructed out of vinyl pipes) her seedlings followed the tremor of the fan, "knowing" it would lead them toward light.

The notion of plant cognition causes considerable unease, especially among traditional scientists. But as Gagliano points out, cognition means "to know, to experience, to distinguish, to solve a problem," and that is precisely what her plants are doing. She asks her readers to set aside their usual assumptions, and open to the possibility that plants can not only hear, see, smell, feel, and taste, but also choose and remember and indeed communicate. "With every breath . . . the plant knows the human as herself," she writes. "At every breath, the human becomes more plant-like than he realizes."

She herself has "become more porous now," she says, braiding together the trained mind of the scientist with the "awe-inspired heart" of the mystic. Each month she conducts a ceremony where she asks the plants what they would like her to know. "I am here," she tells them, "and I am listening."

The Joy of Fishes

There's a famous story about the Chinese sage Chuang Tzu. It's a fine day, and he is walking along the river with a friend. Fish are disporting themselves in the water, light glittering on their scales as they dart and leap. "How wonderfully the fishes are enjoying themselves!" observes Chuang Tzu. His friend is not so sure. "How do you know the fishes are enjoying themselves?" he asks. "You're not a fish!" "And you're not me," responds Chuang Tzu, tartly. "How do *you* know I don't know what the fish are feeling?"

I love this little tale, not least because Chuang Tzu is given the last word, his radiant empathy trumping the authority of his literal-minded friend. I love, too, how it reaches back into the mythic past, to a time when the human and non-human worlds were not so separate, one that is increasingly validated by the cutting-edge science of today. Animals and plants, as we now know, share much of their DNA with human beings. Communication goes both ways. "It's often subtle," writes the independent scholar Stephen Harrod Buhner, "but if you pay close attention, you will notice that, quite often, there is some sort of response. Sooner or later, when you least expect it, something will look back . . . something will touch you in return."

One of my favorite such stories was told to me by Sandy Zepka, who worked for many years at the Center for Environmental Studies at Williams College. It centered on her father-in-law, John Zepka, a well-known local beekeeper. I don't know if someone "told the bees" after he died. But when his family and friends arrived at the cemetery, the bees were there ahead of them, thousands of them, hanging in long swags on the wreaths and floral arrangements, and clinging to the tent above his grave. They remained calm and motionless throughout the final prayers. Not until Zepka's coffin had been lowered into the ground, did the entire swarm take flight again, back to their familiar hives.

Such tales can sound fantastical or esoteric. In fact, they are surprisingly commonplace. Working with third graders at a school in New York State, I heard innumerable stories about their family pets—dogs and cats especially, but smaller creatures too (gerbils, hamsters, guinea pigs, pet mice)—who were delicately attuned to their young owners' joys and sorrows. Nor are such connections limited to domestic animals. The writer Gavin Maxwell maintained just such an expressive friendship with the wild otters he adopted, in particular, his favorite, Mijbil. And the naturalist Sy Montgomery pays similar tribute both to the family pig, Christopher Hogwood, and to her beloved octopus, Octavia.

Whether such cross-species understanding has its roots in ear or eye or body/mind, there is no question that the act of listening can be a powerful point of entry. When Gary Snyder writes from Hawaii that "Lots of pre-dawn meditating has given me a real sense of what the birds say early, which one each, and when," he is teaching himself the rudiments of that tongue. But deep listening can be practiced equally well at home in the Sierra, as he notes to his friends the Berrys on a summer evening.

Dear Wendell and Tanya,
I'm sitting outside here by the fire by the pond listening
to the sharp little slashing sound that bats make when

they swoop down and hit the surface of the water after
insects, along with the bull frog booming, the crickets
in the background and the soft rustling of the fire,
enough music for anybody.

Such a practice can be simple and domestic, modest, unexotic and
at the same time utterly transformative. "Not only does it change
the content of our minds," writes Mark Nepo, "but as water rushing
through an inlet changes the shape of the inlet, letting what we hear
enter us so completely changes the *shape* and *threshold* of our minds."
In time, if we persist, it becomes "a partnership by which we listen
and converse with everything."

Cosmic Sounds

When Laurens van der Post told the Kalahari Bushmen (also known
as Khoisan or !Kung San) that he couldn't hear the stars, they were
unable to believe him.

> *They looked at him*
> *Half-smiling. They examined his face*
> *To see whether he was joking. . . .*

Then two of them led him away from the fire, and they stood together
under the night sky, listening.

> *One of them whispered*
> Do you not hear them now?

Van der Post listened—listened hard—but was obliged to answer,
"No." And the two men walked him back into the circle of firelight,
"slowly / Like a sick man," and told him they were terribly sorry.

This account is taken from David Wagoner's poem, "The Silence
of the Stars," itself drawn from van der Post's own writings. There is
bafflement and yearning in the telling, the compressed anguish of
not-being-able-to-hear, not-understanding-why. And there is mystery too. What is that "singing" that the Khoisan hear so easily? How
might it be to catch our own "fair share of the music of the spheres"?

The Lost World of the Kalahari was published more than sixty years ago; Van der Post died in 1996. In the decades since, new technologies have presented us with a cornucopia of cosmic sounds, from the thunder on Venus to the winds on Saturn's moon, Titan—even the 14 billion-year-old echoes of creation, "a slowly changing mournful sound, as if the universe were having second thoughts." We can now hear more and further than any other species on the planet.

These sounds are not, of course, immediately audible. Rather, they are the "sonification" or translation of electromagnetic waves into acoustic signals, which then (and only then) can be understood by the human ear.

Among such sonic treasures are the Northern Lights, the so-called "Merry Dancers," which flirt and flare across the skies of northern Scotland, all the way to Norway and Alaska. Even on the small screen of the computer their colors are surreal, ranging from acid yellow, grey, and sour plum purple to russet and emerald, turquoise, indigo, and deep electric green. "The sky to me is simply mesmerizing," writes photographer Angela Ruddick from her croft in the Orkneys. She compares the display to an entrancing lady, who "begins her dance with a slow tease, wavering her movements at me, wee turns here and there like the swaying of a long velvet skirt." Some nights she is almost invisible. On others, "She dances out her heart for us. Shimmering across the skies, shooting rays high to the heavens, totally visible to the naked eye."

Ruddick herself has never heard the dancers, which traditionally emit an erratic, crackly sound. They have, however, recently been turned into music by the sound artist and composer Matthew Burtner.

Growing up in a fishing family in Alaska, Burtner heard music in the ice and melting snow, and witnessed the Northern Lights many times—though, like Ruddick, he had never been able to hear them. Only when he was commissioned by the BBC to contribute to a radio documentary, "Songs of the Sky," and provided with a low-frequency VLF recorder, could he suddenly make out an astonishing range of sounds: crackling and snapping, chirps and squeaks, as well as dazzling sweeps of frequency, from high to low, or low to high. Because the VLF recorder is so sensitive, he had to hike or snowshoe out into the tundra, far from any human-generated noise, in order to record the Northern Lights. He spent a lot of time outside, just waiting.

Even then, the recordings weren't especially clear. So Burtner worked out how to re-map them into electronic synthesizers, which could be more easily blended with other electronic and instrumental sounds, including some archival footage from the BBC. He wanted listeners to feel as if they too were witnessing the Northern Lights. "When you're outside," he says, "and it's a clear night . . . it's really quite an amazing experience." The resulting composition—"Auroras"— twists and shimmers like the lights themselves, like Ruddick's cosmic dancer, her garments wafting in the winter wind.

The Roaring Ocean

If you look up at the stars or wander by the ocean on a glittering win-ter day, it is easy to deceive yourself, to believe that the world remains as generous and unblemished as it always was, the soundscape just as rich and multifarious. But alas, this is no longer true. Climate change has altered both the *geophony* of our planet—the wind in the trees, the waves on the shore—and its *biophony* too: the sounds of the liv-ing beings that inhabit it.

Some of these changes are perceptible to the human ear. When sound recordist Martyn Stewart visited the Louisiana coast after the BP oil spill he was struck by the "muted slosh" of the contaminated waves, which he described as having "a slurpy, muddy, sluggish signa-ture, almost as if the water were choking on itself or gasping for air. . . ."

Other changes are more insidious, audible only through special-ized equipment. Unless we have access to a seismometer or a hy-drophone, most of us are oblivious to the sonic violence of today's oceans. Lying awake at night, we turn to water sounds to soothe us, comforted by the recorded sounds of brooks and waterfalls, the swash and pull of ocean waves, or the distant singing of the hump-back whale.

But as David George Haskell writes in his recent book, *Sounds Wild and Broken*, such "authentic nature sounds" are increasingly inaccurate. A professor of biology and environmental studies at Sewanee: The University of the South, Haskell is not afraid to name the brutal truth. "If there is an acoustic hell," he writes, "it is in today's oceans. We have turned the homes of the most acoustically sophisticated and sensitive animals into a bedlam, an inescapable tumult of human sound."

Even the depths of the ocean have become loud, blasted by seismic air guns and defensive sonar devices, exacerbated by the thunder of commercial shipping. Whales and dolphins suffer most. Their own low-frequency sounds can travel over ten thousand miles. But human-generated noise obliterates their chirps and clicks, leaving them unable to communicate with others of their kind. Some species are deafened, like the North Atlantic right whales in Cape Cod Bay, others stop foraging altogether, or strand themselves in a desperate effort to escape, most dying within hours.

The grief is that this could be handled so very differently.

Commercial shipping noise could be reduced by 90 percent, in part by designing more efficient vessels, insulating engines from their metal hulls, and making propellers quieter and more efficient. "It is possible," says Haskell, "to build almost silent ships." Shipping lanes could be rerouted and the ships themselves required to move more slowly. Defensive sonar could be tested outside special breeding and feeding grounds.

It would help too, to alert those of us who benefit from commercial shipping (which is to say almost everyone on the planet) of the far-reaching consequences of our behavior. Were we to invest more energetically in a vibrant local economy, there would be less need for such extensive traffic. If we saw images of the beached whales, heard sound clips of the murky water, or of the ear-blasting misery of the container ships or naval sonar, we would at least have the information we need to stand up for *qwe'lhol'mechen,* as the Lummi Nation call "our relatives under the waves." As it is, most of us remain blithely ignorant of the sonic tumult we leave in our wake.

Last time I visited Plum Island off the Massachusetts coast, the ocean was deep blue under a dazzling sky. Each time a new wave crested it sent up a fringe of white spray, filling with rainbow light as it crashed down. Such glory walking barefoot along that sandy shore! Whale songs too are a delight to all who listen. But entwined with their haunting voices are the sounds of woe. *What would you hear if you had a Bionic Ear that could let you listen to anything, anywhere, any time?* asks the composer Pauline Oliveros. What would you do if you could truly feel the anguish of our relatives under the waves?

Listening School

> We need to listen to each other, more than ever. We need to listen to seniors, to women, to young children, to immigrants and refugees. . . . Right now, in Africa, America, Asia, Europe and the Middle East, millions of people feel invisible, unheard. . . .
>
> Ernesto Pujol

Listening to the plants, listening to the trees, listening to the sky overhead and the ground underfoot, to the birds and fish and other animals, even to the depths of the ocean: there is both joy and grief in listening to the more-than-human world. Whether such listening is grounded in traditional belief, enhanced through language, story, art, and music, or given wisdom and precision by the new technology, there can be no question of its transformative power. But if writing this book has taught me anything, it is that human beings cannot be understood as separate from "all our relations." We also need to listen to each other.

In Praise of Listening began with children listening, with listening inwards, to the human voice. It ends—insofar as anything ever does—with the story of Ernesto Pujol and his Listening School: an ongoing performance piece which is also a profound teaching, reaching past ignorance and anonymity, and offering everyone who encounters it a true chance to be heard.

Pujol is a social choreographer and educator, a handsome man with clear brown eyes and open features, his arms wreathed in elaborate tattoos. Born in Cuba in 1957, he spent time in Spain and Puerto

Rico before moving to the United States. As a young man, he sought training in a Cistercian-Trappist monastery, and that emphasis on interiority and contemplation is still apparent in his work, not least in his latest project, "Listening School."

His first such venture, "The Listeners," opened in Germany in the summer of 2018. It consisted of sixteen volunteers, ranging in age from eighteen to eighty, who took turns sitting in a quiet room in the Osnabruck Town Hall, listening in silence to whomever chanced to happen by. "They listened to what is rarely shared, to what remains unspoken or secret: the memories, dreams, traumas, nightmares, pain, sadness, joy, and happiness of people, who carry these around unseen."

Although part of a city-wide festival (celebrating the 370th anniversary of the Peace of Westphalia), "The Listeners" was not intended as a spectacle. No one witnessed it except the visitors themselves, and of course the volunteers, who sat for as long as sixteen and a half hours, embodying mindfulness and silence. Traditionally, art speaks, while the audience listens. In this case, the usual expectations were turned upside down: the audience spoke and both art and artists listened.

Soon after that first project was completed, Pujol made a list (a litany) of what he'd learned from doing it. He recognized that silence was essential, not just as "a shroud, a shelter for the listeners," but also as a gift to those who spoke:

> We think that if we do not respond verbally, that if we do not give advice, we are engaging in a dangerous disservice. But I say to my performers that the world is full of talk, of predictable advice from family, friends, neighbors, teachers, ministers, priests, nuns, rabbis, imams, astrologers, supervisors, bosses, psychologists, psychiatrists, counselors, social workers, physical therapists, doctors, designers, stylists, financial planners, coaches, lawyers, accountants, and more. We do not lack for advice. What we yearn for is to be listened to in silence, without being interrupted or judged.

Such concentrated listening is not easy, even for the most committed. Because we spend so much time communicating via screen, many of us have grown unused to the sheer physicality of human talk, "the uncontrollable smells of the body, its temperature, moisture, posture, the flow of breath, and the intense proximity of a face." Several of Pujol's volunteers were taken aback by all they learned, "by simply sitting next to each other, in silence." Long-cherished stereotypes fell away. As Pujol explained, "When you listen without labels and filters . . . people come out of the flatness of webpage timelines, acquiring subtlety, likeability, and familiarity. Listening makes people real. Listening makes us real."

The following year, Pujol brought his "Listening School" to the River to River Festival in New York City, offering a series of four lunchtime sessions, as well as a silent evening performance, also called "The Listeners." In the weeks before the event, he shared his project proposal with everyone involved, and created a written manual for them to study. He also hosted a number of free workshops, in which volunteers were encouraged to reflect on their prior experience of listening, and to voice any concerns they might have. Crucial to the project was their willingness to be gentle, open, and transparent—and indeed, vulnerable.

"This is a barefoot practice," Pujol said. "I call it the practice of embarrassment. . . . Regardless of class and color, many people are walking around feeling unheard. And that has generated a collective anger that is destroying us. I do not want us to be abused, but my performers and I are willing to take the risk to listen. I hope participants feel listened to. It may take years."

"Listening School" opened unobtrusively one summer lunchtime, as a bevy of blue-coated artist-volunteers spread out across parks and plazas, courts and atriums, quizzing ambient New Yorkers about the act of listening. *Where should we listen? What should we listen to? To whom should we listen?* The questions served as introduction to the event that followed, though once again, there was no culminating spectacle. The only way to see the piece was to participate, to enter the Federal Memorial Hall for the evening performance, and to speak in private to one of the blue-uniformed listeners, as they sat together in their quiet circle.

"All life needs and wants to be listened to," repeats Pujol. He doesn't underestimate the challenges. But "I am not listening alone," he says. "It is a 'we' who is listening."

Consider the following quotations:

> All day I have been reading
> about the invisible world, the one
> that's always trying to reach us. What
>   if we could hear
> the small round o's of dirt,
> the chant of stars and planets,
> carbon and sulphur, calling to each other, innu-
> merable
> to innumerable, a throat at every blade of grass.
>
> Ellery Akers

Another world is not only possible, she is on her way. Maybe many of us won't be here to greet her, but on a quiet day, if I listen carefully, I can hear her breathing.

Arundhati Roy

Continue to explore:

What sounds have been lost over the course of your life? What sounds delight and inspire you? Make a list of each.

"Sometimes it is only the music of the future to which it is worth listening," wrote Isaac Deutscher. How do you imagine it might sound?

The Music of What Happens

It was an ordinary Saturday in a small New England town. Someone was playing banjo on the porch of the local store, and someone else was playing fiddle. A modest crowd had gathered, most of them elderly or middle-aged. Among them was a pretty, fair-haired child, perhaps four years old, in bright pink leggings and a butterfly T-shirt. *Whose child was she?* I had no idea. The grown-ups smiled and listened, tapped their feet. The musicians went on playing. Meanwhile the child was dancing—delighted, unselfconscious—turning happy circles in the dusty street. Swifts flew back and forth between the wooden pillars of the porch, and out again into the open sky.

It was a moment to be treasured: delicate and transient, like something from a haiku. I thought of it often in the years that followed, when Covid made us wary of the smallest gathering, and even that bright sprite would have been masked.

But the long months of the pandemic had their gifts as well. With schools and colleges almost entirely under lockdown, let alone offices and factories, churches and cinemas, restaurants and galleries and concert halls, listening became ever more essential. *Listening to one's friends and family via phone or Skype or Zoom. Listening inwards, listening to the body, listening to the surrounding world.* Any one of those could open into what one might call "a larger listening"—a way to honor and welcome and slow down and pay attention—until there was nothing and no one that was not of interest.

"What is the finest music in the world?" someone asks, in one of the old Irish folktales. "The cuckoo calling from the highest tree," says the young Oisi'n. "The ring of a spear against a shield," says his son, Oscar. And the other warriors join in: "The belling of a stag, the song of a lark, the laugh of a gleeful girl," until finally it is the turn of the great Fionn mac Cumhaill. "The music of what happens," he declares, "that is the finest music in the world."

Consider the following quotations:

You know, I have come to think listening is love, that's what it really is.

Brenda Ueland

Let go, let fly. . . . You've listened long enough. Now strike your note.

Seamus Heaney

Continue to explore:

"Utterance"

Sitting over words
very late I have heard a kind of whispered sighing
not far
like a night wind in pines or like the sea in the
dark
the echo of everything that has ever
been spoken

still spinning its one syllable
between the earth and silence

W. S. Merwin

ACKNOWLEDGMENTS
With Gratitude to All Who Listened

This book has been long in the making, and there were times I thought I'd never finish it. Heartfelt thanks to Maia for her steady friendship and fine-tuned listening ear, to Simon for his kindness (and his crucial edits), and to Alice and Amy, Davina and Josh for offering home and family here in western Massachusetts.

I would also like to thank my tribe of friends for all the years of rich, wide-ranging conversation, and in several cases, housing, meals, and practical support. Much gratitude to Aileen Alfandary, Barbara Bash, Hosie Baskin, Sarah Bauhan, Laetitia Bermejo, Alice Cozzolino, Edite Cunha, Tess Darwin, Tabita Doujad, Susan Davis, Ruth Gendler, Penny Gill, Don Guttenplan, John Hoffman, Joy Holland, Tine Kindermann, Simon Korner, Phyllis Labanowski, Benjie Lasseau, Maia, Maria Margaronis, Annabel McCall, Nini Melvin, Josh and Davina Miller, Pat Musick, Roz Parr, Susie Patlove, Verandah Porche, Amy Pulley, Sarah Rabkin, Steve Rosenbaum, Joy Seidler, Michelle Spark, Arthur Strimling, Davis Te Selle, Chris Ulrich, Sam Wood, Paki Wieland, and Janey Winter.

And to my family back in the UK: my mother, Brigid McEwen, my sisters Helena and Isabella, my brother John, and my beloved uncle Johnnie, again, many thanks.

Thanks too to both my writing groups for their long patience and encouragement: to Trish Crapo, Edite Cuñha, and Maria Lauenstein for our regular in-person gatherings, and to Pat Musick and Sarah Rabkin for our monthly meetings over Zoom.

And to the members of my weekly writing class past and present, thanks especially to Madeleine Cahill, Rosemary Christoph, David Finacom, Meg Fisher, Anna Maclay, Angel Russek, Hetty Startup, Jennifer Storey, and Chris Ulrich.

Acknowledgments

And to everyone who helped construct the Giant Cosmic Ear and Listening Booth; thanks especially to Phyllis Labanowski, Laura Iveson, Jane Beatrice Wegscheider, Susan Bonthron, and Gilbert Ruff. Thanks too to the staff at Mesa Refuge in Point Reyes, California, for their generosity and welcome.

And to the many writers, naturalists, and musicians whose work has inspired me, thanks especially to Robert Bringhurst, Jay Griffiths, David George Haskell, Robin Wall Kimmerer, Frank London, Jacques Lusseyran, Nóirín Ní Riain, Meredith Monk, Kathleen Dean Moore, Pauline Oliveros, Gary Peacock, Rebecca Solnit, Joseph Stroud, and Sherry Turkle.

I would also like to thank everyone who allowed me to interview them, and, oftentimes, to quote them in this book. Special thanks to Eleanor Adams, Charles Atkinson, Laetitia Bermejo, Mirabai Bush, Alice Cozzolino, Meg Fisher, Andrew Forsthoefel, Steve Gorn, Paula Green, Katinka Haycraft, Allen Hirson, Wendy Johnson, Mariel Kinsey, Frank London, Maria Margaronis, Daisy Mathias, Brigid McEwen, Blair McLaughlin, June Millington, Bonnie Miller, Meredith Monk, Sy Montgomery, Junko Oba, Gary Peacock, Arthur Strimling, Susan von Reusner, and Karen Werner.

My cats, Sophie and Noushka, lived just long enough to accompany me through the first two years of Covid—such lively, subtle presences! They are missed.

The staff at the Meekins Library in Williamsburg were unfailingly kind and efficient; thanks especially to Rochelle Wildfong and Daria D'Arienzo. Thanks too to Chris Allard at Ink & Toner Solutions in Northampton, Massachusetts; Jack Radner and Melissa Tefft in Amherst, Massachusetts; Sandy Dorr in Grand Junction, Colorado; and Mary Bisbee-Beek in Portland, Oregon, for their professional advice and expertise.

And finally, many thanks to Mimi Robinson for her gorgeous color grid, and to everyone at Bauhan Publishing—Sarah Bauhan, Mary Ann Faughnan, and Henry James—for once again producing such a lovely book.

Thanks to the hardworking editors and fine publications where excerpts from *In Praise of Listening* first appeared, sometimes in earlier incarnations:

The American Scholar: "The Beloved Voice."

Channel Magazine: "The Little Sounds of Every Day," "The Voices of the Trees."

Lion's Roar: "The One Who Listens."

Stravaig: "Island Listening."

Teachers & Writers Magazine: "Questions Without Answers," "The Small Sounds of the Past," "Listening Empty," "Listening to the Work," "Willing to Listen," and "What Is Lost."

The Zen Mountain Record: "Playing What You Don't Know."

SOURCES AND NOTES

↭My commentary on the notes is in italic, headed by this ornament.

Introduction

In Praise of Listening

Gay, Ross. *The Book of Delights: Essays.* New York: Algonquin Books of Chapel Hill, a division of Workman Publishing, 2019.

↭ *Poet Ross Gay invented the term "essayette."*

Haupt, Lyanda Lynn. *Mozart's Starling.* New York: Little, Brown and Company, 2017.

Kimmerer, Robin Wall. "Rescuing Human Civilization: What Will It Take?" Public dialogue, Dartmouth College, Hanover, NH, March 31, 2021.

↭ *The Anishinaabe are a group of culturally related indigenous peoples resident in what is now called Canada and the United States. They include the Odawa, Saulteaux, Ojibwe, Potawatomi, Oji-Cree, and Algonquin peoples. Other versions of this story exist in North America, and indeed around the globe.*

Nepo, Mark. *Seven Thousand Ways to Listen: Staying Close to What Is Sacred.* New York: Atria paperback, Simon & Schuster, 2010.

↭ Hlysnan *is Old English for "pay attention to."*

1: Children Listening

The Small Sounds of the Past

↭ *My uncles Rory and Alex McEwen cut three records together, and as children, we played them over and over again:* Rory and Alex McEwen, Scottish Songs and Ballads *(Smithsonian Folkways Records, 1957);* Rory and Alex McEwen and Isla Cameron, Folksong Jubilee *(His Master's Voice, 1958); and* Rory and Alex McEwen, and Carolyn and Dick Farina, Four For Fun *(Waverly Records, 1963).*

Adams, Eleanor. Interview with the author, July 26, 2014.

Kinsey, Mariel. Interview with the author, July 1, 2014.

Mathieu, W. A. *The Listening Book: Discovering Your Own Music.* Boston and London: Shambhala Publications, 1991.

Little Velvet Voice

↳ *"She was delicious like that, listening. . . ." My mother, Brigid McEwen, in the journal she kept of my childhood doings (1956–2020).*

Shakespeare, William. *King Lear*, Act V, scene iii.

A Rush of Memories

Dickens, Charles. *Great Expectations*. New York: Barnes & Noble Classics, 2003.

Fisher, Meg. Interview with the author, January 27, 2020.

Invisible

↳ *Catching fish with my hands: the Scottish term for this is* guddling. *Once caught and killed the trout would be strung up on a sturdy length of grass and brought home to be fried up in oatmeal for tomorrow's breakfast.*

Griffiths, Jay. *Kith: The Riddle of the Childscape*. London: Hamish Hamilton, an imprint of Penguin Books, 2013.

↳ *Jay Griffiths writes beautifully about childhood listening. "Children were traditionally taught to pay . . . attention to the land, 'to listen intently when all seemingly was quiet,' in the words of Luther Standing Bear. Listening lets the outer world be recreated within you. Listening means being willing to let one's borders be porous."*

Left to Our Own Devices

Bermejo, Laetitia. Interview with the author, August 17, 2018.

Carr, Nicholas. *The Glass Cage: Automation and Us*. New York, London: W. W. Norton & Company, 2014.

Mathias, Daisy. Interview with the author, May 21, 2015.

McEwen, Brigid. Interview with the author, July 28, 2021.

Musick, Pat. Communication with the author, February 22, 2021.

What Is Lost

↳ *"75 percent of the time we are distracted while we listen," says Buddhist teacher, Tara Brach. An hour after hearing something, the average person remembers only a fifth of what was said.*

Birkerts, Sven. *Changing the Subject: Art and Attention in the Internet Age*. Minneapolis, MN: Graywolf Press, 2015.

Brach, Tara. *Radical Acceptance: Embracing Your Life with the Heart of a Buddha*. New York: Bantam Books, Random House, 2003.

Carr, Nicholas. *The Shallows: What the Internet Is Doing to Our Brains.* New York, London: W. W. Norton & Company, 2010.

Hari, Johann. *Stolen Focus: Why You Can't Pay Attention—and How to Think Deeply Again.* New York, Crown Publishing, Penguin Random House, 2022.

Harjo, Joy. "The Whole of Time: an interview with Joy Harjo." Interviewed by Krista Tippett. *On Being* (May 13, 2021). See the *On Being* website.

Newport, Cal. *Digital Minimalism: Choosing a Focused Life in a Noisy World.* New York: Portfolio Penguin, Penguin Random House, 2019.

Odell, Jenny. *How to Do Nothing: Resisting the Attention Economy.* Brooklyn, NY: Melville House Publishing, 2019.

Powers, William: *Hamlet's Blackberry: Building a Good Life in the Digital Age.* New York and London: Harper Perennial, HarperCollins, 2011.

Price, Catherine. *How to Break Up with Your Phone: The 30-Day Plan to Take Back Your Life.* Berkeley, CA: Ten Speed Press, 2018.

Sacks, Oliver. "The Machine Stops: The Neurologist on Steam Engines, Smartphones, and Fearing the Future." *The New Yorker,* February 11, 2019.

Stafford, Kim. Communication with the author, Spring 2017.

↬ *The poet Kim Stafford tells a story about a 1930s anthropologist who was traveling through northern California, gathering material for a Native dictionary. "How would you describe my people?" he asks, meaning the white man, the settlers. His local informant looks embarrassed, muttering a short phrase under his breath. "And how does that translate?" asks the anthropologist. The man pauses for a long moment. "Those who do not stop to make relation," he says finally.*

The New Noise

Berendt, Joachim-Ernst. *The Third Ear: On Listening to the World.* New York: An Owl Book, Henry Holt and Company, 1988.

Bhatia, Rajiv Bhatia, "Noise Pollution: Managing the Challenge of Urban Sounds." *Earth Journalism Network,* May 20, 2014.

Carson, Anne. "Saturday Night as an Adult." *The New Yorker,* May 1, 2017.

Cox, Trevor. *The Sound Book: The Science of the Sonic Wonders of the World.* New York and London: W. W. Norton & Company, 2014.

↬ *"Nearly 40 percent of Americans want to change their place of residence because of noise."*

Gentleman, Amelia. *"You're Not Listening* by Kate Murphy—a modern epidemic of self-absorbed talk." *The Guardian,* January 11, 2020.
↬ *"Sound levels now average 80 decibels in restaurants in the U.S., whereas a typical conversation averages about 60 decibels."*

Hammer, Monica S., Tracy K. Swinburne, and Richard L. Neitzel. 2014. "Environmental Noise Pollution in the United States: Developing an Effective Public Health Response." *Environmental Health Perspectives* 122 (2).

Horowitz, Seth S. *The Universal Sense: How Hearing Shapes the Mind.* New York and London: Bloomsbury Publishing, 2012.
↬ *On noisy bars, casinos, etc.: "The sound levels in these places are not the result of poor design or acoustic accident. The point . . . is to increase your arousal, to activate your sympathetic nervous system. You can't control the sound, but you can control something—so you buy a drink, or you gamble."*

Krause, Bernie. *The Power of Tranquility in a Very Noisy World.* New York: Little, Brown and Company, 2021.
↬ *"Any sound over 85 decibels is considered harmful." Krause notes that planting trees—especially larch trees—can be very helpful.*

LeClaire, Anne D. *Listening Below the Noise: The Transformative Power of Silence.* New York and London: Harper Perennial, HarperCollins, 2009.
↬ *"We are 46 percent more likely to have a heart attack if we live on a noisy street, and 34 percent more likely if we live in a noisy environment. Noise has also been linked to cardiovascular disease, high blood pressure, gastrointestinal problems, premature birth, immune suppression, and sleep disruption."*

Monk, Meredith. Spring 2020. "The Earth needs a lullaby. . . ." Quote from an online event.

Owen, David, "Volumetrics: Why noise pollution is more dangerous than we think." *The New Yorker,* May 13, 2019.
↬ *OSHA (the Occupational Safety and Health Administration) "allows workers to be exposed to 95 decibels for four hours a day, five days a week, for an entire forty-year career."*

Waldstein, David. "Scientists Say You Can Cancel the Noise but Keep Your Window Open." *New York Times,* July 11, 2020.

ও *Researchers in Singapore have come up with a new system to reduce external noise. Operating on the same technological principles as noise-canceling headphones, their apparatus consists of twenty-four small speakers, each about two inches in diameter. When this is set in an open window, it can neutralize the incoming racket by as much as 10 decibels.*

Williams, Terry Tempest. *Erosion: Essays on Undoing.* New York: Sarah Crichton Books, Farrar, Straus and Giroux, 2019.

ও *Loudness or intensity is measured in decibels, named after the inventor Alexander Graham Bell. One study revealed that a volume of 65 decibels affects memory and the recall of auditory information. The rustle of leaves registers at 10 decibels, a whisper at 30 decibels, a typical conversation at about 60 decibels. But decibels are logarithmic, so a 100-decibel sound isn't twice as intense as a 50-decibel sound; it's a hundred thousand times as intense. And therein lies the rub.*

Listening for the Muse

Bermejo, Laetitia. Interview with the author, August 17, 2018.

2: Listening Inwards

Inner Noise

Burkman, Oliver. "Change Your Life, Sit Down and Think." *The Guardian,* July 20, 2014.

Chödrön, Pema. "Taking the Leap." In *The Best Buddhist Writing, 2010.* Edited by Melvin McLeod. Boston and London: Shambhala Publications, 2010.

ও *Not everyone agrees with Pema Chödrön. For example, His Holiness the Dalai Lama and Archbishop Desmond Tutu claim that fear lasts for an average of thirty minutes, and sadness for as much as 120 hours or almost five days.*

Dass, Ram, and Paul Gorman. *How Can I Help? Stories and Reflections on Service.* New York: Borzoi Books, Alfred A. Knopf, Inc., 1987.

Grumbach, Doris. *Fifty Days of Solitude: A Memoir.* Boston: Beacon Press, 1995.

ও *After years of enduring the sound of her own thoughts, "embedded in that old omniscient voice," the writer Doris Grumbach simply ceased to listen. Once she started up again, she felt appalled by what she might discover. "What if I found not so much a great emptiness as a space full of unpleasant contents, a compound of long-hidden truths, closeted, buried, forgotten?"*

HH the Dalai Lama and Archbishop Desmond Tutu, *The Book of Joy*. New York: Penguin Random House, 2016.

Kagge, Erling. *Silence in the Age of Noise*. New York: Pantheon Books, Random House, 2017.

⮥ *Participants were left alone for six to fifteen minutes without music, reading materials, or access to their cell phones, or the chance to write. They ranged in age from seventeen to seventy-seven years old and came from a variety of backgrounds. Some were allowed to read or listen to music, which they found helpful. Others looked out of the window. But nearly half the subjects eventually pushed the button administering an electrical shock in order to reduce their silent time, even though they had earlier said they'd pay to avoid it. One pushed the button 190 times.*

Khan, Hazrat Inayat. *The Music of Life: The Inner Nature and Effects of Sound*. New Lebanon, NY: Omega Publications, 2005.

O'Donohue, John. *Anam Cara: Spiritual Wisdom from the Celtic World*. London: Bantam Press, a division of Threshold Publishers, 1997.

Sardello, Robert. *Silence: The Mystery of Wholeness*. Berkeley, CA: North Atlantic Books, 2008.

A Back Shop All Our Own

Bakewell, Sarah. *How to Live: A Life of Montaigne in One Question and Twenty Attempts at an Answer*. New York: Vintage, 2011.

Merton, Thomas. *The Way of Chuang Tzu*. New York: New Directions, W. W. Norton & Company, 1969.

Moon, Susan. Conversation with the author, February 2019.

Wayne, Teddy. "The End of Reflection." *The New York Times,* June 11, 2016.

A Meditation on Sound

Epstein, Mark. *Advice Not Given: A Guide to Getting Over Yourself*. New York: Penguin Books, Random House, 2018.

———. *The Trauma of Everyday Life*. New York: Penguin Books, Random House, 2014.

Rumi, Jalal Al-Din. *The Illuminated Rumi*. Translated and with commentary by Coleman Barks. New York: Broadway Books, 1997.

The Ear in Fear

Berensohn, Paulus. "Whatever We Touch Is Touching Us: Craft Art and a Deeper Sense of Ecology," *The Studio Potter*, 32, no. 1, December 2003.

↢ *Once noticed, the word EAR shows up with surprising frequency in the English language, shining out from NEAR and DEAR and HEART and HEARTH, from EARTH and SEARCH and CLEAR and DISAPPEAR. There is an EAR in WEARINESS and TEARS, in WEAR and TEAR, in EARNESTNESS, in LEARNING and in PEARL. As I tracked this through my own mind's maze, I began to wonder what it might mean to listen to one's sorrow and one's exhaustion, to attend, full-hearted, to one's bewilderment and loss.*

> *Listen to your tears and tend your sorrow.*
> *Listen to your weariness and greet fatigue.*
> *Listen to your search and set your course.*
> *Listen to the clouds until they clear.*

The Joy of Reading

Birkerts, Sven. *Changing the Subject: Art and Attention in the Internet Age*. Minneapolis, MN: Graywolf Press, 2015.

Boston, L. M. *The Children of Green Knowe*. Illustrated by Peter Boston. London, England, Faber and Faber, 1954.

Burnett, Frances Hodgson. *The Little Princess: The Story of Sara Crewe*. Illustrated by Margery Gill. Harmondsworth, Middlesex, England: A Puffin Book, Penguin Books, 1963.

Jansson, Tove. *Finn Family Moomintroll*. Illustrated by Tove Jansson. Harmondsworth, Middlesex, England: A Puffin Book, Penguin Books, 1964.

Leese, Germaine. "Have a lover, have friends, read books." *The Guardian*, May 24, 2017.

↢ *Reading can reduce stress levels by as much as 68 percent.*

Nesbit, E. *The Story of the Treasure Seekers*. Harmondsworth, Middlesex, England: A Puffin Book, Penguin Books, 1963.

Travers, P. L. *Mary Poppins*. Illustrated by Mary Shepard. Harmondsworth, Middlesex, England: A Puffin Book, Penguin Books, 1962.

Turkle, Sherry. *Reclaiming Conversation: The Power of Talk in a Digital Age*. New York: Penguin Press, Penguin Random House, 2015.

↢ *"Now we know that literary fiction significantly improves empathetic capacity, as measured by the ability to infer emotional states from people's facial expression."*

Winterson, Jeanette. *Why Be Happy When You Could Be Normal?* New York: Grove Press, 2011.

Questions Without Answers

Neruda, Pablo. *The Book of Questions.* Translated by William O'Daly. Port Townsend, WA: Copper Canyon Press, 1991.

Dream Work

↬ *The dream dates from January 2016, soon after I learned my sister Isabella had been diagnosed with ovarian cancer.*

Stevens, Wallace. "Domination of Black." In *Selected Poems.* London: Faber and Faber, 1965.

And There Was Light

Lusseyran, Jacques. *And There Was Light.* New York: Parabola Books, 1987.

———. *What One Sees Without Eyes: Selected Writings of Jacques Lusseyran.* Edinburgh, Scotland: Floris Books, 1999.

O'Donohue, John. *Beauty: Rediscovering the True Sources of Compassion, Serenity, and Hope.* New York: Harper Perennial, HarperCollins Publishers, 2005.

Additional recommended reading:

Haskell, David George. *Sounds Wild and Broken: Sonic Marvels, Evolution's Creativity, and the Crisis of Sensory Extinction.* New York: Viking Press, an imprint of Penguin Random House, 2022.

Moore, Kathleen Dean. *Earth's Wild Music: Celebrating and Defending the Sounds of the Natural World.* Berkeley, CA: Counterpoint, 2021.

Murphy, Kate. *You're Not Listening: What You're Missing and Why It Matters.* New York: Celadon Books, a division of MacMillan Publishers, 2019.

Turkle, Sherry. *Reclaiming Conversation: The Power of Talk in a Digital Age.* New York: Penguin Press, 2015.

3: The One Who Listens

Arthur's Aunt Annie

Strimling, Arthur. Interview with the author, May 24, 2015.

How We Listen

Cox, Trevor. *The Sound Book: The Science of the Sonic Wonders of the World.* New York, London: W. W. Norton & Company, 2014.

⤳ *No "ear-lids:" We are, of course, capable of covering our ears with our hands. But even then, "[w]e cannot physically stop the eardrum, the tiny bones in the middle ear, or the tiny hair cells in the inner ear, from vibrating."*

Mathieu, W. A. *The Listening Book: Discovering Your Own Music.* Boston and London, Shambhala Publications, Inc., 1991.

The One Who Listened

⤳ *The letters quoted here were written by my grandmother, Bridget Mary McEwen, between September 1969 and September 1971.*

Katie's Letters

⤳ *The letters quoted here were written by my sister, Katie McEwen, between 1972 and 1974.*

⤳ *Sheffield has long been celebrated for its cutlery trade, based largely upon stainless steel.*

Gifted Listeners

Dostoyevsky, Fyodor. *The Brothers Karamazov.* Translated by Constance Garnett. Harmondsworth, Middlesex, England: Penguin Books, 1982.

Doyle, Brian. "His Listening." In *One Long River of Song: Notes on Wonder.* Forward by David James Duncan. New York: Little, Brown and Company, 2019.

Oz, Amos. *A Tale of Love and Darkness.* Translated by Nicholas de Lange. Boston: Harcourt Books, 2004.

Distant Neighbors

Berry, Wendell, and Gary Snyder. *Distant Neighbors: The Selected Letters of Wendell Berry and Gary Snyder.* Edited by Chad Wriglesworth. Berkeley, CA: Counterpoint, 2014.

Bishop, Elizabeth and Robert Lowell. *Words In Air: The Complete Correspondence Between Elizabeth Bishop and Robert Lowell.* Edited by Thomas Travisano with Saskia Hamilton. New York: Farrar, Straus and Giroux, 2008.

Snyder, Gary. *Gary Snyder: Dimensions of a Life.* Edited by Jon Halper. San Francisco, CA: Sierra Club Books, 1991.

↬ *The poet Gary Lawless said of Gary Snyder that he "had a way of easily drawing out useful and exciting conversations."*

Warner, Sylvia Townsend, and William Maxwell. *The Element of Lavishness: Letters of Sylvia Townsend Warner and William Maxwell, 1938–1978.* Edited by Michael Steinman. Berkeley, CA: Counterpoint, 2001.

The Harpist and His Friend

Zen Flesh, Zen Bones. Compiled by Paul Reps. Harmondsworth, Middlesex, England: Penguin Books, 1973.

↬ *My paraphrase of "The Harpist and His Friend."*

Chekhov's "Grief"

Beckham, Jessica. Conversation with the author, February 23, 2020.

Chekhov, Anton. *The Stories of Anton Tchekov*, edited by Robert N. Linscott. New York: The Modern Library, 1932.

↬ *My paraphrase of the story "Grief."*

Gentleman, Amelia. "*You're Not Listening* by Kate Murphy—a modern epidemic of self-absorbed talk." *The Guardian*, January 11, 2020.

↬ *"Sound levels now average 80 decibels in restaurants in the U.S, whereas a typical conversation averages about 60 decibels."*

Haupt, Lyanda Lynn. *Rooted: Life at the Crossroads of Science, Nature and Spirit.* New York: Little, Brown, Spark, 2021.

↬ *"The effects of [such] chronic social isolation are grim, including a 26 percent higher mortality rate."*

4: The Beloved Voice

Vocal Nourishment

Berendt, Joachim-Ernst. *The Third Ear: On Listening to the World.* New York: An Owl Book, Henry Holt and Company, 1985.

↬ *The first sense: "Within a few weeks of impregnation the embryo develops its ears. The child in the womb hears its mother's heartbeat and later the sound of the world outside . . . before a human being can perceive the world with any other sense, he or she hears it."*

Levitan, Daniel J. *This Is Your Brain on Music: The Science of a Human Obsession.* Boston: E. P. Dutton, 2007.

↬ *"During the first six months . . . the regions of the brain that will become the auditory cortex, the sensory cortex, and the visual cortex are functionally undifferentiated. . . ." Levitan also writes "The fetus hears music, as was recently discovered by Alexandra Lamont of Keele University in the UK. She found that, a year after they are born, children recognize and prefer music they were exposed to in the womb."*

Madaule, Paul. *When Listening Comes Alive.* Toronto: Moulin Publishing, 1994.

Mithin, Stephen. *The Singing Neanderthals.* Cambridge, MA: Harvard University Press, 2006.

↬ *"Baby talk, 'motherese,' and infant-directed speech (IDS) are all terms used for the way we talk to infants, from zero to three years old. They include a higher overall pitch, a wider range of pitch, longer, hyperarticulated vowels and pauses, shorter phrases, and greater repetition than normal speech."*

Snyder, Gary. *Gary Snyder: Dimensions of a Life.* Edited by Jon Halper. San Francisco, CA: Sierra Club Books, 1991.

↬ *The writer Will Baker said of Gary Snyder that he had "a guitar of a voice, meant to calm and thrill alternately."*

Strout, Elizabeth. *My Name Is Lucy Barton.* New York: Random House, 2016.

Tomatis, Alfred A. *The Conscious Ear: My Life of Transformation Through Listening.* Barrytown, NY: Station Hill Press, 1991.

Vedantam, Shankar. "Shhh, the Kids Can Hear You Arguing (Even When They're Asleep)." National Public Radio, April 29, 2013.

↬ *What happens when vocal nourishment is lacking? Psychologists Alice Graham, Philip Fisher, and Jennifer Pfeifer decided to find out. They learned that infants as young as two or three months old respond to tense or angry voices, even when they are fast asleep. Children from so-called "higher-conflict" homes were especially reactive. fMRI scanners showed that their brains were altered by witnessing a fight in ways that could affect their emotional well-being, possibly far into the future.*

Coming to Our Senses

Buchbinder, Amnon. "Out of Our Heads: Philip Shepherd on the Brain in Our Belly." *The Sun* magazine, April 2013.

Jung, Carl. *C. G. Jung Speaking: Interviews and Encounters.* Edited by R. F. C. Hull and William McGuire. Princeton, NJ: Princeton University Press, 1987.

The Family Voice

conversation: *The Oxford Dictionary of Word Histories: The life stories of over 12,000 words.* Edited by Glynnis Chantrell. Oxford: Oxford University Press, 2002.

Horowitz, Seth S. *The Universal Sense: How Hearing Shapes the Mind.* New York and London: Bloomsbury, 2012.

ᗌ *"Hearing something numerous times actually rewires the synapses in your auditory system to improve efficiency of response to those specific traits."*

Lee, Hermione. *Virginia Woolf.* New York: A Borzoi Book, Alfred A. Knopf, Inc., 1997.

Manguel, Alberto. *The Library at Night.* New Haven and London: Yale University Press, 2006.

ᗌ *Two hundred and fifty years ago, even a candle could be seen as too much light. "Darkness promotes speech. Light is silent," writes Alberto Manguel. "Or, as Henry Fielding explains in Amelia, 'Tace, madam, is Latin for candle.'"*

Schultz, Kathryn. "What Calling Congress Achieves." *The New Yorker,* March 6, 2017.

ᗌ *Harriott Daley ran the telephone switchboard in the US Capitol building for almost fifty years. By the time she retired, in 1945, she was able to recognize some ninety-six senators, three hundred and ninety-four representatives, and three hundred journalists by the sound of their voices.*

Turner, Frederick. *John Muir: From Scotland to the Sierra.* Introduction by Graham White. Edinburgh, Scotland: Canongate, 1997.

Winterson, Jeannette. "Why I adore the night." *The Guardian,* October 31, 2009.

ᗌ *We sat on in the gloaming: Jeannette Winterson has written beautifully about exactly this. "I have noticed that when all the lights are on, people tend to talk about what they are doing—their outer lives. Sitting round in candlelight or firelight, people start to talk about how they are feeling—their inner lives. They speak subjectively, they argue less, there are longer pauses.*

"To sit alone without any electric light is curiously creative. I have my best ideas at dawn or at nightfall, but not if I switch on the lights—then I start thinking about projects, deadlines, demands, and the shadows and shapes of the house become objects, not suggestions, things that need to be done, not a background to thought."

Another Self

Details of James Lees-Milne's life from his obituary. By James Fergusson. *The Independent,* December 29, 1997.

Lees-Milne, James. *Another Self: Autobiography.* Norwich, England: Michael Russell Publishing, 1970.

ᗌ *Egeria. The name was used to mean a female advisor or counselor.*

The Beloved Voice

Berendt, Joachim-Ernst. *The Third Ear: On Listening to the World.* New York: An Owl Book, Henry Holt and Company, 1985.

↬ *That shared music: "Every person is music, perpetual music, continually going on day and night; and your intuitive faculty can hear that music. That is the reason why one person is repellent and the other attracts you. It is the music he expresses, his whole atmosphere is charged with it."*

Jenkinson, Stephen. *Die Wise: A Manifesto for Society and Soul.* Berkeley, CA: North Atlantic Books, 2015.

↬ *The phrase "witnesses for wonder. . ." is taken from this book.*

Lessing, Doris. *The Golden Notebook.* New York: Ballantine Books, Penguin Random House, 1962.

Nepo, Mark. *Facing the Lion, Being the Lion: Finding Inner Courage Where You Live.* Newburyport, MA: Conari Press, 2007.

Oliver, Mary. *Our World.* Photographs by Molly Malone Cook. Boston: Beacon Press, 2007.

↬ *Mary Oliver writes fondly about her life-partner, Molly Malone Cook. "Dour she could be, but privately," notes Oliver. "She was Irish, after all, and liked to sing and have a good time. Occasionally over the years she would phone a friend she had met in Europe; she would put records on the phonograph, the old songs they both knew, and they would sing together, long-distance, and not necessarily briefly."*

Snyder, Gary. *Gary Snyder: Dimensions of a Life.* Edited by Jon Halper. San Francisco, CA: Sierra Club Books, 1991.

Turkle, Sherry. *Reclaiming Conversation: The Power of Talk in a Digital Age.* New York: Penguin Press, An imprint of Penguin Random House, 2015.

↬ *The phrase "peopled by those . . ." comes from this book.*

Whyte, David. Interviewed by Krista Tippett. *On Being* (April 7, 2016). See the *On Being* website.

Moral Music

Khan, Hazrat Inayat. *The Music of Life: The Inner Nature and Effects of Sound.* New Lebanon, NY: Omega Publications, 2005.

Lusseyran, Jacques. *And There Was Light.* Translated by Elizabeth R. Cameron. New York: Parabola Books, 1987.

————. *What One Sees Without Eyes: Selected Writings of Jacques Lusseyran.* Translated by Rob Baker. New York: Parabola Books, 1999.

Prochnik, George. *In Pursuit of Silence: Listening for Meaning in a World of Noise.* New York: Doubleday, 2010.

↦ *"Hitler used to batter his audience into a submissive state bordering closely on hypnotism. Hitler himself said that without the loudspeakers he could not have conquered Germany."*

A Poetry of the Senses

Monk, Meredith. Interview with the author, November 14, 2015.

5: Learning to Listen

A Space to Be Explored

Ueland, Brenda. "Tell me More: On the Fine Art of Listening." In *Strength to Your Sword Arm: Selected Writings.* Duluth, MN: Holy Cow! Press, 1993.

Hearing One Another into Speech

London Rape Crisis Centre. Conversation with Leonie Rushforth, n.d.

Morton, Nelle. "Beloved Image." In *The Journey Is Home.* Boston: Beacon Press, 1985.

Palmer, Parker. "My Misgivings about Advice." Interviewed by Krista Tippett. *On Being* (April 27, 2016). See the *On Being* website.

Rich, Adrienne. *On Lies, Secrets, and Silence: Selected Prose (1966–1978).* New York: W. W. Norton & Company, 1979.

Turkle, Sherry. *Alone Together: Why We Expect More from Technology and Less from Each Other.* New York: Basic Books, a member of the Perseus Book Group, 2011.

————. *The Empathy Diaries: A Memoir.* New York: Penguin Press, an imprint of Penguin Random House, 2021.

————. *Reclaiming Conversation: The Power of Talk in a Digital Age.* New York: Penguin Press, an imprint of Penguin Random House, 2015.

Just Listening

Cain, Susan. *Quiet: The Power of Introverts in a World That Can't Stop Talking.* New York: Crown Publishing, Penguin Random House, 2012.

Steinem, Gloria. *My Life on the Road* (2015). Quoted online in *Brain Pickings*, October 28, 2015.

Von Reusner, Susan. Interview with the author, September 21, 2015.

The Power of the Pause

Brach, Tara. *Radical Acceptance: Embracing Your Life with the Heart of a Buddha.* New York: Bantam Books, Random House, 2003.

Hendy, David. *Noise: A Human History of Sound and Listening.* London: Profile Books, 2014.

↬ *"Pauses strengthen the voice. They render the thoughts more clear-cut by separating them and give the hearer time to think."*

Iyer, Pico. *The Art of Stillness: Adventures in Going Nowhere.* New York: TED Books, Simon & Schuster, 2014.

———. *A Beginner's Guide to Japan.* New York: Vintage, Penguin Random House, 2019.

Kagge, Erling. *Silence in the Age of Noise.* New York: Pantheon Books, Random House, 2017.

↬ *"To get an important point across, it's wise to introduce a pause before and after the crux. Our brains prefer contrasts. They become attentive when the soundscape changes."*

LeClaire, Anne D. *Listening Below the Noise: The Transformative Power of Silence.* New York and London: Harper Perennial, HarperCollins Publishers, 2010.

↬ *"The pause itself becomes the event," says neuroscientist Vinod Menon of Stanford's School of Medicine. "A pause is not a time when nothing happens."*

Picard, Max. *The World of Silence.* Southlake, TX: Gateway Books, 1972.

Prochnik, George. *In Pursuit of Silence: Listening for Meaning in a World of Noise.* New York: Doubleday, 2010.

Sardello, Robert. *Silence: The Mystery of Wholeness.* Berkeley, CA: North Atlantic Books, 2008.

Listen Empty

James, William. *The Principles of Psychology.* Open Library: Pantianos Classics, 1890.

Jamison, Leslie. *The Empathy Exams: Essays.* Minneapolis, MN: Graywolf Press, 2014.

Lewis, Patricia Lee. "While talking with her on the phone." In *High Lonesome.* Amherst, MA: Levellers Press, 2011.

↪ *The full poem reads:*

I fill the cast iron pot with water
from the well, listen to her weep
and add the salt. She tells me
how she cannot leave her room.
I light the burner, set the pot,
the lid. I say I love you, tearing
cellphone. You are perfect in my
eyes. Did you dream last night?
The pasta sticks. And when the woman
in your dream picked up the knife?
I add some virgin olive oil. She isn't
crying now. She says, I think I'd better cut
if off with him. I'm looking for the
colander, the one with larger holes.
Steam clings to windows. Yes, I say,
and take the grater from its nail.
The parmesan is sweet and makes
a fragrant mountain on the cutting board.

Maslow, Abraham H. *The Psychology of Science: A Reconnaissance.* Chicago: Henry Regnery Company, 1969.

Pinney, Rachel. *Creative Listening.* Emeryville, CA: Creative Listening, Ltd., Alibris, 1983.

Tolle, Eckhart. *The Power of Now: A Guide to Spiritual Enlightenment.* Novato, CA: New World Library, 1999.

Generous Listening

Hanh, Thich Nhat, *The Path of Emancipation: Talks from a 2-Day Mindfulness Retreat.* Berkeley, CA: Parallax Press, 2000.

O'Rourke, Meghan. *The Invisible Kingdom: Reimagining Chronic Illness.* New York: Riverhead Books, Penguin Random House, 2022.

Ostaseski, Frank. *The Five Invitations: Discovering What Death Can Teach Us About Living Fully.* New York: Flatiron Books, an imprint of Macmillan Books, 2017.

Remen, Rachel Naomi. Interviewed by Krista Tippett. *On Being* (July 29, 2010). See the *On Being* website.

———. *Kitchen Table Wisdom: Stories that Heal.* New York: River-head Books, Penguin Random House, 1996.

———. *My Grandfather's Blessings: Stories of Strength, Refuge, and Be-longing.* New York: Riverhead Books, Penguin Random House, 2001.

Sacks, Oliver. *On the Move: A Life.* New York: Alfred A. Knopf, Inc., 2015.

Saying No

Anhoury, Mia. "Borough mayor still knitting to show men speak a lot at Montreal City Hall meetings." *Montreal Gazette,* August 20, 2019.

Murphy, Kate. *You're Not Listening: What You're Missing and Why It Matters.* New York: Celadon Books, a division of Macmillan Publishing, 2019.

Totenberg, Nina. *Dinners with Ruth: A Memoir on the Power of Friendships.* New York: Simon & Schuster, 2022.

↬ *Men out-talk women—or often, just don't listen—even at the highest levels. After Sandra Day O'Connor retired, Ruth Bader Ginsburg was the only woman on the US Supreme Court. Occasionally, she would find herself sitting with her colleagues, men she had worked with for more than a decade. "She would make a comment, and it would go entirely unremarked," writes Nina Totenberg. "Fifteen minutes later, a male justice would make the same point, and the response around the table would be 'That's a good idea.' That day-to-day dismissal of a smart woman's voice—which so many women have experienced—happened even on the Supreme Court." But as Totenberg points out, "it never happened when both Sandra and Ruth were seated at the table."*

Walking to Listen

Forsthoefel, Andrew. Interview with the author, December 18, 2018.

———. *Walking to Listen.* New York and London: Bloomsbury, 2017.

↬ *Also see his website of the same name.*

Haupt, Lyanda Lynn. *Rooted: Life at the Crossroads of Science, Nature and Spirit.* New York: Little, Brown, Spark, 2021.

↬ *Andrew Forsthoefel's willingness to walk has become increasingly rare. "North Americans spend over 93 percent of their waking hours indoors or in cars (and the other 7 percent walking between buildings and cars)."*

Krause, Bernie. *The Power of Tranquility in a Very Noisy World* New York: Little, Brown and Company, 2021.

↬ *Andrew Forsthoefel's "little courtyards in the forest" are reminiscent of shin-rin-yoku: Japanese forest bathing, which Bernie Krause describes as a simple yet powerful practice. "Forest bathing can offer relief from anxiety and depression," he writes, "bestow a deeper sense of mental relaxation, better sleep, and an increased feeling of gratitude for being alive. . . ."*

Peace Pilgrim. *The Sun* magazine, February 2020.

Li, Qing, *Forest Bathing: The Japanese Art and Science of Shinrin-Yoku.* New York: Viking Press, an imprint of Penguin Random House, 2018.

6: The Little Sounds of Every Day

Noisy Flowers

⤏ *Back in Summer 2015, strange popping sounds were reported in some British gardens. A cool early June followed by a sudden hot spell had led to so-called "cauliflower creak"—the sound of the cauliflower florets rubbing together as they grow—the loudest outbreak in a quarter century. The Week, July 4, 2015.*

Bailey, Elisabeth Tova. *The Sound of a Wild Snail Eating.* Chapel Hill, NC: Algonquin Books, 2010.

Berendt, Joachim-Ernst. *The World Is Sound: Nada Brahma: Music and the Landscape of Consciousness.* Merrimac, MA: Destiny Books, 1987.

⤏ *"There are sounds . . . in the realm of vegetation. In Israel, Great Britain, and the United States, photo-acoustic spectroscopy has been used to make the sound of a rose audible at the moment when the bud bursts into blossom: it is an organ-like droning, reminiscent of the sounds of a Bach toccata or Messiaen's Ascension for organ . . . a spread succession of chords."*

Eliot, George. *Middlemarch.* Harmondsworth, Middlesex, England: Penguin Books, 1972.

Kakuzo, Okakura. *The Book of Tea.* Rutland, VT: Charles E. Tuttle Co., 1956.

Listening Out

Kuusisto, Stephen. *Eavesdropping: A Memoir of Blindness and Listening.* New York and London: W. W. Norton & Company, 2006.

Oliver, Mary. "Stars." In *West Wind: Poems and Prose Poems.* Boston: Houghton Mifflin, 1996.

Stafford, William. "Listening." In *West of Your City.* Georgetown, CA: Talisman Press 1960.

Hey, Sweetie!

↜ *Spending time outside: It is a painful fact that 25 percent of the American population currently gets no exercise at all. We don't walk to work or to school, don't chop wood or carry water or even plant a garden. Exercising for as little as twenty minutes a day, three days a week, provides an immediate boost of energy and wellbeing, improving memory and attention, promoting new links between brain cells, and increasing the volume of the hippocampus (crucial for memory).*

Dolesh, Richard J. "The 'Soft Fascination' of Nature." National Recreation and Parks Association (NRPA), April 1, 2013.

McLaughlin, Blair. Interview with the author. June 23, 2021.

↜ *At the time of the interview, McLaughlin was a professor of environmental studies at Hampshire College in Amherst, Massachusetts.*

Nepo, Mark. *Seven Thousand Ways to Listen: Staying Close to What Is Sacred.* New York: Atria paperback, Simon & Schuster, 2010.

Shaw, Martin Shaw. *Scatterlings; Getting Claimed in the Age of Amnesia.* Ashland, OR: White Cloud Press.

Alice's Kitchen

Cozzolino, Alice. Interview with the author, November 9, 2014.

↜ *The French word* fond *translates as "depth, foundation, background, substance," so by refusing to stir Cozzolino is choosing to protect the essential depth and flavor of the onions.* ↜ *One Christmas (December 24, 2016), Molly Birnbaum and Dan Sousa were interviewed by Allison Aubrey on National Public Radio. They had just published an article called "Taste with Your Ears: How Sound Can Change the Way We Eat," which Cozzolino would have loved. It taught people to distinguish between "the very soft, almost muffled" sound of hot water being poured into a mug, and the "much crisper" sound of cold water and helped them attend to the "really sharp sizzle" of a perfectly butter-basted rib eye steak.*

Madison, Deborah. Quoted by Laura Fraser in "The Joy of Mindful Cooking." In *The Best Buddhist Writing 2010.* Edited by Melvin McLeod. Boston and London: Shambhala Publications, 2010.

↜ *"Whenever you're doing something with awareness, it's a two-way street: things talk back to you. . . . Cooking, is a wonderful opportunity to observe— the food, yourself, and the magic that can happen between the two."*

Nepo, Mark. *Seven Thousand Ways to Listen: Staying Close to What Is Sacred.* New York: Simon & Schuster, 2012.

Listening Behind the Noise

Hirson, Allen. Interview with the author, January 17, 2022.

The Voices Return

Balbuena, Diego. "Monitoring the Sound of Human Quarantine." *Lifeology,* April 13, 2020.

Beardsley, Eleanor. "Human Life Is Literally Quieter Due to Coronavirus." National Public Radio, April 14, 2020.

Cox, Trevor. *The Sound Book: The Science of the Sonic Wonders of the World.* New York and London: W. W. Norton & Company, 2014.

⤦ *For years, good friends in Park Slope, Brooklyn, had a pair of cardinals resident in their backyard. But with the lessening of traffic on their street, the cardinals moved to the tree in front of the house, clearly exulting in the opportunity to be heard. Trevor Cox writes, "Great tits in cities such as London, Paris, and Berlin sing faster and higher in pitch compared with those living in forests. Urban nightingales sing louder when there is traffic, and robins now sing more at night, when it is quieter."*

Griffiths, Jay. *Why Rebel.* New York: Penguin Books, Penguin Random House, 2021.

⤦ *"When asked their single favorite thing about lockdown, many people answered in one word: birdsong."*

Koren, Marina. "The Pandemic Is Turning the Natural World Upside Down: Widespread social-distancing measures have produced some jarring effects across land, air and sea." *The Atlantic,* April 2, 2020.

"Listening to the pulse of nature." *Provincetown Banner,* April 9, 2020.

McCarthy, Michael. "The Sound of Silence: The Cuckoo Is Vanishing." *The Independent,* March 22, 2009.

⤦ *A friend in the Scottish Highlands, Joyce Gilbert, described the cuckoos calling to one another in April 2020. Hearing such cuckoos is a special delight. Since the 1980s, the number of British cuckoos has diminished by 65 percent. See the British Trust for Ornithology website.*

Winter, Janey. Conversation with the author, April 2020.

An Audible Gift

"At one border crossing into Poland, those fleeing Ukrainians are met with music." National Public Radio, *All Things Considered,* March 23, 2022.

↪ *In March 2022, soon after the Russian invasion of Ukraine, the German musician Davide Martello hitched his baby grand piano to his car and towed it fifteen hours to the Medyka border crossing, the busiest one between Poland and Ukraine. Volunteers gave out hot tea, food, clothes, and toiletries, and Martello, bless his heart, provided the music.*

Bocelli, Andrea. "Amazing Grace: Music for Hope." YouTube, April 16, 2020.

Fry, Naomi. "What's the Frequency?" *The New Yorker*, November 25, 2019.

Schafer, W. Murray. "Music and the Soundscape." *The Book of Music and Nature: An Anthology of Sounds, Words, Thoughts.* Edited by David Rothenberg and Marta Ulvaeus. Middletown, CT: A Terra Nova Book, Wesleyan University Press, 2001.

↪ *Raking, etc.:The Japanese are especially alert to such pleasures, for which they employ the term* ongaku: *"the enjoyment of sounds." Even now, traditional gardeners place rocks in the beds of streams to alter the music of their flow, or set up decorative bamboo pumps which tip when filled with water, then fall back with a pleasant hollow pitch against the stones.*

In years past, they would also bury a series of "resounding jars" under the rock basins where visitors paused to wash their hands before entering the tea house. These were arranged to create "a melodic cascade of hollow pitches" as the spilled water dropped down from one to the next.

The Thunder Mutters: 101 Poems for the Land. Edited by Alice Oswald. London: Faber and Faber, 2005.

"Yo-Yo Ma plays cello in the vaccine waiting room in Massachusetts." YouTube. *Guardian News*, March 14, 2021.

↪ *In Spring 2021, after receiving his second Covid shot, Yo-Yo Ma played cello in a Pittsfield, Massachusetts, waiting room: a lovely example of an audible gift.*

A Gift for Listening

Oba, Junko. Interview with the author, November 8, 2015.

7: Listening to the Wild

Island Listening

Barkham, Patrick. "This island is not for sale: how Eigg fought back." *The Guardian*, September 26, 2017.

Cox, Trevor. *The Sound Book: The Science of the Sonic Wonders of the World.* New York and London: W. W. Norton & Company, 2014.

Dressler, Camille. *Eigg: The Story of an Island*. Edinburgh, Scotland: Birlinn Ltd., 2007.

Krause, Bernie. *The Great Animal Orchestra: Finding the Origins of Music in the World's Wild Places*. New York: Back Bay Books, Little, Brown and Company, 2012.

The Invitation

Berry, Thomas, et al. *Befriending the Earth: A Theology of Reconciliation Between Humans and the Earth*. Waterford, CT: Twenty-Third Publications, 1991.

↬ *"If we do not hear the voices of the trees, the birds, the animals, the fish, the mountains and the rivers, then we are in trouble. . . . That, I think, is what has happened to the human community in our times. We are talking to ourselves. We are not talking to the river, we are not listening to the river. We have broken the great conversation."*

Clark, Thomas A. *Distance & Proximity*. Edinburgh, Scotland: Pocketbooks, Morningstar Publications, Canongate Venture, 2000.

Lopez, Barry. "The Invitation." In *Granta* 133, November 2015.

↬ *This essay is reprinted in Embrace Fearlessly the Burning World: Essays by Barry Lopez. New York: Random House, 2022.*

Nelson, Richard. "Forgotten Voices, Natural Sounds and the Lost Art of Listening." YouTube. Sydney Environment Institute, University of Sydney, Australia, April 2, 2014.

↬ *"People in traditional cultures were in constant reciprocal communication," writes naturalist Richard Nelson. "They spent time listening to the plants, to the wind, to the birds, to other animals." Such focus was for them extremely purposeful. To this day, when Eskimo (Inupiaq) hunters are intent on catching a seal off the Alaskan coast, they drift silently in a skin-covered boat, rest their wooden paddle in the water, and tilt an ear to the wood. This transmits the voice of the seals as they swoop and plunge in the depths below.*

They also locate bears by means of sound. Black bears live in dens deep underground, each with a number of branching tunnels. When the men go out to hunt in early winter, they work their way into the tunnels, poking ahead with a long pole. If the bear is a young one, they will be able to hear the pounding of its heart.

Mountain Truths

↬ *How to encourage close listening to the natural world? In 2015, a group of architecture students came up with an answer, in the form of three enormous megaphones (six feet long by three feet in diameter) set deep in the Estonian forest, not far from the border with Latvia and Russia. The megaphones are made of larch wood, each one large enough to sit and play and even sleep inside. Standing midpoint between the three, one hears a gorgeous amplification of the usual forest sounds: the scurrying of rabbits, squirrels, foxes; the wind in the pine trees; the call of a passing owl. Visitors are drawn by the art installation and return for what the students call "a Public Forest Library," where the only book is nature, and reading means to listen. See the Atlas Obscura website.*

Cox, Trevor. *The Sound Book: The Science of the Sonic Wonders of the World*. New York and London: W. W. Norton & Company, 2014.

Hanh, Thich Nhat. *Cultivating the Mind of Love*. Berkeley, CA: Parallax Press, 1996.

✧ *After the atomic bomb was dropped on Hiroshima, the Japanese considered that the rocks in the park were dead. So, they "carried them away and brought in living rocks."*

Muir, John. *The Unpublished Journals of John Muir*. Edited by Linnie Marsh Wolfe. Madison, WI: University of Wisconsin Press, 1979.

Turner, Frederick. *John Muir: From Scotland to the Sierra*. Edinburgh, Scotland: Canongate, 1997.

The Voices of the Trees

Hardy, Thomas. *Under the Greenwood Tree*. London: Penguin Books, 2012.

Muir, John. *The Wild Muir: Twenty-two of John Muir's Greatest Adventures*. Selected by Lee Stetson. San Francisco, CA: Yosemite Association, 1994.

Snyder, Gary. *Gary Snyder: Dimensions of a Life*. Edited by John Halper. San Francisco, CA: Sierra Club Books, 1991.

✧ *As a boy, Gary Snyder had a special friendship with the cedar tree behind his house. "I used to climb to the top of it all the time," he reported. "I asked it questions and listened to the wind give answers; now it would give you answers, but not in language. I drew a lot of comfort from that."*

Thoreau, Henry David. *Excursions*. New York: Corinth Books, 1962.

———. *Walden or, Life in the Woods*. New York: Signet Classic, New American Library, 1960.

The Inside Story

✧ *The city of Melbourne, Australia, assigned trees email addresses so that citizens could report problems they noticed. Instead, people wrote thousands of love letters to their favorite trees. (LaFrance, Adrienne. "When You Give a Tree an Email Address," The Atlantic, July 10, 2015.)*

Haskell, David George. *The Songs of Trees: Stories from Nature's Great Connectors.* New York: Viking, Penguin Random House, 2017.

Kimmerer, Robin Wall. *Braiding Sweetgrass: Indigenous Wisdom, Scientific Knowledge, and the Teachings of Plants.* Minneapolis, MN: Milkweed Editions, 2013.

Oliver, Mary. *West Wind: Poems and Prose Poems.* Boston: Houghton Mifflin, 1997.

Powers, Richard. *The Overstory.* New York: W. W. Norton & Company, 2018.

Simard, Suzanne. *Finding the Mother Tree: Discovering the Wisdom of the Forest.* New York: Knopf, Doubleday, 2021.

Wohlleben, Peter. *The Hidden Life of Trees: What They Feel, How They Communicate.* Vancouver: Greystone Press, 2015.

⇢ *Wohlleben uses the phrase "wood wide web," which was apparently coined by Suzanne Simard.*

Stop and Listen

Armbrecht, Ann. *Thin Places: A Pilgrimage Home.* New York: Columbia University Press.

Johnson, Willard L. *Riding the Ox Home: History of Meditation from Shamanism to Science.* Boston: Beacon Press, 1982.

Kimmerer, Robin Wall. *Braiding Sweetgrass: Indigenous Wisdom, Scientific Knowledge, and the Teachings of Plants.* Minneapolis, MN: Milkweed Editions, 2013.

Kimmerer, Robin Wall and Richard Powers. "Tales of Sweetgrass and Trees." Conversation with Terry Tempest Williams, Harvard Divinity School, March 26, 2019.

Macfarlane, Robert. *Underland: A Deep Time Journey.* New York: W. W. Norton & Company, 2019.

Shepherd, Philip. *New Self, New World: Recovering Our Senses in the Twenty-First Century.* Berkeley, CA: North Atlantic Books.

The Language of the Wild

Abram, David. *The Spell of the Sensuous: Perception and Language in a More-than-Human World*. New York: Vintage Books, Knopf Doubleday, 1996.

B. B., *The Little Grey Men: A Story for the Young at Heart*. Illustrated by Denys Watkins Pitchford. Harmondsworth, Middlesex, England: Penguin Books, 1967.

Berendt, Joachim-Ernst. *The Third Ear: On Listening to the World*. New York: Henry Holt and Company, 1985.

Dahl, Roald. *The BFG*. Harmondsworth, Middlesex, England: Puffin Books, 1982.

Grahame, Kenneth. *The Wind in the Willows*. Illustrated by Ernest H. Shepard. New York: Charles Scribner's Sons, Simon & Schuster, 1960.

Travers, P. L. "John and Barbara's Story." In *Mary Poppins*. Illustrated by Mary Shepard. Harmondsworth, Middlesex, England: A Puffin Book, Penguin Books, 1962.

Their Listening

Cox, Trevor. *The Sound Book: The Science of the Sonic Wonders of the World*. New York and London: W. W. Norton & Company, 2014.
‹∂ *"The loudest purr of a domestic cat has been tracked at 67.7 decibels."*

De Waal, Frans. *Are We Smart Enough to Know How Smart Animals Are?* New York: W. W. Norton & Company, 2016.
‹∂ *On elephants: "An elephant brain has three times as many neurons as we do—257 billion. Most of these are in the cerebellum. . . . They can hear infrasound, which are sound waves far below human hearing." On dolphins: "Dolphins produce signature whistles, unique to each individual." On ravens: "Ravens recognize each other's voices and pay close attention to dominant and subordinate calls."*

Donahue, Michelle Z. "Flowers can hear buzzing bees—and it makes their nectar sweeter." *National Geographic*, January 15, 2019.

"Fun Facts about Hearing: Animal and Insect Edition," April 27, 2017. Signia website, USA.

"The top 10 animals with the best hearing," May 15, 2023. Hidden Hearing website, UK.

"World's most extreme hearing animal: It's a moth." *Earth*, May 9, 2013.

A Wider Listening

De Waal, Frans. *Are We Smart Enough to Know How Smart Animals Are?* New York: W. W. Norton & Company, 2016.

↬ *"The octopus has the largest and most complex brain of all invertebrates."*

Haupt, Lyanda Lynn. *Rooted: Life at the Crossroads of Science, Nature, and Spirit.* New York: Little, Brown, Spark, 2021.

↬ *"In 2012 . . . an international consortium of scientists signed the Cambridge Declaration of Consciousness, proclaiming that all animals, from birds to apes to coyotes to fish to octopuses, possess consciousness worthy of ethical consideration."*

Montgomery, Sy. Interview with the author, April 7, 2015.

————. *The Good Good Pig: The Extraordinary Life of Christopher Hogwood.* New York: Ballantine Books, Penguin Random House, 2006.

————. *Journey of the Pink Dolphins: An Amazon Quest.* White River Junction, VT: Chelsea Green Publishing, 2009.

————. *The Soul of an Octopus: A Surprising Exploration into the Wonder of Consciousness.* New York: Atria Books, Simon & Schuster, 2015.

8: Sound Healing

The Earliest Music

Limón, Ada. "Instrumentation." *The Hurting Kind: Poems.* Minneapolis, MN: Milkweed Editions, 2022.

Mathieu, W. A. *The Listening Book: Discovering Your Own Music.* Boston and London: Shambhala Publications, 1991.

↬ *Mathieu's house, his stairs and tabletops, glasses and silverware are all* idiophones: *objects that make music simply by vibrating or being vibrated.*

Mithin, Stephen. *The Singing Neanderthals: The Origins of Music, Language, Mind, and Body.* Cambridge, MA: Harvard University Press, 2006.

↬ *"The musicologist Stephen Brower believes there was a single precursor both for music and language, which he calls* musilanguage. *. . . According to Brower, at some unspecified date in the past, musilanguage became differentiated into two separate systems, each of which then acquired additional unique properties. One became music, while the other became language."*

Sacks, Oliver. *Musicophilia: Tales of Music and the Brain.* New York: Vintage Books, Penguin Random House, 2007.

Shaw, Martin. *Scatterlings: Getting Claimed in the Age of Amnesia.* Ashland, OR: White Cloud Press, 2016.

Totenberg, Nina. *Dinners With Ruth: A Memoir on the Power of Friendships.* New York: Simon & Schuster, 2022.

↵ *In a recent memoir, NPR legal affairs correspondent Nina Totenberg remembers her own childhood home. Her father, Roman Totenberg, was a virtuoso violinist. When he wasn't rehearsing or playing for fun, he would practice for hours on end. "The house didn't just come alive with music," writes Totenberg, "it reverberated, the floorboards literally vibrated from the sounds of the violin." When she moved into her first apartment, she described herself as "almost undone by the silence, the music so abruptly gone."*

The Rhythms of Nature

Krause, Bernie. *The Great Animal Orchestra: Finding the Origin of Music in the World's Wild Places.* New York: Little, Brown and Company, 2013.

Schafer, W. Murray. "Music and the Soundscape." *The Book of Music and Nature: An Anthology of Sounds, Words, Thoughts.* Edited by David Rothenberg and Marta Ulvaeus. Middletown, CT: A Terra Nova Book, Wesleyan University Press, 2001.

↵ *Gershwin's* Rhapsody in Blue *was similarly inspired by a train journey. "It was on a train, with its steely rhythms, its rattlety-bang that is so often stimulating to a composer (I frequently hear music in the very heart of noise) that I suddenly heard—even saw on paper—the complete construction of the Rhapsody from beginning to end. . . . I heard it as a sort of musical kaleidoscope of America—of our vast melting pot, of our incomparable national pep, our metropolitan madness."*

Stein, Gertrude. *How Writing Is Written.* Boston: Black Sparrow Press, 1974.

Pan Pipes

↵ *The earliest known wind instruments are two elegant flutes, made of bird-bone and ivory, found in a cave called Geissenkloesterle in southern Germany, and thought to be some 42,000 to 43,000 years old. The best preserved is made of a vulture's wing bone and has a V-shaped notch at one end and five finger holes. I feel confident Thoreau would have loved them.*

Alcott, Louisa May. "Thoreau's Flute." In *Harper's Magazine*, September 1863.

Emerson, Edward Waldo. *Henry Thoreau: As Remembered by a Young Friend*. Concord, MA: Thoreau Foundation, Inc., 1968.

↬ *Edward's father, Ralph Waldo Emerson, wrote to a distant friend around this time, hoping to lure him to Concord, and using Thoreau as bait. "If old Pan were here, you would come: and we have young Pan here under another name, whom you shall see, and hear his reeds, if you tarry not."*

Thoreau, Henry David. *The Journal of Henry David Thoreau*. Vol. II, September 19, 1850. [various editions]

Breath Becoming Sound

Gorn, Steve. See the extended biography on the artist's website. n.d.

———. Interview with the author, July 8, 2014.

———. "The Universe Hangs on Sound," Zoom presentation, Sky Lake, Rosendale, NY, March 16, 2021.

↬ *Sonic visualization fascinates him, Gorn says. "Each raga has a landscape, has a mandala, you could say a family constellation of notes, all in relation to the fundamental drone, and to each other. When the image-making settles in, when I become one with the music, I can really dance in that space. The specific colors and energy become my friends."*

Sound Healing

Sacks, Oliver. *Awakenings*. New York: Vintage Books, 1990.

———. *The Man Who Mistook His Wife for a Hat and Other Clinical Tales*. New York: Summit Books, Vintage, 1985.

———. *Musicophilia: Tales of Music and the Brain*. New York: Vintage Books, 2007.

———. *On the Move: A Life*. New York: Alfred A. Knopf, Inc., 2015.

↬ *Oddly enough, Sacks had a similar experience of internally generated sound healing. In 1974, he broke his leg in several places, and at first walking felt painfully foreign to him, "like manipulating a robot limb." He had, however, been given a Mendelssohn tape by his good friend Jonathan Miller, and those first days in the hospital, had played it constantly. Now, as he was struggling to walk, he suddenly "'heard,' with hallucinatory force, a gorgeous, rhythmic passage from Mendelssohn's Violin Concerto," and at that moment was able to walk again, or rather, "to regain . . . the 'kinetic melody' of walking." Within an hour, he had recovered all his usual ease and fluidity.*

Storr, Anthony. *Music and the Mind.* New York: The Free Press, Simon & Schuster, 1992.

Styron, William. *Darkness Visible.* New York: Random House, 1990.

Restorative Chant

Berendt, Joachim-Ernst. *The World Is Sound: Nada Brahma: Music and the Landscape of Consciousness.* Merrimac, MA: Destiny Books, 1987.

↦ *"Saying or singing OM has a powerful effect on the pineal and pituitary glands, which pass on the vibrations to the interior glandular system, and thus to the entire organism."*

Doidge, Norman. *The Brain That Changes Itself: Remarkable Discoveries and Recoveries from the Frontiers of Neuroplasticity.* New York: Viking Press, 2015.

Schumacher, Michael. *Dharma Lion: A Critical Biography of Allen Ginsberg.* New York: St. Martin's Press, 2016.

O Rare Delight!

Kinsey, Mariel. Interview with the author, July 1, 2014.

Sacks, Oliver. *Musicophilia: Tales of Music and the Brain.* New York: Vintage Books, 2007.

Schneider, David. *Crowded by Beauty: The Life and Zen of Poet Philip Whalen.* Berkeley, CA: University of California Press, 2025.

Song of the Union

↦ *The Burns Monument was designed by Scottish architect Thomas Hamilton and originally contained a white marble statue of Robert Burns (1759–1796), now in the Scottish National Portrait Gallery. The foundation stone was laid in 1831.*

Emeka Ogboh (b. 1977) is best known for his Lagos soundscapes, but his 2015 installation, "The Song of the Germans," in which ten African immigrants (now resident in Berlin) sing the German national anthem in their first language, is an obvious precursor to "Song of the Union."

Sound Fishing

Anthology of Essays on Deep Listening. Edited by Monique Buzzarté and Tom Bickley. Kingston, NY: Deep Listening Publications, 2012.

Oliveros, Pauline. *Sounding the Margins: Collected Writings 1992–2009.* Kingston, NY: Deep Listening Publications, 2010.

Listen with Everything

London, Frank. Interview with the author, October 30, 2014.

9: Writers Listening

Moments of Being

McEwen, Christian. *Sparks from the Anvil: The Smith College Poetry Interviews.* Peterborough, NH: Bauhan Publishing, 2015.

Muir, Edwin. *An Autobiography.* London: The Hogarth Press, 1954.

Woolf, Virginia. *Moments of Being: Unpublished Autobiographical Writings.* New York and London: Harcourt Brace Jovanovich, 1976.

Listening to the Radio, Listening to the Page

Heaney, Seamus, *Opened Ground: Selected Poems 1966–1996.* New York: Farrar, Straus and Giroux, 1999.

———. *Preoccupations: Selected Prose 1968–1978.* New York: The Noonday Press, Farrar, Straus and Giroux, 1980.

The Writer's Voice

Bringhurst, Robert. *The Tree of Meaning: Language, Mind & Ecology.* Berkeley, CA: Counterpoint, 2006.

Heaney, Seamus. *Preoccupations: Selected Prose 1968–1978.* New York: The Noonday Press, Farrar, Straus and Giroux, 1980.

Kunitz, Stanley, with Genine Lentine. *The Wild Braid: A Poet Reflects on a Century in the Garden.* New York: W. W. Norton & Company, 2005.

Double-Tongued

Reid, Alastair. *Inside Out: Selected Poetry and Translations.* Introduction by Douglas Dunn. Edinburgh, Scotland: Polygon, Birlinn Ltd., 2008.

———. *Outside In: Selected Prose.* Introduction by Andrew O'Hagan. Edinburgh, Scotland, Polygon, Birlinn Ltd., 2008.

Simic, Charles. "The Difficult Art of Translation." Library of Congress, June 2008.

✧ *Simic moved to New York in 1960, and soon discovered the Slavic section of the New York Public Library. As he explained "Translating poetry is an act of love, an act of supreme empathy."*

The Musical Wave

Griffin, Susan. *The Eros of Everyday Life: Essays on Ecology, Gender, and Society.* New York: Anchor Books, Knopf Doubleday, 1995.

Joyce, James. *Ulysses.* London: Penguin Books, 2000.

Maia. Communication with the author, 2009.

The Thunder Mutters: 101 Poems for the Planet. Edited by Alice Oswald. London: Faber and Faber, 2005.

Early Morning

Temple, Stanley. "Sounds Heard by Aldo Leopold." Interviewed by Steve Curwood. *Living on Earth* (September 28, 2012). See the *Living on Earth* website.

Learning to Wait

Buhner, Stephen Harrod. *Ensouling Language: On the Art of Non-Fiction and the Writer's Life.* Rochester, VT: Inner Traditions, 2010.

Hughes, Ted. *Winter Pollen: Occasional Prose.* London: Picador, Pan Macmillan, 1994.

Ted Hughes & the Classics. Edited by Roger Rees. Oxford: Oxford University Press, 2009.

McEwen, Christian. *Sparks from the Anvil: The Smith College Poetry Interviews.* Peterborough, NH: Bauhan Publishing, 2015.

Soft Imagined Voices

Campbell, James. *Talking at the Gates: A Life of James Baldwin.* Berkeley, CA: University of California Press, 1991.

↤ *Baldwin may have told Studs Terkel that he was alone in Switzerland, but in fact he was living with his then-lover, a man called Lucien Happersberger. They stayed in a small chalet in the village of Loeche-les-Bains, not far from Lausanne. Baldwin was the first black person the villagers had ever seen, "and the locals were not shy of showing their curiosity. They wanted to touch his hair, to see if it was prickly. They wanted to touch his skin, to see if the blackness rubbed off." Nor had they ever seen a typewriter before. "Happersberger recalls that it made a great deal of noise for the people who lived down below, and he had to bring them upstairs to gaze on the wondrous machine and the strange little black man who operated it." By then, Baldwin had been working on his book for more than eight years. But it was there, with Lucien, in the Happersberger family chalet, that he was finally able to finish it.*

Cep, Casey. "Book of Revelation: Marilynne Robinson's essential American stories." *The New Yorker,* October 5, 2020.
↪ *Marilynne Robinson's most recent novel, Jack, also began with listening. Cep quotes her: "I heard these two people walking around in the dark. I heard them talking in this sort of otherworldly environment, and they were talking freely in the way that people do when they are killing time."*

Dickens, Charles. *Our Mutual Friend.* Ware, Hertfordshire, England: Wordsworth Editions, 1997.

Le Guin, Ursula K. *The Wave in the Mind: Talks and Essays on the Writer, the Reader, and the Imagination.* Boston and London: Shambhala Publications, 2004.

Robinson, Marilynne. *Authors Guild Bulletin,* Winter 2016.

———. *When I Was a Child I Read Books: Essays by Marilynne Robinson.* New York: Farrar, Straus and Giroux, 2012.

Smiley, Jane. *Charles Dickens.* New York: Viking Penguin, 2002.

Terkel, Studs. *Voices of Our Time: Five Decades of Studs Terkel Interviews.* The Chicago Historical Society, WFMT Chicago, 1993.
↪ *James Baldwin told Terkel, "Bessie had the beat. . . ." Strangely enough, Bessie Smith also provided the soundtrack to Marilynne Robinson's novel* House-keeping, *according to Casey Cep in the article cited above.*

Listening to the Work

Bringhurst, Robert. *The Tree of Meaning: Language, Mind, and Ecology.* Berkeley, CA: Counterpoint, 2006.

Buhner, Stephen Harrod. *Ensouling Language: On the Art of Non-Fiction and the Writer's Life.* Rochester, VT: Inner Traditions, 2010.

Doty, Mark. Elizabeth Bishop in a letter to Anne Stevenson. In *The Art of Description.* Minneapolis, MN: Greywolf Press, 2010.

Mandelstam, Nadezhda. *Hope Against Hope: A Memoir.* Harmondsworth, Middlesex, England: Penguin Books, 1975.

The Poet's Work: 29 Masters of 20th Century Poetry on the Origins and Practice of their Art. Edited by Reginald Gibbons. Boston: Houghton Mifflin, 1979.

Rich, Adrienne. *Arts of the Possible: Essays and Conversations.* New York: W. W. Norton 2001.

————. *What Is Found There: Notebooks on Poetry and Politics*. New York: W. W. Norton & Company, 1993.

Stroud, Joseph. "Cathedral." *Country of Light: Poems by Joseph Stroud*. Port Townsend, WA: Copper Canyon, 2004.

Listening Across Time

꙳ *My mother's mother was Veronica Turleigh (1899–1971).*

Stroud, Joseph. *Country of Light: Poems by Joseph Stroud*. Port Townsend, WA: Copper Canyon Press, 2004.

————. "Riding the Dragon: An Interview with Joseph Stroud." Interviewed by Barbara March. *Poetry Flash*, June 2016.

————. "Translating Neruda the Year My Father Was Dying." In *Everything That Rises*. Port Townsend, WA: Copper Canyon Press, 2019.

10: Communing with the Dead

Communing with the Dead

꙳ *Each year, my friend Edite Cuñha plants roses or dahlias in honor of her grandmother. Maria Candida Nogueira lived as a subsistence farmer in a small village in Portugal, and for her, flowers were a luxury. She grew olives, potatoes, corn, wheat, rye, kale, beans, and all manner of greens; also grapes, apples, gifs, peaches, cherries, and pears. She had a kitchen garden too, where she grew roses and rose campion, larkspur, and lemon verbena. But she loved dahlias, and they need much more water. She planted them in distant hills and hollows, around the moist edges of the watering wells. But there were never quite enough. So, each year, on the anniversary of her birthday, Edite plants new flowers in her own garden—roses and dahlias, flax and calendula—"to feed her grandmother's soul." (Conversation with Edite Cunha, October 15, 2022.)*

Alexievich, Svetlana. *Voices from Chernobyl: The Oral History of a Nuclear Disaster*. Translated by Keith Gessen. London: Picador, Pan Macmillan, 2006.

Serrano, Miguel. *C. G. Jung and Hermann Hesse: A Record of Two Friendships*. Translated by Frank MacShane. Milton Park, Oxfordshire, England: Routledge and Kegan Paul, 1966.

Swinton, Tilda (director). 2016. *The Seasons in Quincey: Four Portraits of John Berger*, "Harvest," Part IV.

The Wind Telephone

꙳ *My friend Janey Winter described her own experience with a wind phone on Cape Cod, soon after her mother died. "I was very glad of the black rotary phone which was a clone of my childhood phone," she wrote. The lack of dialtone took her aback, but was also very powerful, "because the phone, in fact, was dead too." She dialed her mother's number in Connecticut, which she still knew by heart, even after ten years. "I remember being caught between total self-consciousness, wanting to believe, and knowing that a phone call wasn't possible any more. I chose to do it anyway. I said, 'Why are you still dead? I wish you weren't. I love you.' It moved me even without total belief. The whole point." (Communication with the author, November 8, 2021.)*

Fontaine, Tessa. "The Phone of the Wind: A Pilgrimage to a Disconnected Phone in Otsuchi, Japan." *The Believer*, July 25, 2018.

↬ *"In 2010, Mr. Sasaki learned that his cousin, a calligrapher and martial arts instructor had stage 4 cancer. He was given three months to live."* ↬ *The 2011 Fukushima earthquake was the most powerful ever recorded in Japan; the fourth most powerful in the world since recordkeeping began in 1900.*

Meek, Miki. "Really Long Distance" (NHK Sendai #702). *This American Life* (September 23, 2016). See the *This American Life* website.

Saito, Mari. "Japan's tsunami survivors call lost loves on the phone of the wind." Reuters, March 3, 2021.

↬ *The wind phone still attracts visitors from all over Japan. It is used not just by survivors of the tsunami, but by those who have lost friends and family to sickness, suicide, and of course, the coronavirus. Sasaki was recently approached by organizers who want to set up similar phones in Britain and Poland, so people could call loved ones who had died in the pandemic.*

The Voices of the Dead

↬ *The story about Nadine Gordimer was told to me by writer Don Guttenplan, to whom many thanks.*

Manguel, Alberto. *The Library at Night.* New Haven, CT: Yale University Press, 2006.

Listening to the Ancestors

Silko, Leslie Marmon. *Yellow Woman and a Beauty of Spirit: Essays on Native American Life Today.* New York: Simon & Schuster, 1996.

Presences, Visible and Invisible

Lumley, Katharine Isobel (McEwen). Private notebook, unpublished.

Parry, Richard Lloyd. *Ghosts of the Tsunami: Death and Life in Japan's Disaster Zone.* New York: Farrar, Straus and Giroux, 2017.

Listening to the Dead

Judah, Ben. *This is London: The Stories You Never Hear, The People You Never See.* London: Pan Macmillan, 2016.

Luhrmann, T. M. "The Sound of Madness: Can we treat psychosis by listening to the voices in our heads?" *Harper's Magazine*, June 2018.

The Conversation Continues

Bourgeault, Cynthia. *Love is Stronger than Death: The Mystical Union of Two Souls.* New York: Bell Tower, 1999.

Dass, Ram, and Mirabai Bush. *Walking Each Other Home: Conversations on Loving and Dying.* Louisville, CO: Sounds True, 2018.

↪ *The spiritual teacher Ram Dass had just such a relationship with his own root teacher, Neem Karoli Baba or Maharaj-ji. "After he died, he became an invisible, loving companion to me. He was an imaginary inspiration and rascally playmate who still loved me unconditionally. I took walks with him. I had long conversations. . . ."*

↪ *Such ideas continue to percolate. At a memorial for Les Patlove (October 15, 2022), his son Will spoke of wanting to share his eyesight with his father, "as a gift from him to me, and from me to him." Will's wife, Katie, spoke powerfully of death "as a dazzling portal to who we really are," and of Les's continuing presence, "not in his body, but in himself."*

Strange Radio

Gordon, Avery F. *Ghostly Matters: Haunting and the Sociological Imagination.* Minneapolis, MN: University of Minnesota Press, 2008.

Kaplan, Aryeh. *Sefer Yetzirah: The Book of Creation.* San Francisco, CA: Weiser Books, 1997.

Werner, Karen. Interview with the author, May 28, 2019.

11: The Sounds of Silence

The Not-So-Silent Night

tinnitus. Wikipedia uses the words "ringing, hissing, chirping, cheeping . . ." to describe this condition that, according to the National Center for Health Statistics (NCHS) affects approximately 32 percent of American adults. See the NCHS website.

Cox, Trevor. *The Sound Book: The Silence of the Sonic Wonders of the World.* New York: W. W. Norton & Company, 2014.

↪ *"Medics define tinnitus as perceiving sound when there is no external source.*

. . . The auditory cortex doesn't go to sleep. It always wants some input. So especially if you have a hearing loss due to noise, [and] there's an area where the ear isn't getting as much input, the brain turns up the volume, and says, 'I'm listening for something. I'm listening for something. Where is it?'"

The Essential Haiku: Versions of Basho, Buson, & Issa. Edited and with verse translations by Robert Hass. New York: The Ecco Press, HarperCollins, 1994.

The Sea and the Honeycomb: A Book of Tiny Poems. Edited by Robert Bly. Boston: Beacon Press, 1971.

The (Many) Sounds of Silence

Goodman, Paul. *Speaking and Language: Defense of Poetry.* New York: Random House, 1972.

Larson, Kay. *Where the Heart Beats: John Cage, Zen Buddhism, and the Inner Life of Artists.* New York: Penguin Press, 2012.

McCann, Colum. *Apeirogon.* New York: Random House, 2020.
↪ *"[Cage's] original intention was to replicate the length of a typical piece of canned music and to call his composition Silent Prayer." . . . "Cage said afterwards he wanted to make the opening thirty-three seconds as seductive as the shape and fragrance of a flower."*

Shepherd, Chuck. "Deafening Silence, Hi Def." *The Advocate,* February 28, 2013.

The Silent Brain

Beris, Rebecca. "Science Says Silence Is Much More Important to Our Brains Than We Think." *Lifehack,* June 6, 2019.

Center for Health and Wellness, David Lynch Foundation.
↪ *Increasing numbers of US schools now incorporate some version of "Quiet Time," leading to a 10 percent improvement in test scores, a 40 percent decrease in stress, anxiety, and depression, an 86 percent drop in suspensions over two years, and a 65 percent decrease in violent conflict. Students at the Brooklyn Urban Garden School (BUGS) enjoy fifteen minutes of Quiet Time at the beginning and end of each school day. Some put up their hands to cover their face or lay their heads down on their desks. Some repeat a silent mantra; others don't. But all remain silent for the allotted quarter of an hour. "Your mind goes to rest, and we need that," one girl said.*

Gregoire, Carolyn. "Why Silence Is So Good for Your Brain." *Science,* March 5, 2016.

Gross, Daniel A. "This Is Your Brain on Silence." *Nautilus*, August 21, 2014.

Kaleem, Jaweed. "Reading, Writing, Required Silence: How Meditation Is Changing Schools and Students." *Huffington Post*, June 12, 2015.

Lachs, Jenifer Lachs, "Why Silence Is Good for Your Brain." *InformED*, October 22, 2016.

Oliveros, Pauline. *Sounding the Margins: Collected Writings 1992–2009*. Church Lawton, Cheshire, England: Lawton Hall, 2010.

Prochnik, George. *In Pursuit of Silence: Listening for Meaning in a World of Noise*. New York: Doubleday, 2010.

Sardello, Robert. *Silence: The Mystery of Wholeness*. Berkeley, CA: North Atlantic Books, 2008.

The Charm of Quiet

Fisher, Meg. Interview with the author, January 27, 2020.

Krause, Bernie. *The Power of Tranquility in a Very Noisy World*. New York: Little, Brown, and Company, 2021.
꙳ *"When children can't hear a reflection of their own voices, they tend to be much quieter, more focused, and more respectful toward the environment. . . . Teachers aren't as exhausted by the end of the day."*

Private, Secret, and Anonymous

Dillard, Annie. *Teaching a Stone to Talk: Expeditions and Encounters*. New York: Harper and Row, 1982.

Iyer, Pico. "The Eloquent Sounds of Silence." *Time* magazine, June 24, 2001.

King, Martin Luther Jr., *Stride Toward Freedom: The Montgomery Story*. New York: Harper and Row, 1958.

Rich, Adrienne. *Arts of the Possible: Essays and Conversations*. New York: W. W. Norton & Company, 2001.

Woolf, Virginia. Letter to Ethel Smyth, September 17, 1938, in *The Letters of Virginia Woolf 1936–1941*. Edited by Nigel Nicolson and Joanne Trautman. Vol. 6. New York and London: Harcourt Brace Jovanovich, 1979.

The Quiet Activist

꙳ *The Quiet Garden Movement was founded almost thirty years ago by an*

Anglican priest called Father Philip Roderick. It offers people space for prayer and reflection, whether in private gardens, retreat centers, churches, hospitals or schools. Hosts are encouraged to welcome visitors into their gardens and their buildings too, especially on cold or rainy days, giving everyone a chance to "step back and experience a sense of stillness and wonderment."

Silent Space was founded more recently, in 2016. Its organizers contact parks and gardens that are already open to the public and ask them to reserve "a quiet place" where visitors can switch off their phones and cameras, and simply stop talking for a while. Already more than 300 gardens have agreed to participate, and the numbers continue to increase.

Goodman, Leslee. "Quiet Please." *The Sun* magazine, September 2010.

Hempton, Gordon. "Gordon Hempton Wants to Save Silence from Extinction." TEDx Talk, May 25, 2011.

———. "Silence and the Presence of Everything." Interviewed by Krista Tippett. *On Being* (May 10, 2012). See the *On Being* website.

Hempton, Gordon, and John Grossman, *One Square Inch of Silence: One Man's Search for Natural Silence in a Noisy World.* New York: Free Press, Simon & Schuster, 2009.

Moore, Kathleen Dean. "Silence Like Scouring Sand." *Orion* magazine, November–December 2008.

✧ *Hempton defines a quiet place as one where it's possible to listen interrupted for a full quarter of an hour, without hearing one human-created sound, According him, there are no quiet places left in Europe or the Eastern United States, and only ten or twelve in the American West.*

Quiet Parks International website.

Wright, Chris. "A Quest to Protect the World's Last Silent Place." *The Nature Conservancy*, June 19, 2019.

A Breath of Life

Lusseyran, Jacques. *What One Sees Without Eyes: Selected Writings of Jacques Lusseyran.* New York: Parabola Books, 1999.

Remen, Rachel Naomi. *Kitchen Table Wisdom: Stories that Heal.* New York: Penguin, 2006.

Room Sound

Eno, Brian. "Ambient Music." In *The Book of Music and Nature: An*

Anthology of Sounds, Words, Thoughts. Edited by David Rothenberg and Martha Ulvaeus. Middletown, CT: Wesleyan University Press, 2001.

Grumbach, Doris. *Fifty Days of Solitude.* Boston: Beacon Press, 1995.

Remnick, David. "Into the Clear: Philip Roth puts turbulence in its place." *The New Yorker*, May 8, 2000.

Playing What You Don't Know

Peacock, Gary. Interview with the author, September 13, 2015.

↬ *Peacock called the process of silent rehearsal* ideation. *"Instead of you intentionally plucking the string or bowing," he said, "you simply ideate it. You allow your body to do it without getting in the way." He told me he'd seen such a rehearsal described only once, and that was in* New Pathways to Piano Technique: A Study of the Relations Between Mind and Body with Special Reference to Piano Playing *by the Italian–American conductor Luigi Bonpensiere. (New York: Philosophical Library, Inc., 1953).*

See too, this little story about Liu Chi Kung, who had placed second to Van Cliburn in a Tchaikovsky piano contest back in 1958. "Not long after, during the Chinese Cultural Revolution, he was imprisoned. He lived alone in a cell for seven years. When he was released, he almost immediately played a series of highly acclaimed concerts. The public was amazed that none of his virtuosity had been lost, despite seven years without a piano. When asked how he had retained such a high level of skill with no piano to practice on, he replied, 'I practiced every day in my mind.'" (Davey, H. E. Living the Japanese Arts & Ways: 45 Paths to Meditation and Beauty. *Albany, CA: Stone Bridge Press, 2002.)*

12: Listening to the Spirit

Only Listen

Biblical references: "Samuel, Samuel. . . ." Samuel 1:3; "a still small voice. . . ." 1 Kings 19:11–13; "This is my beloved Son. . . ." Matthew 3:17.

Groopman, Jerome. "The Voices in Our Heads: Why do people talk to themselves?" *The New Yorker*, January 9, 2017.

O'Donohue, John. *Anam Cara: Spiritual Wisdom from the Celtic World.* New York: Bantam Books, Penguin Radom House,1999.

O'Riordain, John J. *The Music of What Happens.* New York: The Columbia Press, 1996.

Steindl-Rast, Brother David. *A Listening Heart: The Spirituality of Sacred Sensuousness.* Chestnut Ridge, PA: Crossroad Publishing Company, 1999.

Listening Angels

Wenders, Wim, Peter Handke, and Richard Reitinger. *Wings of Desire* (1987).

The Ones Who Listen to the Cries of the World

Alexander, Elizabeth. *The Light of the World: A Memoir.* New York: Grand Central Publishing, 2015.

⟿ *Saint Francis too, had the ability to address each person in his or her own language, as Elizabeth Alexander relates. "St. Francis spread his arms like wings, and a flock of birds landed here, doves and larks and sparrows and owls. A crowd gathered, and though they all spoke many different languages, they all understood him. . . . Each bird repeated the words Saint Francis uttered, but each bird spoke a different language, so that each listener could understand."*

Blofield, John. *Bodhisattva of Compassion: The Mystical Tradition of Kuan Yin.* Boston and London: Shambhala Publications, 1988.

Hanh, Thich Nhat. *The Heart of the Buddha's Teaching: Transforming Suffering into Peace, Joy, and Liberation.* Berkeley, CA: Parallax Press, 1998.

———. *Cultivating the Mind of Compassion: The Practice of Looking Deeply in the Mahayana Buddhist Tradition.* Berkeley, CA: Parallax Press, 1996.

Mipham Rinpoche, Sakyong. "True Listening," *Lion's Roar*, October 14, 2016.

A Hundred Thousand Voices

Abram, David. *Becoming Animal: An Earthly Cosmology.* New York: Pantheon Books, 2010.

⟿ *"Prayer, in its most ancient and elemental sense, consists simply in speaking to things—to a maple grove, to a flock of crows, to the rising wind—rather than merely about things. As such, prayer is an everyday practice common to oral, indigenous peoples the world over."*

"East Meets West in Anoushka Shankar's Latest Album." National Public Radio, June 5, 2021.

Hendy, David. *Noise: A Human History of Sound and Listening.* London: Profile Books, 2013.

↬ *According to the Chukchi people of Siberia, everything in nature is potentially alive, and spirits are always lurking, even in inanimate objects.*

Mitchell, John Hansen. *Ceremonial Time: Fifteen Thousand Years on One Square Mile.* Addison-Wesley Publishing Co., 1997.

↬ *The speaker here is a man called Fred Williams, who is in fact part Pawtucket and part Micmac. "His 'real' name, he says, is* Nompenekit, *or Man Born Twice."*

O'Donohue, John. *Anam Cara: Spiritual Wisdom from the Celtic World.* New York: Bantam Books, Penguin Random House, 1997.

Schneider, David. *Crowded by Beauty: The Life and Zen of Poet Philip Whalen.* Berkeley, CA: University of California Press, 2025.

↬ *Gary Snyder's friend, the poet Philip Whalen, had a visceral sense of this. According to his biographer, Whalen "did not pray to the Christian God: he prayed all over the place—to the elements, the plants, animals, the Greek gods, other writers. 'Eagle, mimosa, juncos & sunshine, be my help.'"*

The Way We Lived: California Indian Stories, Songs, and Reminiscences. Edited by Malcolm Margolin. Berkeley, CA: Heyday Books, 1993.

Tibetan Medicine

Dass, Ram, and Paul Gorman. *How Can I Help? Stories and Reflections on Service.* New York: Alfred A. Knopf, Inc., 1987.

A Double Listening

Kinsey, Mariel. Interview with the author, July 1, 2014.

Staying Open

Atkinson, Charles. Interview with the author, October 19, 2018.

———. *Poems: New and Selected.* Santa Cruz, CA: Hummingbird Press, 2022.

———. *Skeleton, Skin, and Joy.* Georgetown, KY: Finishing Line Press, 2017.

Rippling Out

There are parallels here with what Pauline Oliveros called "Global Listening."

Barbezat, Daniel P., and Mirabai Bush. *Contemplative Practices in Education: Powerful Methods to Transform Teaching and Learning.* San Francisco, CA: Jossey-Bass, 2014.

Berendt, Joachim-Ernst. *The World Is Sound: Nada Brahma: Music and the Landscape of Consciousness.* New York: Destiny Books, Simon & Schuster, 1987.

13: All Our Relations

Lost Sounds

⇴ "Over the past half-century, North America has lost more than a quarter of its entire bird population, or around 3 billion birds. That's according to a new estimate published in the journal Science by researchers who brought together a variety of information that has been collected on 529 bird species since 1970." National Public Radio, September 19, 2019.

MacLeish, William. *The Day Before America: Changing the Nature of a Continent.* Boston: Houghton Mifflin, 1994.

All Our Relations

Griffiths, Jay. *Why Rebel.* London: Penguin Books, 2021.
⇴ "In Costa Rica, a suburb of San José has given citizenship to every bee, bat, hummingbird, and butterfly."

Kimmerer, Robin Wall. "Rescuing Human Civilization: What Will It Take?" Public dialogue, Dartmouth College, Hanover, NH, March 31, 2021.
⇴ Robin Wall Kimmerer credits the naturalist Gary Paul Nabhan for the term re-story-ation.

———. "Speaking of Nature: Finding language that affirms our kinship with the natural world." *Orion,* March/April 2017.
⇴ Kimmerer's Potawatomi grandfather had his language stolen from him at the Carlisle Indian School, as did so many others.

Russell, Ruby. "Rights of nature: Can Indigenous traditions shape environmental law?" February 5, 2020. See the Deutsche Weller website.

Smith, Anna V. "Some Indigenous Communities Have a New Way to Fight Climate Change: Give Personhood Rights to Nature." *Mother Jones,* September 29, 2019.
⇴ "In essence, the Yurok resolution means that if the river is harmed, a case can be made in the Yurok tribal court to remedy the problem. Currently, says the Yurok Tribe General Counsel Amy Cordalis, laws like the Clean Water or

Endangered Species acts can be used to protect rivers by addressing symptoms of problems like diseased fish or pollution. But the Yurok resolution seeks to address the river's problems directly and holistically, including the impacts of climate change."

The Way We Lived: California Indian Stories, Songs and Reminiscences. Edited by Malcolm Margolin. Berkeley, CA: Heyday Books, 1981.

When the Light of the World Was Subdued, Our Songs Came Through: A Norton Anthology of Native Nations Poetry. Edited by Joy Harjo. New York: W. W. Norton & Company, 2020.

A Mutual Listening

Buber, Martin. *I and Thou.* Translated by Ronald Gregor Smith. New York: Charles Scribner's Sons, Simon & Schuster, 1958.

Klein, Kerry. "Mariposa Grove: Seeking Balance Between Humans and Their Environment." Valley Public Radio (KVPR), June 19, 2018.

Paulson, Steve. Transcript of interview with Gary Snyder on *The Practice of the Wild,* July 15, 2014. See Modern American Poetry website. ↔ The title of the poem is "They Are Listening."

Williams, Terry Tempest. *Erosion: Essays of Undoing.* New York: Macmillan, 2019.

Zen Master Ikkyu

Berendt, Joachim-Ernst. *The World Is Sound: Nada Brahma: Music and the Landscape of Consciousness.* Merrimac, MA: Inner Traditions, 1987.

↔ *This is my paraphrase of Berendt's story.*

Thus Spoke the Plant

Gagliano, Monica. "From Marine Biology to Plant Science: Plant Cognition and Bioacoustics." Interviewed by Nikki Trott. *Going Conscious,* December 28, 2020.

———. *Thus Spoke the Plant: A Remarkable Journey of Groundbreaking Scientific Discoveries and Personal Encounters with Plants.* Berkeley, CA: North Atlantic Books, 2018.

The Joy of Fishes

Berry, Wendell, and Gary Snyder. *Distant Neighbors: The Selected Letters of Wendell Berry and Gary Snyder.* Edited by Chad Wriglesworth. Berkeley, CA: Counterpoint, 2014.

Buhner, Stephen Harrod. *Ensouling Language: On the Art of Nonfiction and the Writer's Life.* Rochester, VT: Inner Traditions, 2010.

Kakuzo, Okakura. *The Book of Tea.* Foreword by Elise Grilli. Rutland, VT: Charles E. Tuttle Co., 1956.

Nepo, Mark. *Seven Thousand Ways to Listen: Staying Close to What Is Sacred.* New York: Atria paperback, Simon & Schuster, 2010.

"Telling the Bees: Maria Margaronis surrenders to the life of the hive, exploring the ancient folk customs around telling the bees." British Broadcasting Corporation (BBC), March 21, 2021. See the BBC website.
⤳ *There is a longstanding tradition of "telling the bees" when someone dies.*

Zepka, John. "Bees Join Mourners at Funeral Today." *The North Adams Transcript* (North Adams, MA, April 27, 1956.

Cosmic Sounds

Burtner, Matthew. "The Music of the Northern Lights." Interviewed by Lulu Garcia-Navarro, National Public Radio, January 3, 2021.

Horowitz, Seth S. *The Universal Sense: How Hearing Shapes the Mind.* London: Bloomsbury, 2012.

Ruddick, Angela. "Chasing the Merry Dancers." See the Orkneyology website.

Van der Post, Laurens, *The Lost World of the Kalahari.* New York: Harcourt Brace & World, Inc., 1958.

Wagoner, David. "The Silence of the Stars." *Traveling Light: Collected and New Poems.* Champaign, IL: University of Illinois Press, 1999.

The Roaring Ocean

Andrews, Robin George. "Hear the sounds of climate change—with earthquake monitors." *National Geographic,* October 17, 2019.

Haskell, David George. *Sounds Wild and Broken: Sonic Marvels, Evolution's Creativity, and the Crisis of Sensory Extinction.* New York: Viking Press, a division of Penguin Random House, 2022.
⤳ *"To be* authentic," *writes Haskell, "a whale soundtrack ought to suffuse our blood with alarm chemicals and steep our mind in anxiety and dread, distress rooted in the infernal noise that we pump into the whales' world. Instead, we feed ourselves the aural equivalent of synthetic tranquilizers, manufactured anodynes for the senses and soporifics for ethical discernment and action." He notes, "The largest container ships blast at around 190 underwater decibels or more, the equivalent on land of a thunderclap or the takeoff of a jet."*

Krause, Bernie. *The Great Animal Orchestra: Finding the Origin of Music in the World's Wild Places.* New York: Little, Brown and Company, 2013.

————. *The Power of Tranquility in a Very Noisy World.* New York: Little, Brown and Company, 2021.

↤ *The terms geophony and biophony were invented by soundscape ecologist Bernie Krause. He defines geophony as "sounds present for the entire lifespan of the earth—about 4.5 billion years," and biophony as "the collective sound produced by all non-human organisms at one period of time," first appearing about 550 million years ago.*

Listening School

Pujol, Ernesto. "Hearing the Audience with 'The Listening School' and 'The Listeners' (Q&A) A Conversation with Ernesto Pujol about the upcoming interactive event series." Interviewed by Kathryn Yu. *No Proscenium: The Guide to Everything Immersive,* June 21, 2019.

Afterword

The Music of What Happens

The Faber Book of Irish Verse. Edited by John Montague. London: Faber and Faber, 1974.